DAVID CRYSTAL is one of th[e most] respected commentators on la[nguage. He] has been a consultant, contributor or presenter on all the important radio and television programmes and series about language, including *The Story of English* and *The Routes of English*. He is the author of over a hundred books, including *How Language Works* and, most recently, *Think on my Words: Exploring Shakespeare's Language*. He was Sam Wanamaker Fellow at Shakespeare's Globe in 2003–4, and was Honorary President of the Johnson Society for 2005–6. He received an OBE for services to the English language in 1995, and was made a Fellow of the British Academy in 2000.

From the reviews of *By Hook or by Crook*:

'Rambling essays patched together from notebook gleanings, informed digressions, and anecdotes. The book reads like a donnish Bill Bryson, a Bryson possessed with a maniacal passion for the *Cambridge Encyclopedia of the English Language* . . . This is stream of consciousness linguistics, a pied-piper-led dance down the byways of language'   *Independent*

'Crystal is more than just the Dr Johnson of our age, a linguistic expert who never takes a day off from considering language in all its aspects, and even hears sheep bleat in a Welsh accent'   *Sunday Herald*

'Every page of Crystal's book contains some linguistic curiosity or flight of fancy. He should go walkie-talkie more often. Another 100 books of this kind would not be too many'   *Financial Times*

DAVID CRYSTAL

By Hook or by Crook

A JOURNEY IN SEARCH OF ENGLISH

HARPER PERENNIAL
London, New York, Toronto, Sydney and New Delhi

Harper Perennial
An imprint of HarperCollins*Publishers*
77–85 Fulham Palace Road,
Hammersmith, London w6 8jb

www.harperperennial.co.uk
Visit our authors' blog at www.fifthestate.co.uk

This edition published by Harper Perennial 2008

1

First published in Great Britain by Harper*Press* 2007

A catalogue record for this book is available from the British Library

ISBN 978-0-00-723557-5

Map by Leslie Robinson

Set in Linotype Granjon with Trajan display by
Rowland Phototypesetting Ltd, Bury St Edmunds, Suffolk

Printed and bound in Great Britain by Clays Ltd, St Ives plc

Mixed Sources
Product group from well-managed
forests and other controlled sources
www.fsc.org Cert no. SW-COC-1806
© 1996 Forest Stewardship Council

FSC is a non-profit international organisation established to promote the
responsible management of the world's forests. Products carrying the FSC
label are independently certified to assure consumers that they come
from forests that are managed to meet the social, economic and
ecological needs of present and future generations.

Find out more about HarperCollins and the environment at
www.harpercollins.co.uk/green

For Hilary,
who did most of the driving

Contents

Illustrations

Preface

The inspiration for this book came from reading W.G. Sebald's *The Rings of Saturn*, an atmospheric semi-fictional account of a walking tour throughout East Anglia, in which personal reflections, historical allusions, and traveller observations randomly combine into a mesmerizing novel about change, memory, oblivion, and survival. The metaphor of the title – Saturn's rings created from fragments of shattered moons – captures the fragmentary and stream-of-consciousness flow of the narrative.

I was frequently reminded of the serendipitous nature of language study, when reading that book. Around the next corner is always a new linguistic experience, waiting to be observed. Language is in a state of constant change, with each day bringing new developments. Any linguistic study is a search for the impossible – to say something sensible about the 'whole' of a language. I have spent my entire professional life as a university teacher and researcher in linguistics trying to make valid statements about language and languages – and about the English language in particular. Every now and then I feel I have come close to it, and then it leaves me behind, like the soldiers chasing the Ghost in *Hamlet* – ' 'Tis here! 'Tis here! 'Tis gone.' I feel I am always dealing in linguistic half-truths.

My subtitle has other echoes, chiefly of the series of explorations carried out by H.V. Morton in the 1920s and '30 – *In Search of England*, *In Search of Scotland*, *In Search of Wales* ... This is what he writes, in the preface to *In Search of England*:

I have gone round England like a magpie picking up any bright thing that pleased me. A glance at the route followed will prove that this is not a guide book, and a glance at the contents will expose me to the scorn of local patriots who will see, with incredulous rage, that on many an occasion I have passed silently through their favourite village. That is inevitable. It was a moody holiday, and I followed the roads; some of them led me aright and some astray. The first were the most useful; the others were the most interesting.

This has been my experience too: the linguistic side roads always proved more interesting. And writing this preface having finished the book, I can see that its spirit – and certainly its style – is far more Morton than Sebald.

Both Sebald and Morton had reasons for starting their journeys. I did not. The idea for this book had been wandering around my head for several months, but I had no particular motive to go off on a linguistic journey. After all, where should I go? There was everywhere to choose from, and that was too much. A journey needs a structure, and I didn't have one.

Then, out of the blue, I was given a reason, and a structure. In 2002 the BBC had initiated an ambitious project to record and celebrate the whole range of present-day British English accents and dialects. The project was called, quite simply, 'Voices', and it came to fruition in August 2005, when broadcasters all over the country presented a wide range of programmes in 'Voices Week'. I had been the project's linguistics consultant.

It was mainly a radio experience, but a few television programmes were also being made, and in May I was asked to help present one of them, for BBC Wales. The idea was to travel around the principality to find out what was happening to the English accents in the region. My impression was that Anglo-Welsh accents were becoming increasingly diverse. Was this so? And what did people feel about the changes which were taking place? The programme would find out.

And that is how I found myself suddenly faced with a series of ports-of-call, dotted around Wales. Several of them coincided with plans I had already made to visit places in nearby England, such as the Hay Festival, and one week in particular, at the beginning of June, stood out as an especially wide-ranging opportunity. The events of that week, I decided, would act as my structure.

In making a television documentary, there are long chunks of time when there is nothing for a presenter to do, other than wait for the moment when the producer and the film crew have everything ready – the right light, the right angle, the right background . . . I imagine some presenters read a novel at that point. With me, the linguistic bit of my mind goes walkabout. The spoken and written paraphernalia around me – voices, place-names, signs, noticeboards – trigger all kinds of questions, reflections, and memories. Everything goes into a notebook. My book includes those moments too. They took me all over the English-speaking world.

By Hook or by Crook is a linguistic travelogue. It is an attempt to capture the exploratory, seductive, teasing, quirky, tantalizing nature of language study. Certainly, in both structure and style, it is unlike anything I have written before. My previous published encounters with the English language have ranged from the research monograph to the school textbook, and from highly illustrated encyclopedias to the most unillustrated of dictionaries. But everything, hitherto, has had a tight structure. In each case, I knew where I was going, and where my book would end.

As I began to write *By Hook or by Crook*, I realized it was not going to be like that. In piecing together my journey, telling my 'Voices' story, and researching the answers to my notebook questions, I found still more linguistic side roads that I could not resist exploring. A surprising number of questions have more than one answer. This book includes them all. I suppose it might be called 'stream-of-consciousness linguistics'.

DAVID CRYSTAL
Holyhead, 2006

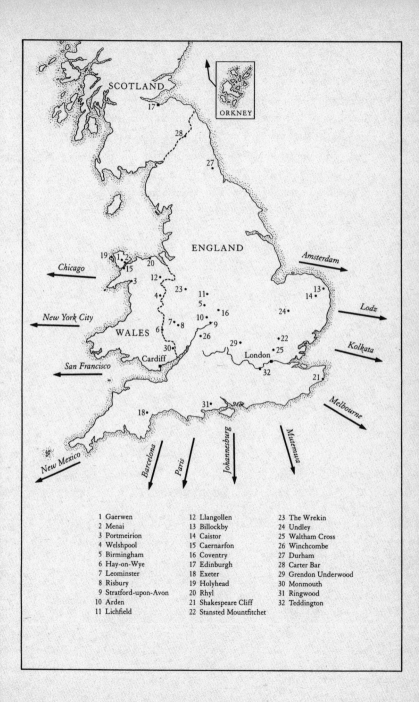

SCOTLAND

ORKNEY

ENGLAND

Amsterdam

Chicago

WALES

New York City

Lodz

Kolkata

Cardiff

London

San Francisco

Melbourne

New Mexico

Barcelona

Paris

Johannesburg

Mutemwa

1 Gaerwen
2 Menai
3 Portmeirion
4 Welshpool
5 Birmingham
6 Hay-on-Wye
7 Leominster
8 Risbury
9 Stratford-upon-Avon
10 Arden
11 Lichfield

12 Llangollen
13 Billockby
14 Caistor
15 Caernarfon
16 Coventry
17 Edinburgh
18 Exeter
19 Holyhead
20 Rhyl
21 Shakespeare Cliff
22 Stansted Mountfitchet

23 The Wrekin
24 Undley
25 Waltham Cross
26 Winchcombe
27 Durham
28 Carter Bar
29 Grendon Underwood
30 Monmouth
31 Ringwood
32 Teddington

BY HOOK
OR BY CROOK

1

By Hook or by Crook

GAERWEN

'It's a Welsh accent, ye see.'

I looked again at the sheep, and then at the farmer. Was he having me on? His face was old, lined, and very serious. The price of sheep was down today, and he had six ewes at auction. He was not in a joking mood.

All I had wanted to do was start a conversation. I was in Gaerwen sheep market, in the east of Anglesey in North Wales, on a Wednesday morning in June 2005, looking for regional accents. *Gaer – wen*. That's 'fort white' in Welsh, though there's no trace of any fort now. The Romans passed through once, so maybe it was one of theirs.

I was travelling all around the country, as part of the BBC 'Voices' project, and this was one of the days in the north. The programme researcher had been tasked to find some local people who would interview well. She had found one, in the form of Simon, the Gaerwen auctioneer, and we had arranged to meet him before the day's auction started. And thus I found myself in the stockyard, surrounded by 1,500 noisy sheep.

The producer wanted 'actuality'. She gave me a digital tape recorder and suggested I wander round and find interesting people to talk to with typical local voices. That suited me fine. I know what an Anglesey accent sounds like. I was brought up in the county as a child, and live there again now. But it's one thing knowing an accent, and quite another seeing it in the faces around you. From a phonetic point of view, all faces look the same.

I spotted a good prospect. A tall, craggy man, aged I thought about seventy, who was shepherding some sheep into a pen with his staff. He was one of the oldest farmers there – a classic local accent if ever I saw one. I switched on the tape recorder, and squelched my way towards him, suddenly aware why everyone else in the yard was wearing boots.

He pushed the last ewe into the pen and lugged the gate shut behind it. What should I talk about? I decided to ask him about his staff, which was puzzling me. It was a long, thin pole, and it didn't have a curved end. I don't know much about sheep, but I do know that shepherds' sticks are supposed to have crooks. That's their name. A shepherd's crook. Why wasn't his curved?

He looked at me and my tape recorder and my splattered trousers without any evident emotion.

'Good morning,' I said. 'Nice day.'

'Ay,' he replied, 'it's a brave morning.' In a broad Scots voice.

I temporarily lost the power of speech. My crook question fled. I was definitely in Gaerwen, not in Glasgow. If my tape recorder could have spoken, it would have said, in the manner of Hal, the onboard computer in *2001*, 'I don't think you want to be doing this, Dave.' Certainly my producer wouldn't want me collaborating with non-Welsh accents. We were short of time as it was. I looked around. She was nowhere to be seen, so I reckoned I could get away with a few moments of surreptitious conversation.

I just had to find out what was going on. I switched my machine off and took the ram, as it were, by the horns.

'I'm here making a programme about Welsh accents, but I don't think I'm asking the right person!'

He laughed. 'Yee're right theere, laddie.'

Laddie! I couldn't remember the last time I was called *laddie*. Have I *ever* been called laddie? Still, at age sixty-five, if someone offers you a youth credit, you accept it gladly.

'So where *are* you from?' I asked him.

'Llanfairpwll,' he said.

Now, in case you are wondering, Llanfairpwll is not in Scotland. It is a small village in the east of Anglesey. Lots of sheep-farming over that way. A very Welsh area. Its name has archetypal status, as in its full form it is the longest name in the British Isles, with fifty-eight letters. Not in the world – a place in New Zealand is longer.

Place-names like that don't come up naturally. The historical name of the village was already quite long – *Llanfair Pwllgwyngyll* – but that was because of the way names work in Wales. I know two men near where I live, Dick Jones who drives a taxi, and Dick Jones who works on the ferry-boats. One is called *Dick Jones Taxi* and the other *Dick Jones Ferry*, or *Dick Taxi* and *Dick Ferry* for short. It's the same with place-names. There are lots of places called *Llanfair*. *Llan* in Welsh means 'church'; *fair* is a form of *Mair*, 'Mary'. Together the words mean 'Mary's Church'. To distinguish them, something gets added on. The Anglesey Mary's Church was located by a hollow (*pwll*). In fact, by a hollow near a white hazel (*pwll* – *gwyn* – *gyll*). So that's what they called it.

That's how it was for centuries. Then in the 1800s, the railway was built between Chester and Holyhead, and Llanfair Pwllgwyngyll was on the route. A local committee was formed to think of ways of encouraging the trains, travellers, and tourists to stop there. A cobbler from the nearby town of Menai Bridge came up with the fifty-eight-letter name:

Llanfairpwllgwyngyllgogerychwyrndrobwll-llantysiliogogogoch

The town council adopted it. It was one of the most successful travel marketing ploys ever.

When you live in Anglesey, learning the name by heart is a child rite of linguistic passage. You can then spend the rest of your life correcting English-speakers who say it all wrong apart from the last three syllables. But it isn't so hard if you remember that *w* and *y* are vowels in Welsh, *f* is pronounced like an English *v*, and the double-*l* is exactly like an English *l*, but without any buzzing of the vocal cords. Try it. Say *l*, and notice where your tongue is – hard against the ridge behind your top teeth. Keep it there, and just push the air past the sides of your tongue. That's the Welsh double-*l*. Then you can go for the name, splitting it up into its meaningful bits:

Llan	*fair*	*pwll*	*gwyn gyll*
Church (of)	Mary	(in the) hollow	(of the) white hazel

goger y	*chwyrn drobwll*	*llan*	*tysilio*	*gogo goch*
near the	rapid whirlpool	(and) church	of (St) Tysilio	(by the) red cave.

Locals never use the long name. Life is too short. They even avoid the official shorter version. Instead they abbreviate it, and say either *Llanfairpwll* or *Llanfair P.G.*

The full name is actually used as a valid domain name on the Internet. A domain name can have up to sixty-seven characters. They have to be *o* to *9*, *a* to *z*, or the hyphen. The dot and what follows it count in the total – so, for instance, if your domain name ends in *.com*, that would be four characters, leaving you with sixty-three. In fact, someone has already registered Llanfair's full name with an additional five letters in it, making up the sixty-three. The extra five letters are *uchaf*, which means 'higher' in Welsh. It would be like saying 'Upper Llanfair . . .' – like Upper Slaughter in the Cotswolds.

Actually, technically, the full Llanfair name has only fifty-one letters, as the double-*l* counts as a single letter in Welsh. But Internet software usually assumes that all languages work like English.

You can't beat the ingenuity of the people of Llanfairpwll, though you can try. Years later, another Welsh town, further south, in Cardiganshire, decided to do the same thing, and thought up a sixty-six-letter name. It never caught on. A country can only get away with this kind of creative name-building once.

There's a joke told about an American tourist who bought a postcard in Llanfairpwll, and stopped for a coffee at the nearby Little Chef. She studied the full name on the card intently, then asked the waitress, 'Can you tell me how to pronounce the place we're in?' And the waitress said, slowly and distinctly: 'Lit – tle Chef.'

English doesn't go in for long place-names. Indeed, the language as a whole doesn't go in for long words. I know there are competitions to find 'the longest word in English', and the winners always earn a place in the *Guinness Book of Records*. But that makes the point, really. Long words are the exceptions, so they fascinate us. Even quite young kids play with them. I learned to say *antidisestablishmentarianism* when I was nine. I still don't know what it means. There's no special interest in long words in Greenland Eskimo, where most of the words are lengthy.

Nobody knows what the longest word in English really is, anyway. That would be a scientific term – probably one of the terms in chemistry for some unbelievably complex molecule. No scientist would ever say it, of course. So when people hold competitions, there is usually a rider – the 'longest word in an English dictionary'. Which is also a cheat. Dictionaries don't always agree. If it's the *Oxford English Dictionary* (*OED*), it would be the forty-five-letter

pneumonoultramicroscopicsilicovolcanoconiosis

sometimes spelled with a *k* instead of its last *c*. It is a lung disease caused by breathing in particles of siliceous volcanic dust. It is another cheat. It was coined in 1935 by Everett Smith, the president of the US National Puzzlers' League, purely for the purpose of making sure he had found the longest word.

You can look for the longest word for ever, and not reach agreement about it. Does *supercalifragilisticexpialidocious* from *Mary Poppins* count? Or is that excluded because it is a nonsense word? I don't know.

Llanfairpwll may be recognized as having the longest place-name in the UK, but it isn't the longest one in English. There are lakes in the USA, named in American Indian languages, which are much longer. And there is the eighty-five-letter monster in New Zealand, coming from Maori. But there's nothing to match it in the UK. The nearest is the eighteen-letter *Blakehopeburnhaugh*, a hamlet in the Redesdale Forest in Northumberland. The name is a combination of four words of Old English origin – 'black' + 'valley' + 'stream' + 'area of flat riverside land'. I think it's the longest. I haven't found anywhere longer with Anglo-Saxon (as opposed to Celtic) origins – yet.

If you go there – as a linguist would, just to see – you might notice a sign to *Cottonshopeburnfoot*, half a mile up the valley, and think to yourself, wait a minute, that's got nineteen letters. But spaces and hyphens aren't usually allowed to count, when you're searching for long place-names. It has to be a single word. And on the Ordnance Survey map this place is written *Cottonshopeburn Foot*.

You could cheat, of course, and let hyphens in. Then you will find *Stratton-on-the-Fosse* in Somerset, *Winchester-on-the-Severn* in Maryland, and a host of others. I don't know what the longest hyphenated place-name is in England. Someone will probably write and tell me. I'd like to know. It would be another piece fitted into the jigsaw puzzle of facts that make up the English language.

The valley of Redesdale is an interesting place. It has for centuries been an important route from England into Scotland. Today it contains the A68, winding its way towards Jedburgh and Edinburgh. Spectacular scenery, well worth a leisurely drive. The road crosses the border six miles to the north-west of Carter Bar.

Carter Bar was the scene of one of the last battles fought between the English and the Scots – the so-called Redeswire Fray. A fray is a 'fight'. It's a shortened version of the word *affray*. Neither word is used much now, except in legal contexts. But it may be getting a new lease of life. It is the name of a US rock band as well as of a fantasy comicbook by Joss Whedon, the creator of the TV show *Buffy the Vampire Slayer*.

The fight was in 1575. The Warden of the English Marches had an argument with the Keeper of Liddesdale, and it escalated into a violent confrontation. Several men were killed. The English had the worst of it. The irony is that the meeting took place on a day of truce, and both men had been employed to keep the peace on their own side of the border.

I knew my Scottish farmer was local when he said 'Llanfairpwll'. Only locals say that. Moreover, he said the Welsh 'double-*l*' very accurately. He had obviously lived here long enough to master it. But that didn't make sense. How could he have lived here so long and yet kept his Scottish accent so strong?

'How long have you been in Anglesey, then?' I asked him.

'I came here in '65.'

I did a swift calculation. That's *forty years*.

'And where did you grow up?'

'Near Galashiels.'

I'd been there. It's just a few miles north of Jedburgh. On a road off the A68.

'How come you've not lost your accent?'

'I reckon I was too old to change. I was in me forties when I got here.'

In his forties. How old *was* this man!

He was right. An accent would be thoroughly established by then, and it would take a huge change in circumstances to shift it. Accents exist to express your identity. They tell people where you are from. And they get established very early in life. Children have them by the age of three. New accents come easily during childhood and into the teenage years. When a family moves from one part of the country to another, it's invariably the children who pick up the new accent first.

But no accent is immune from its surroundings. And, indeed, in the old farmer's voice I could hear the occasional Welsh lilt. I wanted to hear more of it. So I asked him about his stick.

'I always thought shepherds had crooks,' I said.

'Ay,' he said, 'that's true, but I haven't meself for quite a while.'

He paused. 'Did ye know that there are different kinds of crooks?'

He said the word with a long *oo*, as in *croon*.

I had to confess I didn't. My definition of *crook* would be a stick with one end bent into a hooked sort of shape. I was vague about why. The linguist in me suggested a link with *by hook or by crook*, but I couldn't immediately think of a good reason why this phrase should have come into existence.

The next five minutes was a tutorial on crooks. I hadn't realised crook-making was such a precise craft. And I hadn't realised that classic crooks have hooks at both ends, one larger than the other. One end is large enough to catch hold of a sheep's neck; the other end is smaller, for catching hold of the hind foot. He called it a 'leg cleek'. I heard it as 'clayk', and only established the spelling when I looked it up later. Not an everyday word. It took me three dictionaries to find it. Never an easy matter finding a word in a dictionary if you don't know how to spell it. *Cleak*? *Cliek*? *Cleke*?

It seems to have been a Scottish word originally, in the fifteenth century. A hook for catching hold of something, or pulling something, or hanging something up. Fishermen used it a lot. And then it turned up again in the nineteenth century, in golf, referring to a type of club. There's an early instance recorded in 1829: golfers at St Andrews are described as swinging their 'drivers and cleeks'. At that time it was spelled *cleques*.

In parts of Scotland, to this day, if someone calls you *cleeky*, they mean you're grasping, captious.

And in the jazz era it turned up again, meaning a wet blanket at a party, a party-pooper. Beatniks in the US used it in the 1960s for any sad or melancholy person. Could that be the same word? Did it cross the Atlantic with some Scots emigrants?

I learned from my farmer friend that the space between the shank and the nose of a neck crook was usually the width of the four fingers of a person's hand. It should be wide enough to comfortably slip over the forearm. The leg cleek has a width of one old English penny. That would make it about three centimetres.

He also mentioned that the crook had been used for fighting in the old days. He didn't say how old those days were, or who were the fighters. English and Scots shepherds at Carter Bar, perhaps? Later, I recounted this conversation to a friend who's into martial arts in a big way, and he wasn't at all surprised. He'd used sticks in some fights, and he could see the value of having one with two hooks, especially if they were good at trapping necks and legs. And then he asked me: 'Is that where *by hook or by crook* comes from?'

I was at home at the time, so wordbooks were everywhere. I found references to the phrase in three books straight away – and found three different explanations. That's the trouble with folk idioms. The origins of many of them are lost, and people have to start guessing where they came from. Quite often there are some nice pieces of real evidence from literature or history.

The first use of *hook and crook* seems to have been in the writing of the Bible translator John Wiclife – or Wycliffe, as he is usually spelled today. That was around 1380. He wrote about the sale of sacraments and people being made to buy them 'with hook or crook'. Plainly the phrase already had its modern meaning, 'by all possible means, fair or foul'. The modern expression, with *by* used twice, is known from at least 1529.

When a dictionary says a word was first recorded at such-and-such a date, you have to take it with a pinch of salt. It might mean that the word was invented in that year, but it usually doesn't. People have generally been using a word for a while before it gets written down. In the Middle Ages, when things weren't written down all that often, a phrase like *hook and croo*k would probably have been in everyday speech for decades before the 1380s. Wycliffe had a good ear for common idiom, and tried to make his translation of the Bible as down-to-earth as possible. If *he* used the phrase, it was certainly out on the street.

The two words *hook* and *crook* had already been in English for several hundred years. *Hook* is found in Old English, in the tenth century, with the same meaning that it has today. *Crook* comes into the language in the early thirteenth century, with a meaning very similar to *hook*. The sense used in shepherding can be traced from the early 1400s. All sorts of other meanings followed. The 'criminal' sense grew up in US slang towards the end of the nineteenth century. And in Australia and New Zealand, the word developed a general sense as an adjective meaning 'bad', 'useless', 'unsatisfactory', 'malfunctioning'.

When I was last in Australia I didn't feel so well at one point. Somebody said: 'You feelin' a bit crook?' He was asking if I felt ill.

The most likely origin of *by hook or by crook* lies in a medieval countryside practice. The forests of medieval Britain belonged to the king, and trees could not be cut down without permission. The penalties were ferocious. So how would people get wood for their fires? They were allowed to use branches that had fallen on the ground. And they were also allowed to cut any dead wood from a tree if it could be reached with a shepherd's crook or the hooked tool used by a reaper. The Bodmin Register of 1525 refers to local people being allowed to 'bear away upon their backs a burden of lop, crop, hook, crook, and bag wood'.

If you go to the New Forest, you will see a plaque, the Rufus Stone, just off the A31 near Ringwood, marking the place where King William II was killed. There are clear signposts on the main road. Its inscription reads:

> Here stood the oak tree on which an arrow shot by Sir Walter Tyrrell at a stag glanced and struck King William II surnamed Rufus on the breast of which stroke he instantly died on the second day of August anno 1100. King William thus slain was laid on a cart belonging to one Purkess and drawn from hence to Winchester, and buried in the Cathedral Church of that City.

Nearby, in the Sir Walter Tyrrell pub, you can reflect on the fact that Purkess was rewarded with permission to gather all the wood he could reach 'by hook or crook'. Several generations of the Purkess family are buried in the cemetery of All Saints Church in Minstead, and the Purkiss name is still known in the area.

If you visit the churchyard, prepare to be distracted by Sherlock Holmes enthusiasts. Behind the church, under an oak, is the grave of Sir Arthur Conan Doyle.

An Irish origin has also been claimed for the phrase. In 1170 Richard de Clare, 2nd Earl of Pembroke, known as 'Strongbow', sailed into Waterford harbour as part of Henry II's Irish campaign. He saw a tower on one side and a church on the other. On being told that it was the 'Tower of Hook' (in County Wexford) and the 'Church of Crook' (in County Waterford), he is reported to have said, 'We shall take the town by Hook and by Crook.' There are several variations of the story in Irish folklore. Cromwell is supposed to have said the same thing in 1650 when he was attacking Waterford.

I never got a chance to ask my Scottish-Welsh farmer if he had any opinions about the origins of *by hook or by crook*. My BBC producer, apparently sensing that something was not going as expected, appeared from within a flock of sheep-farmers. She had found somebody she wanted me to talk to. I thanked my friend for his company, and was just walking away from him when I felt my arm being tugged backwards. I looked down at it. There was a crook round it, holding it tight. I looked back at the farmer.

'You should be interviewing the sheep, ye know,' he said.

'Excuse me?'

'They don't bleat the same down here as they do in Scotland.'

'You don't say.'

'Ay, it's a Welsh accent, ye see.'

2

Making a Beeline

MENAI

Later, as I got into my car, I looked out at the sheep, thousands of sheep, and ruminated about their accents. Five sheep for every person in the county, so they say. The face of my Gaerwen shepherd had been unmoving as he said it, no sign of a wink or a smile. Had he been joking? The notion wasn't totally absurd. Why shouldn't sheep have accents? If farmers can distinguish their breeds by the way they look, why not by the way they sound? I wonder if Karl von Frisch ever studied sheep?

Probably not. Bees were his thing. And fish. But mainly bees. I still have the copy of a *Scientific American* article he wrote in 1962: 'Dialects in the Language of the Bees'. It led me to his book, written a few years before, translated into English as *The Dancing Bees*. Von Frisch was director of the Zoological Institute at Munich University, and in the 1920s he began a lifelong series of experiments into the way bees communicate with each other. It got him a share of the 1973 Nobel Prize for Physiology/Medicine.

Observers of nature know that when a single forager bee finds a good source of nectar, within an hour or so dozens, maybe hundreds, of bees will have found their way to the place. Evidently, the pioneer bee has returned to the hive and 'told' the others about the location of the food. But how? Von Frisch and his colleagues discovered that the information was being conveyed through a pattern of repeated body movements which he called 'dancing'.

It was taking a while to get out of the sheep-market car park. I had to negotiate my way through a slow reversing dance of Range Rovers and sheep trailers, as they manoeuvred to offload their noisy contents into the sheep pens. A bee floated indecisively across my windscreen, plainly not on a von Frisch mission.

How had he worked it out? The researchers' method was to put a small dish of sugar water some distance from the hive. The dish might not be discovered for several days, but as soon as one bee found it, and returned to the hive, others soon emerged and made their way to *exactly* the place where the dish was. It seemed to be precision navigating.

The first time I read about this research, I remember thinking: how on earth could you keep track of a single bee within a hive? But there was a simple solution. The researchers marked the pioneer forager with a coloured dot while it was feeding, so that they could track its movements when it returned. The hive had glass walls so that they could see what was happening inside. And there they saw the dance – a 'round' dance, with the bee turning in circles alternately to the left and the right.

The behaviour has now been observed by hundreds of researchers. It's been filmed, and – these days – computer-analysed. The dance is evidently saying, 'Hey, everyone, come and see what I've found, not far away!' If the nectar source is especially rich, the dance language is especially lively. 'Hey, you *really* have to see this!'

I finally got out of the sheep-market, and followed the little back road around to the junction with the A5 at the edge of Gaerwen, near where the Lit – tle Chef used to be. It's a quiet road now. The new dual-carriageway A55 across Anglesey took most of the traffic away, and the café went with it. But there are enough points of interest along the A5 to keep the tourists coming. Llanfairpwll is just a couple of miles away, on the edge of the Menai Straits that separate Anglesey from the Welsh mainland. I always have a linguistic compulsion to avoid the bypass and drive along its main street, just to take in the long name outside the railway station.

Things have changed in Llanfairpwll. During the later decades of the last century you would see navy cadets (of both sexes) walking around the village. They were from the Royal Navy shore-based training school on the edge of the Menai Straits. The name of the school, inherited from a famous training vessel of the past, was on the front of their caps. It said simply *Indefatigable*. The school closed in 1995, and with it went an era of risqué jokes.

These days Llanfairpwll has another magnet as well as the name: Pringle's knitwear store – though its racks of souvenir mugs, books, and teatowels have added fresh nuances to the definition of 'knitting'. Several tourist buses were lined up outside, and their contents were dancing to and fro at the entrance, excitedly pointing out things in the shop to one another. 'Hey, you *really* have to see this!'

A busload of Japanese tourists was posing for a photograph in front of the long name on the shop and trying to pronounce it. The one at the railway station has a pseudo-phonetic transcription underneath it, which I suppose helps.

One of the buses was having some difficulty negotiating the turn into the car park, so a small traffic jam built up. While I waited for it to clear, I looked across at the buzzing forecourt. Just inside the door of the shop there is one of those signposts which gives distances and directions to major cities. It tells you that it is 6,879 miles to Buenos Aires that way (past Aberystwyth and keep going) and 5,923 miles to Tokyo this way (via Benllech). It is also 9,898 miles from Llanfairpwll to the South Pole.

I expect when the tourists get back home they will tell their friends about where they have been, and more will come.

That seems to be what happened to von Frisch's bees. When the forager did its round dance, the nearby bees got the message, detected the scent of the kind of flower on the forager's body, and flew off to look for it. When they found it, they too returned to the hive and did a similar dance. And so it went on, with more and more bees making the visit, until most of the nectar had been drained from the source. Late arrivals at the flower then found little to feed on, so when they returned to the hive they had, quite literally, nothing to make a buzz and dance about. Their dancing movements were slow or they stopped altogether. 'Don't bother going!' And the other bees, noting the inactivity, stayed put – until the next excited forager arrived with news of a fresh source of nectar.

There was no danger of the Pringle's source being totally drained. Indeed, as I waited for the traffic to clear, I could see a delivery van unloading fresh supplies. Nectar yesterday, nectar tomorrow, and always nectar today.

The round dance is enough to indicate the source if it's fairly near to the hive – von Frisch thought within about 275 feet or so – but if it's a lot further away, such as a mile or more, something more precise is needed. That's when the bees do the 'tail-wagging' dance. Inside the hive, the forager runs a short distance in a straight line, wagging its abdomen from side to side, then returns in a semi-circle to the starting point. It repeats the run, and comes back in a semi-circle on the opposite side. Then it does the whole cycle again – and again . . .

It's the tempo of the dance that signals the distance from the source. For instance, in one experiment, a feeding dish was placed a thousand feet away, and the bee that discovered it performed fifteen complete cycles of the dance in thirty seconds. When the dish was placed two thousand feet away, the number dropped to eleven. The further away, the fewer the cycles.

And how do they work out the direction of the food? That's shown by the straight-line part of the dance. If the dance is done on the platform in front of a hive, in the light of day, the orientation of the bee's body along the line with respect to the sun is enough to point other bees directly towards the goal. Inside the hive, where it's dark, the bee's sense of gravity allows it to make an upwards movement against the honeycomb wall. It's as if the bee draws a straight vertical line on the wall. If it then runs straight up the line, this tells the others that the food is in the same direction as the sun. If the food is, say, forty degrees to the left of the sun, the run points forty degrees to the left of this line.

It's an amazingly sophisticated system, with modifications built in to allow for the sun's movement across the sky. And it works. When other bees fly out, they know that the nectar source is, say, about half a mile away at a bearing of forty degrees left, and – from the excitement of the dance – how much nectar is likely to be there. And that's the source they go for, ignoring everything else on the way. In one series of experiments, von Frisch placed other food dishes between the hive and the nectar source that the pioneer forager had found. The other bees flew straight over them, making a beeline, as it were, only for the source they'd been told about.

The bus that had been causing all the trouble finally made it into its parking bay, but my little traffic jam stayed put. A tractor was trying to follow it in, and that was now blocking the road. What on earth was a farmer doing at Pringle's at this time of day? As it slewed around, I could see it was pulling a trailer with two sheep in it. Now that's what I call service. Out of the field, into the Gaerwen auction, and onto a Pringle's shelf, all in one afternoon.

I could hear the sound of the sheep above the noise of the traffic. Were there Welsh-English bleatlects? I fantasized about an article: 'Dialects in the Language of the Sheep'. Von Frisch's first experiments had used black Austrian honeybees. He then carried out some further experiments using Italian honeybees. The Italians restricted their round dances to distances of only thirty feet. For intermediate distances they performed a 'sickle-shaped' dance, which the Austrians did not do. Then, for distances over 120 feet they did the tail-wagging dance, but rather more slowly than the Austrians.

As a result, when the Austrian and Italian bees were placed in the same hive, the wagging dance of the Italians made the Austrians search for the feeding place too far away. And vice versa. They seemed to understand each other, but not exactly. Just like the dialects of human language, really, von Frisch thought.

If he'd studied the buzzing, he might have said accents too. I wonder if the sound of the buzz alters in proportion to the excitement?

The bee-dancing hypothesis was received with considerable scepticism at first. Later observations showed that the time it took for bees to arrive at the source was usually longer than von Frisch had predicted. Maybe it was all a mixture of chance, sight, and scent after all? But in 2005 a research team made more precise measurements to show that von Frisch's dancing theory was right.

They used a method called harmonic radar – a system first used to track the location of avalanche victims. A tiny transponder was attached to a bee, and this returned radar signals enabling its flight path to be plotted. The team was able to demonstrate that the waggle dance was enough to enable most of the bees to reach the vicinity of the food. But they then needed sight and odour to pinpoint the final destination.

That was why von Frisch's bees took longer than expected to reach the food. The dance got them to the railway station, as it were, but they had to find the right platform for themselves.

The busload of Japanese tourists had found their way onto the station platform and had lined up under the name sign. They were having trouble working out how to stand in front of it without obscuring the letters. The photographer was having trouble too, getting everybody into his shot. He backed away, momentarily forgetting that the railway line was right behind him. An eruption of Japanese – which, roughly translated, said, 'Excuse our temerity in troubling you, Hiro, but you are about to fall onto a railway track and there is a train coming' – kept him safe.

After the train had passed he solved his problem by taking the photograph from the opposite platform. And his subjects solved theirs by having some of their party sit down on the ground in front of the name sign. It looked as if the letters were sprouting out of their heads.

Suddenly the jam cleared, and I drove on, leaving the sheep and Japanese behind. The road out of Llanfairpwll runs alongside the Menai Straits, and if you pull into a lay-by there is a splendid view of the two bridges – Thomas Telford's fine Menai Suspension Bridge to the north, and the later Britannia Bridge, originally built by Robert Stephenson, a mile and a half to the south.

The suspension bridge was opened on 30 January 1826. It was one of the highest bridges of its day, because the Admiralty insisted that there should be room beneath it to allow the passage of sailing ships. It's a hundred-foot drop to the water below. It carried the A5 from London to Holyhead – the first British road instituted by an Act of Parliament. The Irish Act of Union had been passed in 1801. Once the link was completed, Irish MPs would be able to make the journey down to the Houses of Parliament in two days instead of four.

Before the bridge there were only ferries – six main services, running at different points along the Straits, each under the control of a local landowner. A highly competitive business it was, I suppose much like the local taxi businesses in the area today. Apart from the time involved, and the danger from the strong currents, it could be expensive. Who pays the ferryman? You did – and sometimes twice! Some boatmen would charge you when you got onto the boat, and then charge you again before they let you off.

The ferry owners were totally against the project, but they were overruled by London, and work started on the bridge in 1819. Limestone was quarried at Penmon a few miles north, and carried down by boat. The ironwork was made at a Shrewsbury foundry. To prevent rust, it was immersed in warm linseed oil.

Lewis Carroll had a different idea. In Chapter 8 of *Through the Looking Glass* he has the White Knight come up with a unique preservation scheme. The Knight has been singing a song to Alice about the life-story told to him by 'an aged, aged man, a-sitting on a gate'. Then, quite out of the blue, he reflects:

> I heard him then, for I had just
> Completed my design
> To keep the Menai Bridge from rust
> By boiling it in wine.

A-sitting. That use of *a-* goes back to the Middle Ages. It is historically a form of *on*, which came to be used to emphasize the duration of an action, and especially its repeated character. If you were 'a-shouting', as Casca says the people do at the beginning of Shakespeare's *Julius Caesar*, you would be engaged in that activity for longer than if you were just 'shouting'. You would be shouting over and over.

Why does Carroll use it here? *Sitting* isn't a verb which needs an *a-* prefix. It is already expressing a continuous duration. The aged man wasn't sitting repeatedly on his gate. So you wouldn't expect to find an *a-* used.

What happened was that poets started to use the prefix to make up the 'te-tum-te-tum' rhythm of a line. It was a bit cheeky, really, but the nuance added by *a-* was so slight that it hardly made any difference. And it was an easy 'fix'.

The stratagem was a boon to anyone making up simple rhymes:

> *Bye, baby bunting. Daddy's gone hunting.*

Doesn't work.

> *Bye, baby bunting. Daddy's gone a-hunting.*

Works.

So, 'A-hunting we will go . . .', 'Here we come a-wassailing . . .' – and 'an aged, aged man, a-sitting on a gate'.

That day in June 2005, as I passed by, they were preserving the bridge again, but totally ignoring Carroll's advice, for there was no wine in sight. They were three months into the painstaking task of stripping off the old paint down to the bare metal and repainting. It would take them several months to finish, and in the meantime one side of the bridge was covered with scaffolding. Only one lane of the bridge was open. In the morning it took the traffic across from Anglesey to the mainland, and then at 2 p.m. the flow reversed. Hard luck if you arrived at the Anglesey side at one minute past two. You had to find another way – or wait a day, of course.

Fortunately, there is another way. Just a few years after Telford's bridge was opened, plans were drawn up by Robert Stephenson for a bridge to carry the London–Holyhead railway across the Straits. To take the weight of a train, he designed a bridge consisting of two rectangular wrought-iron tubes, ten feet apart, one of which enclosed the up-line and the other the down-line. A protective wooden roof was added, covered with hessian and coated with tar, along the whole length of the bridge. There was a gap of a couple of feet between the roof and the top of the tubes.

The tubes were 150 feet above the water, supported by five tall masonry towers, again using Penmon limestone. Each tower was surmounted by a stone structure, which gave the bridge a distinctive fort-like silhouette. Four limestone lions, about thirteen feet in height, guarded the bridge, two at each end. They were carved by John Thomas, who had previously worked at the Houses of Parliament and Buckingham Palace.

Would the tubes take the weight of a train? To be on the safe side, Stephenson allowed for suspension chains in his design, and put slots into the top of the arches above the bridge. But it proved to be an unnecessary precaution. A model of the bridge was built and tested, and the tubular construction went ahead without chains. The bridge was opened on 5 March 1850, and trains passed comfortably to and fro for 120 years. The slots now look rather ominous as you approach them – like pairs of beady eyes.

I remember travelling by steam train through the bridge in the 1950s, to and from Holyhead. If the window of your compartment was open – and as a child you tried to make sure it was – you would soon be covered with wonderful smoke and ash, and your ears would ring with the whistle of the engine as it entered the tunnel and the deafening noise of the train in the confined space.

Then, on the evening of Saturday, 23 May 1970, the bridge burned down. A group of local teenagers had gone into the tunnel on the Caernarfonshire side to see what it was like, and lit some paper for illumination a few yards inside. They dropped it accidentally, and other rubbish alongside the track caught fire. The mixture of wood, hessian, and tar, and the draught tunnel formed by the roof space, did the rest.

The problem for the fire brigade was that the entrance to the tubes was difficult to access – they had to negotiate three-quarters of a mile of rough track. There were no pressure water supplies in the area, and the nearest static water was the Menai Straits, 450 yards away down a one-in-three gradient.

By the time they got some water onto it, the fire had taken hold. One of the red-hot girders even snapped in half when water was sprayed upon it. It was a raging inferno inside the roof space – though curiously, because of the enclosed nature of the bridge, for some time no fire could be seen from the outside. But once it broke through, the line of flames extending across the Straits was as spectacular as it was horrific. You can see a video clip, and an interview with one of the teenagers, at a BBC Wales website.

One estimate of the damage was over £1 million, but as the bridge cost over £600,000 to build in 1850, that was surely a low guess. The railway was out of action for four years. Irish ferries to and from Holyhead had to be diverted to Morecambe. The economy of the area took years to recover.

A new single-track railway bridge was back in action in 1974, supported by arches, and they put a road on top of it in 1980. It's now the main link between Anglesey and the mainland, carrying the A55. Three of the imposing towers are still there, and the road passes underneath them, right on top of the railway line.

You can't see the lions from the road, but they're still there too, beside the railway. You can visit the two on the Anglesey side if you take a path by the Carreg Bran Hotel. A small section of the original tubular bridge is also displayed on the Bangor side. You can see it from the train.

I was planning to head south into mid-Wales, where I had my next appointment with Welsh accents, so I took the Britannia Bridge out of Anglesey, and turned towards Caernarfon past the thousand-acre Vaynol estate. The Old Hall there dates back to Elizabethan times, and maybe earlier. These days they hold major cultural events in the park. Local boy Bryn Terfel started a glittering annual music festival there in 2000, and regularly performs there. They say that when he's singing you can hear him in Cardiff. Only when the wind's in the right direction, mind.

If you look carefully at the wall near the entrance, you can still see the faded image of a piece of anonymous biblical graffiti text, whose original white-paint impact has long been erased. I photographed it when it first appeared. It reads: *ALL SHALL BE WELL!*

All was well, and it was a fine sunny day when I stopped to eat a sandwich at the top of a hill overlooking the Straits. A lovely view back across Anglesey, and plenty of opportunity to observe bees – and wasps – out in force, and especially interested in my sandwich.

Dylan Thomas got it right about wasps. In his short story 'Conversation about Christmas' he tells a small boy about his childhood

Christmas presents. Some of them were books, he says, 'that told me everything about the wasp, except why'.

A bee meandered into view. It must have been the general impression of bees flying directly to their food or to the hive which led to the emergence of that phrase, *making a beeline*. In fact, radar – or for that matter, common observation – shows that there's nothing particularly straight about the flight-path at all. Bees wobble about a lot. Nor do they have the sense of urgency or rapid movement that is usually intended when someone is said to 'make a beeline' for something.

The earliest recorded usage of the phrase is 1830, but it must still have felt very new a decade later. When Edgar Allen Poe used it in one of his short stories, 'The Gold Bug', published in 1843, he felt he had to explain it. His character Legrand describes how he worked out where some pirate treasure was hidden. What he did, he says, was draw 'a bee-line, or, in other words, a straight line' from one point to another. That's a sure indication that a usage is recent. People don't bother explaining the sense of a word if it's well established.

It's hardly ever possible to say when a word first comes into a language. Who knows when *king* was first used, or *eggshell*, or *inconsequential*? Or *by hook and by crook*?

Just occasionally we can be in on a word-birth.

One such moment was in New York in 1907 at a publishing trade association dinner. Huebsch had just published a successful book by the American humorist Gelett Burgess, called *Are You a Bromide?* (A *bromide* was Burgess's word for a dull, conventional person.) Free copies were given out to those present, printed – as was the association's custom – in a special jacket.

Burgess was there, and he didn't like the jacket. He felt it was much too conventional. A much better idea, he thought, was the practice of contemporary lurid novels, which always had a delicious damsel posing on the front cover. So he decided to draw one. He sketched out a buxom blonde on one of the jackets, and labelled her 'Miss Belinda Blurb'.

The name caught on. Any excessive testimonial for a book, on front or back covers, was soon being called a *blurb*. In a little wordbook he wrote a few years later, he defined his own term:

> 1 A flamboyant advertisement; an inspired testimonial.
> 2 Fulsome praise; a sound like a publisher.

Blurbs have been with us ever since.

Actually, *blurb* was quite fortunate. Most of the words we make up on the spur of the moment never catch on. It doesn't matter even if you're gifted and famous. Shakespeare is the first recorded user of about two thousand words, but nearly half of them fell out of use sooner or later. From his list, we continue to use *abhorred*, *abstemious*, *accessible*, and *accommodation*; but nobody uses *adoptious*, *aidance*, *allayment*, or *annexment* any more.

Why did *abstemious* stay and *adoptious* go? One of the great mysteries of language change is why people decide to use one word and not another.

Sometimes you can sense the nature of the choices available. For instance, *frequency* is recorded in English from 1553. A century later, *frequentness* appeared. This is something which happens quite a lot. A word with a good Anglo-Saxon ending (such as *–ness*) is put into competition with an already existing word with a foreign ending (the Latin/French *–ency*, in this case). Which won? Today the dictionaries all include *frequency* and only occasionally even bother to mention *frequentness*.

Perhaps it was the shorter length of *frequency* which made it appeal. Or the desire to sound educated. Or the fact that it was recognized in the leading dictionaries. Or perhaps it wasn't so much that people preferred *frequency* as that they disliked *frequentness*. Maybe it was the slightly awkward pronunciation, as they tried to get their tongues around the *–ntn –* sequence in the middle. Maybe they didn't like the sound of the two *n*'s.

But *frequentness* didn't totally disappear. If you listen out in everyday conversation, you will quite often find the Anglo-Saxon constructions being used in place of the expected forms. I have heard *immenseness*, *immediateness*, and *delicateness* as well as *frequentness*. None of them is a recommended dictionary form. The dates of their earliest and latest recorded uses, according to the *OED*, are:

> immenseness: 1610–1798
> frequentness: 1664–1862
> delicateness: 1530–1873
> immediateness: 1633–1882

They should be dead; but they live on.

It's an interesting exercise to explore the use of suffixes, trying them out to see the different meanings and effects they convey. I tried it once with a school group. The idea was to see how many suffixes could attach to a noun like *bee*. Modern dictionaries usually don't give any. I found *bee-like* in one, and that was all.

Within minutes they had concocted a story about an imaginary *beedom* (from *kingdom*), in which a queen bee (*your beeness*) had offered *beehood* (from *knighthood*) to a brave worker who had saved the hive from attack. They went on to form a *beeocracy*. Outsiders who criticized their way of life were displaying *beeism* and considered *beeist*. The heroic worker was eventually *beeified*. And so it went on. It was like the unwritten script for an animal cartoon – the stuff of *Antz*.

The students weren't the first to think up *beedom*. The *OED* editors had already found an instance of it in 1868. They also found one use of *beeishness* in 1674. *Beedom* turns up several times in the writing of the missionary poet John Bradburne. It is the sort of word that gets repeatedly invented.

I wonder if von Frisch was ever stung? An occupational hazard of an entomologist, I imagine. And if I ever had the chance to do some detailed work on the languages and dialects of animals, I think I'd prefer sheep to bees, having been stung more than once.

Of course, all this talk of language and dialects is metaphorical when applied to animals. Von Frisch knew this very well. We can hardly compare the infinite possibilities of expression and comprehension mediated through human language to the limited set of instinctive reactions that we find in a bee, whose brain, he pointed out, is the size of a grass seed. And we would find huge limitations of communication, similarly, if we were to investigate the communicative patterns of larger-brained animals, such as we find in gull cries, thrush songs, ape calls – or sheep bleats.

We do keep underestimating the ability of animals to learn facets of language, though. For a long time, it was thought there were certain properties of language that animals could never learn, and this may still be true. Maybe the defining characteristic of humanity is indeed being 'Homo loquens', the speaking animal. But animal researchers have been steadily chipping away at the idea that there is a major evolutionary gap between humans and other species.

Some animals may not be able to speak, write, or sign in the way humans can; but they can do more than we might expect. Chimps can be taught manual signs. Parrots imitate a remarkable range of vocal sounds. Dogs recognize subtle tones of voice. There was even news, in

2006, of a species of African monkey that varied the sequence of calls in order to express different meanings – much as we vary word order in English. And in the same year a research team in California reported that they had taught some starlings to tell the difference between the song equivalent of simple sentences and those containing a song into which another bit of song had been inserted – in effect, a subordinate clause.

Actually, 2006 was quite a year, because in August there was a report suggesting that cows have regional accents too. Apparently some Somerset dairy farmers had noticed that cows have different moos, depending on which herd they come from. Mooolects. Maybe bleatlects aren't such a fantastic idea after all.

A huge flock of starlings flew towards me and then turned back at the last minute, as if they were wanting to keep out of Gwynedd. Maybe starlingese syntax is different there. Or maybe they understand more about human dialects than we give them credit for. If so, any especially sensitive starlings would steer well clear of the town I was about to pass through, Caernarfon.

There is an English four-letter taboo word beginning with the letter *c* which is so sensitive still, in the minds of many, that if I were to print it in full in this book I would cause unknown quantities of upset and complaint. So, not being in the business of upsetting readers, I will rely on folk memory to supply the missing word. And in case there are any who do not know what I am talking about, I will provide a clue in a couple of paragraphs' time.

In Caernarfon, this same word is used among some sections of the population as an amiable form of address. Much as you might hear 'Hello, mate' as a friendly greeting, so in the streets of Caernarfon you can hear an affable 'Hello, c——.' Anywhere else in the UK, such a greeting would earn you a black eye at least. But not here.

Book publishers are able to eliminate such words at an early stage, if they want to. But what do you do with the Internet? The search engines had a real problem when they first tried to devise filters which would identify pages containing offensive words or images. They thought that all they had to do was have a piece of software search through a page, and if it found a string of letters which added up to a potentially sensitive word, they would block access to it.

The only thing was, the software didn't make a distinction between the string of letters when it was a separate word and the string when it was part of a word. So, the search engine having decided that *sex* was a 'bad word', the residents of Sussex and Essex found they were unable to access many web pages relating to their counties. Not to mention the good citizens of Scunthorpe.

Software is a bit more advanced these days, but it still lacks the kind of linguistic sophistication which is needed to ensure that basic blunders are avoided. A couple of years ago, there was an Internet news page that reported a street stabbing in Chicago. The automatically-generated ads down the side of the screen said 'Buy your knives here' and 'Get cheap knives here'. The dumb software had spotted the word *knife* and assumed that this was what needed to be plugged. It wasn't clever enough to analyse the content of the page and see that, if there were to be any ads at all, they should be about personal protection.

Publications go to extraordinary lengths sometimes to protect their readers from the shock of encountering a taboo word. Even dictionaries. In the 1940s, Eric Partridge's *Dictionary of Slang and Unconventional English*, the first to pay full and detailed attention to all four-letter words, was banned by some libraries and placed on the reserved shelves by others. If you were interested in slang and asked to see it, the librarian would look you up and down as if you were a pervert.

Modern dictionaries generally include all taboo words, marking them with a stylistic label such as 'taboo' or 'offensive'. But even these sometimes back away from a full frontal presentation. I have a dictionary, published not very long ago, where the last word on the right-hand page to be given a definition is *fuck*. This should therefore appear as the guide-word (or 'running head') at the top right-hand corner of the page. But it doesn't. Instead we see its alphabetical predecessor, *fuchsia*.

As I drove through Caernarfon, past the castle, I stopped at a zebra crossing to let a young man cross. He had just stepped onto the crossing when a car coming from the opposite direction zipped past in front of him, giving him a bit of a fright. He shouted after the miscreant. It was the *c*-word again, but not at all affable this time.

3

We Want Information

The road south from Caernarfon into mid-Wales runs along the Lleyn peninsula then cuts across through Porthmadog and past the Italianate village created by Clough Williams-Ellis in the 1920s in loving memory of his visits to Portofino, on the coast of north-west Italy. Portmeirion. I had to go and worship there, for a little while, because it was chosen as the location for *The Prisoner*, the 1960s cult television series starring Patrick McGoohan. I am of the generation that watched it assiduously, week by week, and puzzled over what on earth it was all about.

Portmeirion was 'the Village' where (it seemed) kidnapped spies and agents of all descriptions were kept for interrogation, so that whatever data they had in their heads might be extracted for use by those (whoever they were) who were in charge. McGoohan's character has suddenly resigned from his job in British intelligence. He is followed home, put to sleep with a gas spray, and taken to the Village. Each episode begins with his character, now a prisoner, waking up in his new bedroom and having an exchange with the Village's current second-in-command ('Number 2').

PRISONER: Where am I?
NUMBER 2: In the Village.

PRISONER: What do you want?

NUMBER 2: Information.

PRISONER: Whose side are you on?

NUMBER 2: That would be telling. We want information. Information. Information.

PRISONER: You won't get it.

NUMBER 2: By hook or by crook, we will.

PRISONER: Who are you?

NUMBER 2: The new Number 2.

PRISONER: Who is Number 1?

NUMBER 2: You are Number 6.

PRISONER: I am not a number. I am a free man!

Despite their hook and crook, the Village guardians don't get their information. And at the end of the series, McGoohan triumphs (possibly).

The surreal location, and the ingenious, ambiguous 'Big Brother is watching you' plots, a combination of thriller, fantasy, and science fiction, reinforced by quirky music, clever camerawork, crisp editing and colourful design, resulted in a series now acknowledged to have been well ahead of its time. I especially admired the quickfire dialogue, with its contagious catch-phrases, and forty years on still find myself saying 'Be seeing you' as a farewell – the *au revoir* that all brainwashed inmates of the Village had been programmed to say.

Catch-phrases are notoriously difficult things to pin down, as they rarely get into dictionaries. Often, by the time lexicographers come to be aware of them, they are already on their way out, so they are never recorded at all. In any case, they don't easily fit into a dictionary format. A dictionary is not the obvious place to put 'Be seeing you,' for instance. Or Victor Meldrew's 'I don't beLIEVE it!' from *One Foot in the Grave*.

Many catch-phrases are generated by particular radio or television series, or by TV advertising slogans, and last only as long as the transmissions take place. 'Can I do you now sir?' from the radio show

ITMA in the 1940s. 'Are you sitting comfortably?' from *Listen with Mother* in the 1950s. 'There's no answer to that,' from *The Morecambe and Wise Show* in the 1960s. 'And now for something completely different,' from *Monty Python* in the 1970s.

There can be huge generational gaps in communication – teenagers not understanding adult catch-phrases and, even more so, adults not understanding the latest teenage linguistic fashions. Nor are catch-phrases much recognized outside the country in which they originate. Most British catch-phrases are not known in America, and vice versa. PC Dixon's 'Evenin' all,' from the 1950s and '60s television series *Dixon of Dock Green*, never travelled across the Atlantic. Nor did 'Gissa job' (= 'Give us a job' in Liverpool dialect), from Alan Bleasdale's 1980 television play *Boys from the Blackstuff*, and the series it inspired.

A favoured few phrases catch the public linguistic imagination, and live on. Some of them eventually become part of the mainstream of English usage, and their origin is lost to memory. Who now knows which film Western originally inspired 'A man's gotta do what a man's gotta do'? And how many of us are aware that it was Al Jolson, in the first talking film, *The Jazz Singer* (1927), who gave us 'You ain't heard nothin' yet'? Such phrases have refreshed parts of our linguistic intuition that other phrases have not reached.

For some (especially younger) readers, that last sentence will seem to be an original piece of literary expression, perhaps admired for its metaphorical ingenuity, more likely condemned as a piece of intellectual self-indulgence. Others (slightly less young) will nod wisely, and remember the original lager slogan which ran from the 1970s for some twenty years: 'Heineken refreshes the parts other beers cannot reach'.

A significant amount of our daily language is a matter of recalling our individual past linguistic experiences, reflecting old interests and habits. Catch-phrases tell others what we have watched or listened to. If you have experienced the same happenings, you recognize the allusions and respond with pleasure. If you haven't, you would probably think the behaviour puerile. Nudge, nudge, wink, wink. Say no more. Know what I mean?

When phrases are consciously taken from literature or high oratory, they are usually called 'quotations'. Some people sprinkle them throughout their speech and writing. They may not know their origins, of course. 'A thing of beauty is a joy for ever.' 'O, what a tangled web we weave . . .' 'You're a better man than I am, Gunga Din.' If they escape your memory, a book of quotations will tell you that these are from John Keats, Walter Scott, and Rudyard Kipling, respectively.

Some quotations have become so familiar that they have entered the standard everyday language. 'The plot thickens', from George Villiers' play *The Rehearsal*. 'Ships that pass in the night', from Longfellow's poem-saga *Tales of a Wayside Inn*. 'Having your pound of flesh' and 'to the manner born' from Shakespeare. 'Six of one and half a dozen of the other' from Frederick Marryat's novel *The Pirate* – or, of course, from *The Prisoner*.

Misquotations enter the standard language too. Sherlock Holmes never said 'Elementary, my dear Watson.' Ingrid Bergman never said, 'Play it again, Sam' (in the film *Casablanca*). Tarzan never said 'Me Tarzan, you Jane.' In each case, something similar *was* uttered, but it is the misremembered versions which have come down to us.

Catch-phrases help people to bond. Conversely, a difference of taste in catch-phrases, as George Eliot nearly said, 'is a great strain on the affections'. Only the most successful advertising campaigns, or the most reported public statements, manage to reach out to everyone, and transcend individual tastes. 'A diamond is forever,' from a campaign of 1939. 'Clunk, click, every trip,' from a 1971 road safety campaign. The slogan 'Drinka pinta milka day,' from 1958. That brought the word *pinta* into English.

You can, of course, keep linguistic memories alive artificially. This is what fanclubs and anniversary gatherings and appreciation societies do.

There is a *Prisoner* Appreciation Society. The society has a shop in

Portmeirion, in a building called the Round House, where they sell *Prisoner* books, recordings, and memorabilia. Each year they have a get-together in the village, and there is a tradition of re-enacting one of the scenes – the chess-match on the lawn from the episode called *Checkmate* in which the pieces are represented by Village inmates. Proper *Prisoner* dress is the order of the day. Everyone says 'Be seeing you,' when they leave. The appropriate response is 'And you.'

To reach the village you follow the A487 out of Porthmadog, past the station where the Ffestiniog steam railway begins, and across the mile-long embankment built by local landowner William Madocks in 1811, known as 'the cob', to reclaim land from the Traeth Mawr ('great beach') estuary. Madocks had hoped that the embankment, along with the new model village of Tremadog, which he was building nearby, would provide an attractive road route between London and Dublin. Unfortunately for him – though fortunately for Holyhead and Llanfairpwll – the commissioners decided on a northern route, across the Menai Straits, and, as we have seen, eventually got Thomas Telford to build it.

High tides in the winter of 1812 breached the cob. Hundreds of local men turned out to carry material to fill the gap, and the embankment was saved. But the disaster closed the cob for two years, and placed Madocks in serious financial trouble. He received welcome and un-expected support from the poet Shelley, who was passing through Wales at the time and looking for a place to escape the attentions of the authorities, who were concerned about his radical political views. Shelley was hugely enthusiastic about the Tremadog project, which he saw as a bold experiment in forming a new social community, so he decided to stay in the area and fund-raise on Madocks' behalf. He lived in a cottage in the grounds of Madocks' house. Much of his long philosophical poem 'Queen Mab' was written there.

The collaboration didn't last long. One night in February 1813, Shelley claimed that an attempt had been made on his life, and he immediately left the area. The event – if it was not simply hallucination

– has attracted endless speculation. Was it a government-inspired assassination attempt? Had his radical views upset local businessmen? Some think it was a clever scheme by local shepherds to drive him away. They had become upset at Shelley's practice of shooting any injured sheep which he encountered on his mountain walks. So one story goes.

Madocks' house, Plas Tan-yr-Allt, is now a hotel. The rooms are named after Madocks' guests. One is called Shelley's Theatre.

Madocks was saved by the development of the new slate quarries at Blaenau Ffestiniog, which used his embankment to export the slate via a nearby harbour, which was called Port Madoc – modern Porthmadog. A railway line was later built along the cob, alongside the road. It's a splendid tourist attraction today.

Cobs turn up in all kinds of places. There's another one on Anglesey, linking Holy Island to the Anglesey mainland. I suppose the most famous one in Britain is at Lyme Regis in Dorset, because it figured in Jane Austen's novels and also starred in the film *The French Lieutenant's Woman*.

Cob – or *cobb*, as it is sometimes spelled – is a curious word. It has a remarkable range of senses, some dating back to the fifteenth century. At one time or another it has referred to a well-built man, a type of gull, a herring, a male swan, a stout horse, and a spider (think of *cobweb*). Small haystacks, loaves of bread, certain types of nut, the tops of maize shoots, and even testicles have also been called *cobs*, as have Spanish dollars (the famous 'pieces of eight'), lumps of building material for walls, and small rounded stones for roadways, more commonly called *cobble stones*.

Which is where Lyme Regis comes in, for the cob there was originally made out of cobble stones.

The *OED* editors must have spent some time puzzling over this set of senses, but without coming to any definite conclusion. Are the meanings all related to each other, or do they have different points of origin? There seem to be three semantic themes involved. The notion of 'large in size' is there in such cases as the large men, swans, and horses – and probably also the pieces of eight, which were bigger than the average coin. The notion of 'head' or 'top' (compare German *Kopf*) is there in gulls and spiders and maize shoots. The notion of 'something rounded or forming a roundish lump' is there in most of the others.

It's hard to disentangle these notions in many instances. Was it the male swan's size relative to the female, or the rounded shape of its head, which caused it to be called a *cob*? And then there are the more abstract or figurative uses of the word, many of which are still found in dialects. To *give someone a cob* can mean to hit them. To *have a cob on* is to be in a bad mood. To *get a cob on* is to become sulky. I remember using those last two in Liverpool, where I lived as a teenager. But are these related to the other senses? Nobody knows.

At the end of the Porthmadog cob, on the left if you're driving towards Portmeirion, is a small house where until recently you had to pay a 5p toll per car – an unusual practice, to say the least, on a British A-class road. It's a legacy of William Madocks' original toll, which helped rescue him from financial difficulty. But it is no more. The road was nationalized by the Welsh Assembly in 2005.

The opening paragraph of the old toll-board is a *Roget's Thesaurus* of early-nineteenth-century vehicle names:

TOLLS TO BE TAKEN AT THIS GATE

For every Horse or other Beast of Draught drawing any Coach, Sociable, Berlin, Landau, Chariot, Vis-a-Vis, Chaise, Calash, Chaise-marine, Curricle, Chair, Gig, Whisky, Caravan, Hearse, Litter, Waggon, Wain, Cart, Dray, or other Carriage, any Sum not exceeding One Shilling:

For every Horse, Mare, Gelding, or Ass, laden or unladen, and not drawing, the Sum of Sixpence: but if there shall be more than one such Horse, Mare, Gelding, Mule, or Ass, belonging to the same Person, then the Sum of Sixpence shall be paid for one of them only, and the Sum of Threepence only for every other of them:

For every Drove of Oxen, Cows, or Neat Cattle, any Sum not exceeding Five Shillings per Score, and so in proportion for any greater or less Number:

For every Drove of Calves, Pigs, Sheep or Lambs, any Sum not exceeding Three Shillings and Sixpence per Score, and so in proportion for any greater or less Number:

And for every Person crossing or passing on Foot, without any beast or Carriage, any Sum not exceeding Two-pence.

The sign shows the eighteenth-century liking for capital letters on nouns considered to be important – *Coach*, *Mare*, *Pigs*, *Horse*, *Berlin*, *Person*, *Chaise* . . . , of course, as these are the critical factors; but also *Number*, *Sum*, and *Foot*, which the sign-writer felt needed extra prominence. The fashion for noun capitalization died out by the end of the century.

After you've crossed the cob, quite suddenly you turn right for Portmeirion. You have to be on your toes not to miss the turning. If you encounter a sign saying Penrhyndeudraeth, you've gone too far. That name means 'headland with two beaches'. In 1998 it became the first broadband-networked village in the UK.

TOLLS TO BE TAKEN AT THIS GATE

Actually, you don't have to go as far as Penrhyndeudraeth. Another sign just after the turning tells you that you've missed it.

The road down to the village winds for a mile through woodland and into the car park by the arched gatehouse which is the entrance to Portmeirion. You pay to get in, unless you're staying there, or dining in the hotel. But it's worth every penny. You'd have to travel to Portofino to have a comparable experience.

In his account of the development of Portmeirion, Clough Williams-Ellis describes his creation as full of 'wilful pleasantries, calculated

naivetes, eye-traps, forced and faked perspectives, heretical constructions, unorthodox colour mixtures, [and] general architectural levity'.
That's exactly what it's like. There is cheeky joy everywhere.

Noël Coward was one of many literary visitors. He stayed for a
week in the Watch House, arriving one Saturday and leaving the next.
In between he wrote *Blithe Spirit*.

I called in to the *Prisoner* shop, and bought yet another book on the
subject. As I left, I said 'Be seeing you,' to the man behind the counter.
He said, 'And you,' through a thin smile. The rest of his face held an
expression of extreme pity.

A sunny day, and Portmeirion was full of tourists. It's a small
place, really, with one steep windy road leading down to the sea,
and innumerable recesses and side turnings beckoning you towards
intricately landscaped gardens and visually teasing ornate façades. On
a tall pedestal, at the head of the long flight of steps leading to the
harbour, is a bronze statue of Hercules, standing in for Atlas, in a
heroic kneeling pose, carrying a huge stone globe on his shoulders.
Prisoner aficionados would of course see this as an allusion to the huge
bouncing balloon-entities, controlled by the Village guardians, that
prevented people escaping.

Thomas Telford turns up in Portmeirion. A tall building overlooking the piazza was erected in honour of the bicentenary of his
birth, in 1957. They call it Telford's Tower. Today it is a self-catering
cottage for three.

The compact layout of Portmeirion tends to push people towards
each other. That day in June it seemed there were more English accents
per square metre here than anywhere else in the world. And foreign
languages too. I heard five in as many footsteps.

I walked down to the water's edge, by the hotel. A group in front
of me were speaking Welsh. Having been listening to so many English
accents, it took me a bit by surprise. And yet this is a corner of the
traditional heartland of Welsh. Once upon a time it would have been

English that caused the surprise on the banks of Cardigan Bay. And indeed, in some Gwynedd villages English is still the exception rather than the rule.

Welsh has been the success story of the twentieth century when it comes to plotting the future of the world's endangered languages. And endangered they certainly are. It is thought that half the languages of the planet, some three thousand in all, are unlikely to survive to the end of the present century.

That's one language dying out somewhere in the world, on average, every two weeks.

About two thousand of those languages have never been written down. That's the savage part. For when a language dies that has never been written down, it is as if it has never been. And that means the irretrievable loss of another unique vision of what it means to be human.

Many of those endangered languages have only a few dozen or a few hundred speakers. Welsh, by contrast, has over half a million. About a fifth of the people of Wales speak Welsh, and the numbers are steadily increasing. It is the only Celtic language to have done so well. The activism of the 1970s and the subsequent Language Acts, giving measures of protection to the language, helped enormously. Plus radio and TV channels in the medium of Welsh.

I sat in the stone boat next to the hotel and looked across the Dwyryd estuary. It was early afternoon, and the tide was coming in. Some people were walking on the estuary sands in the distance. They would have to watch out. The sea comes in very quickly here, and it's easy to get cut off.

When was English first spoken along the banks of this estuary, I wondered. And when Welsh? And what was the language that was here before Welsh? Nobody knows how many languages have been spoken on earth since the human race developed the ability to speak. Some people think as many as 150,000. Maybe more. The six thousand or so we have left today are only a fraction of what may have been.

Sometimes you can see a trace of an earlier period of language inhabitation. In the territory between Spain and France you will find Basque, unrelated to any modern language, and in structure quite unlike the Indo-European languages surrounding it. People think it is the last example of the languages which were spoken in Europe before the invaders from Asia arrived.

The tide had almost reached the group walking on the sands, but they seemed oblivious. Some Portmeirion regulars were sitting nearby, bemoaning the way some people 'don't take any notice of the warnings'. The hotel staff were used to it. A man with a megaphone came out and bellowed. The walkers scuttled. I asked him whether this happened often. 'Not so much these days,' he said. 'The time of the high tide is printed on the ticket.'

His accent wasn't local, and I couldn't immediately place it. 'You don't sound as if you're from these parts, then?' I asked. I can never resist an unfamiliar accent.

Nor an unfamiliar name. Once I was looking for a particular old edition of *Hamlet*, and called an antiquarian book company that I thought might have it. The person who answered the phone said she would look, and asked me to call her back. 'Ask for Lassarina,' she said.

I couldn't stop myself. 'That's a lovely name,' I said. And as I said it, I thought, she'll think this is a come-on, so I hastily added, 'You see I'm a linguist and I'm interested in the history of names and I've not come across that one before and do you know what it means and how do you spell it?' Then I thought, that sounds totally implausible, even more of a come-on! But she reacted equably, and said she'd no idea, but thought it was Irish. She spelled it out, and told me her friends called her Lassie for short.

'Hold on a minute,' I said, and I rushed over to my bookcase, where I had some 'origins of names' books. There she was, *Lassarina*, an anglicized form of Gaelic *Lasairiona*, a combination of *lasair* and *fion*, 'flame' and 'wine'. I picked up the phone and told her. She was delighted. People usually are when you do a bit of etymological digging on their behalf.

I thought that piece of mini-research might get me a discount on my *Hamlet*, but no such luck. Maybe if I'd called her Lassie . . . But I couldn't do that to a non-canine.

Then, in one of those coincidences that make linguistic life worthwhile, I came across the name again a few weeks later. In Irish writer Padraic Colum's collection of stories called *The King of Ireland's Son*, published in 1916, there is a character called Lassarina.

'I'm from near Norwich,' the hotel man replied to my question about his origins. He pronounced it as a single syllable – 'norrch'. He added: 'Little place called Caistor.'

Caistor-by-Norwich. I knew it, Horatio. It's famous – at least to people interested in English historical linguistics. It's the place where they found the earliest runic inscription known in England. Caistor was originally a Roman base – the name comes from Latin *castra*, 'fort' – and in a cremation cemetery there they found the anklebone of a roe deer. It was probably used as a plaything – perhaps as part of a dice game – but what made it special was the inscription on the side: *raihan*, written in Germanic runes. *Raihan* means 'roe deer'.

The shape of the *H* rune attracted especial attention. It has a single cross-bar. This is typical of the kind of runic writing found in northern parts of Europe. Further south they wrote *H* with two cross-bars, ᚺ. This suggests that the person who wrote the inscription came from Scandinavia.

The significance of the find to linguists is that it dates from around the year AD 400. The Anglo-Saxons did not arrive in Britain until 449. This person was using a Germanic language in East Anglia well before the well-known Germanic invasions began.

East Anglia is *the* place to be if you are looking for early evidence of the English language. In 1981 a farmer found a gold bracteate – a kind of medallion, fashioned with eyelets so that it could be worn around the neck – at Undley Common, near Lakenheath in Suffolk. It dates from around AD 475, within a generation of the Anglo-Saxons arriving. It seems to be modelled after an old Roman coin from the time of Constantine the Great in the early fourth century. It shows a helmeted head of the emperor next to a she-wolf suckling two children – presumably a representation of the story of Romulus and Remus.

And there is an inscription: a sequence of runes, written around the edge from right to left. Transliterated into the Latin alphabet, the runes say *gægogæ mægæ medu*. It would have been pronounced roughly 'ga-gog-a ma-ga may-doo'. Inscriptions are often sentences. If so, this is the oldest known sentence in the language which would one day be called English. But what does it mean?

The second and third words aren't a problem. *Mægæ* probably comes from *mæg*, 'kinsman, companion'. Depending on how the ending is interpreted, the sense is either 'of a/the kinsman' or 'to a/the kinsman'. *Medu* is likely to be an early form of the word *med* or *meord* – meaning 'reward'. The closest modern equivalent is the archaism *meed*. An alternative suggestion is that it is something to do with the drink, 'mead'.

Scholars have puzzled over the first word. It has an unusual phonetic shape, with its three *g*s, suggesting it might be a nonsense word – a magical formula, perhaps, or a tribal shout of some kind. The form *gagaga* has been found on a sixth-century spear-shaft from Kragehul in Denmark, suggesting a battle-cry. And lots of magic words use a reduplicated sequence of sounds: *abracadabra*, *alakazam*, *hocus pocus* . . . Wizzo the wizard (aka American magician Marshall Brodien) says 'Doodee, doodee, doodee' to get a trick to work.

On the other hand, it could be a real word. There are words in Old English with three *g*s in them, such as *gegongan* ('conquer'), *gegogud* ('relying on'), *gegegnian* ('meet'). And there are words with similarities in form to which *gægogæ* could relate. The first syllable might be a prefix, an early form of *ge–*, which is common in Old English (as it is in modern German). The root of the word, *–go–*, might be related to a word such as *geomrian*, 'lament'. The ending might be a marker of femaleness. Thinking along these lines, the Swedish linguist Bengt Odenstedt suggested the reading 'howling female wolf', referring to the picture on the bracteate. There have been other interpretations.

If Odenstedt is right, then the inscription could mean 'this howling she-wolf to a kinsman [is] a reward'. It's certainly a plausible interpretation. But it's no more than a well-informed guess.

The Undley Bracteate, as it is called, is now in the British Museum, in the study collection of the Department of Medieval and Modern Europe. Other coins in the museum collection show runic inscriptions too, but they are usually even less decodable. The hope is that, as more finds are made, the semantic clues will increase, and things will become clearer. But often the finds just add even more puzzles.

In August 1997 a man with a metal detector found a gold coin at Billockby, a few miles north-west of Great Yarmouth in Norfolk. It is now in the Fitzwilliam Museum in Cambridge. It was a tremissis – a coin with the value of one-third of a solidus – thought to date from around AD 670. A number of coins of the same general type had been found previously – including one at Caistor – but this was the first to display a runic inscription.

The solidus had been used in the Roman Empire since the time of Emperor Constantine, and would stay in use until the tenth century. We remember it in modern English in several words, such as *solid*, *solidarity* – and *soldier*. Roman soldiers were paid with the solidus.

The inscription is very faint in places – perhaps through wear and tear, or perhaps it was badly stamped when the coin was made. It is possible to make out a sequence of *l*, *t*, *o*, *e*, and *d*, and there may be an *i* at the beginning and an *h* or *g* at the end. Nobody has any idea what this might mean.

'I know Caistor,' I said to the man from the hotel. I should have said 'know of', I suppose, for I have never been there; but it's a curious fact that when you study the linguistic history of a place, you quickly develop a sense of intimacy about it. I do feel I 'know' Caistor. It's much more than 'know of'.

I was spared an interrogation, however, because a loud bell sounded, and the man dashed away to deal with it. Maybe it was a fire alarm. People at the Portmeirion hotel would be especially sensitive to that. The present hotel isn't the one that was originally developed by Clough Williams-Ellis. That burned down during the night of 5 June 1981. It didn't reopen until 1988.

'Fire' was the symbolic meaning of one of the runes: ⟨, called *cen* (pronounced 'cane'). An Old English poem has been preserved, in which each symbol in the runic alphabet is given a poetic gloss. This is what the poet has to say about *cen*. (The þ and ð letters are pronounced as modern 'th'.)

> Cen byþ cwicera gehwam, cuþ on fyre
> blac ond beorhtlic, byrneþ oftust
> ðær hi æþelingas inne restaþ.

'The torch is known to everyone alive by its pale, bright flame; it always burns where princes sit within.'

Time was passing, and I had to move on. I had to be in Hay-on-Wye that evening. The sands in the estuary were rapidly disappearing. The family that had been walking there had reached the harbour wall, and were talking furiously amongst themselves. I didn't recognize the language. Maybe it was Basque.

As I walked up the hill towards the car park a man passed me wearing a huge *Prisoner* badge with a penny-farthing bicycle and a number 6 on it. That was another mysterious thing about the Village. A penny-farthing bike would appear here and there for no apparent reason.

There is something especially dehumanizing when people are given numbers instead of names. It doesn't take a television programme to tell us that. We have seen it in the form of the labels and tattoos which identify incarcerated victims everywhere.

I suppose the practice of giving names to houses arose from a desire to avoid the impersonal effect of house numbering. That's understandable. It's the naming of *streets* by numbers that has always puzzled me. *First Street*, *Second Street*, *Tenth Street*, *Thirty-Eighth Street* ... Why would anyone choose such an unimaginative and mechanical method of locating where they live?

It seems to be an American practice. Europeans don't go in for it. On the contrary. Mainland European cities tend to personalize street locations as much as possible. *Place Victor Hugo* in Paris. *Schillerstrasse* in Berlin. *Queen Caroline Street* in London. *Albert Cuyp Market* in

Amsterdam. The comparative literature critic George Steiner thinks that this is one of the major features of a European – as opposed to a New World – mindset. Europeans, he asserts, 'inhabit echo-chambers of historical, intellectual, artistic, and scientific achievements' as they walk through the streets of the cities of Europe.

Mind you, the Americans make up for it by being highly personal when they name towns and cities. There are twenty-three states in the USA which have a city called *Washington*.

The American practice of multiplying place-names can get confusing, though. There is a *Wyoming* city in Ohio and an *Ohio* city in Illinois. There are *Californias* in Kentucky, Maryland, Missouri, and Pennsylvania. A city called *Iowa* is in Louisiana; the city of *Louisiana* is in Missouri; and *Missouri City* is in Texas.

By contrast, the British tend to shy away from naming towns and cities after people. There is no city in England called *Shakespeare* or *Chaucer* or *George* or *Elizabeth*. And there is certainly no tendency in the UK to follow the Russian fashion, where a whole town might be renamed following someone's special achievement. After the death of the world's first astronaut Yuri Gagarin in 1968, the town of Gzhatsk near his birthplace was renamed *Gagarin* in his honour.

Things were different in Anglo-Saxon times. Then a common way of naming a place was to name it after the tribal chief who lived there. Thus, we have *Reading* – 'the people of Raed' or 'Raeda' – and *Dagenham* – 'Dacca's homestead'. The Danes did the same: *Grimsby* is the village where Grimr lived.

The Welsh go in for person-names too. *Llanfair* – 'Mary's Church'. *Porthmadog* – 'Madog's Harbour'. *Caergybi* – 'Cybi's Fort'.

Portmeirion? *Port + Meirion*, from *Meirionydd* – *Merioneth* in English – the old name of the county in which the village is located. It can be traced back to the name of a fifth-century Welsh prince.

It's always a risky business trying to make a generalization about names. There are always exceptions. For instance, for years I'd laboured under the illusion that if a person's name had an initial in the middle, the letter must stand for a specific name. Then I encountered President Harry S. Truman.

I spent a week once trying to discover what the 'S' stood for. Finally, in his daughter's autobiography, I found out. It appears that Truman's parents had difficulty deciding which of his two grandfathers to name him after. One was called Solomon and the other was called Shippe. The identical initial presented a solution. Harry was called Harry S, and it was left up to the two sides of the family to interpret the initial as they wished.

I looked back across the village before getting in my car. Times have changed since they filmed *The Prisoner*. The green-painted wooden dome which acted as Number 2's residence was replaced in the early nineties by a new copper dome. But all shall be well. It will eventually turn verdigris green once again.

4

Where are You From?

WELSHPOOL

The A487 away from Portmeirion runs alongside the Ffestiniog steam railway for a while, then winds its way through the edges of Snowdonia National Park. It was a clear day, and every now and then I could see the dramatic peaks of the Snowdon range. All highly photogenic, as film companies have repeatedly seen.

Take a left at Penrhyndeudraeth and you soon pass through Carreg Llanfrothen. There you will find Plas Brondanw, the family home of Clough Williams-Ellis. The 'Dr Who' series *The Five Doctors* was shot at the Folly Castle in the grounds. So was some of *Brideshead Revisited*. And, if you could time-travel back to 1958, you would encounter hundreds of Liverpudlian Chinese children marching with Ingrid Bergman across stand-in Chinese mountains for *The Inn of the Sixth Happiness*.

The roads through Snowdonia resound with the echoes of famous films. *Carry On Up the Khyber* was shot along the Watkin Path, one of the routes up Snowdon. *Tomb Raider 2* used the environs of Llyn Gwynant. James Bond was in the area (for *From Russia with Love*), as were Robin Hood and Merlin.

That's North Wales for you. One enormous film set. You can measure out any journey in film locations.

Robin Hood is a bit of a surprise, but you would expect Merlin to be here, in view of his home-grown origins – *Merlin* is an adaptation of *Myrddin*, according to the twelfth-century chronicler Geoffrey of Monmouth in his *Historia Regum Britanniae* ('History of the Kingdom of Britain'). Myrddin in turn comes from *Caerfyrddin*, the Welsh name of the county of Carmarthen, where he is supposed to have been born. Where exactly is a conundrum. I have lost track of the number of places in Wales – let alone elsewhere – which claim his presence, in birth, life, or death. There are several caves and mounds associated with him or his battles. I would pass at least three on the way to Hay.

In the meantime I followed the A470 winding south towards mid-Wales. I soon reached Lake Trawsfynydd, and in the distance, on the lakeside edge, I could see the solid mass of the old power station. It started service in the 1960s, but was decommissioned in 1991. What do you do with a retired power station? Turn it into a film set, of course. It was the location of Camelot in *First Knight*. They built the town on the shore of the lake and transformed the front of the power station into a castle.

Shame they had to build a mock castle, seeing as real castles abound in the region. I had passed four already on my journey from Gaerwen – Beaumaris, Caernarfon, Criccieth, and Harlech.

Every time I see the turning to Harlech, 'Men of Harlech' comes into my head. The song commemorates the men who defended the castle during a long siege in the Wars of the Roses in the fifteenth century. It is one of the few Welsh songs that has crossed the border into England. It achieved worldwide – or at least, Hollywood – fame when it was sung in the film *Zulu* by the men of the Welsh regiment fighting in the Battle of Rorke's Drift.

Did they sing it, really, in 1879? The song was first published in 1860, and the regiment didn't officially adopt it until 1881. It seems unlikely. But it was a great film moment, nonetheless.

I had to make a decision after Trawsfynydd. Should I turn east and cut across through Bala towards Welshpool? Or should I keep going on the A470 south through Dolgellau and on towards Builth Wells? Linguistically, there was no contest. Welshpool is in marcher country. England is just a mile or so away. And marcher country is an excellent breeding ground for interesting accents. But time wasn't on my side. I had to go 'straight down the middle', as they say in Wales.

Marcher has nothing to do with marching. It comes from Old English *mearc*, which meant 'boundary'. That's why people talk about 'the Marches', referring to the land on either side of the Welsh–English border. The modern word *mark* is related. Offa's Dyke closely follows the modern border, going back and forth across it several times.

Offa was the Anglo-Saxon king of Mercia between 757 and 796. He built the dyke to protect his kingdom from invasion by Welsh barbarians. It reaches twenty feet in height in some places along its eighty-mile length. One end is at Prestatyn in the north; as you travel south it passes Llangollen, Chirk, Knighton, Hay, and Monmouth; the other end is at Chepstow. It isn't continuous. Offa may never have finished it; or maybe he decided to save unnecessary labour and let other natural obstacles fill the gaps.

The earthworks are especially prominent at Knighton. Indeed, the town's entrance sign now has the caption: 'The Town on the Dyke'. It boasts an excellent information centre.

Beware. If you look up Offa's Dyke on an Internet search engine, you may need to do two searches. They spell *dyke* with an *i* in American English.

The name *Welshpool* means exactly what it says: 'Welsh' + 'pool'. But the pool in question is not just an area of water. The original thirteenth-century borough was called *Pola*, and this developed into *Pool*. The region was known for its marshy land – the flood-prone River Severn is not far away – and in Welsh the local name is *Y Trallwng*, meaning 'the sinking land'. But when the railways developed in the nineteenth century, the railway companies felt that travellers would get confused with the other Poole, in Dorset – so they changed the name to Welshpool, and it stayed.

I had already visited Welshpool a few weeks earlier, as it happened, as part of the same BBC project which had brought me to the sheep market in Gaerwen. On that visit I ended up in a different kind of market (fruit and veg), in the town centre, talking to one of the stallholders. What I was hoping to record was evidence of a mixed accent – one displaying features of both Welsh and English.

And that's what I found. Here was a man who had lived all his life in Welshpool, but if you didn't know that you might have placed him further south over the border in Herefordshire, or maybe even Gloucestershire. It was the phonetic quality of the *r* sound after the vowels in such words as *car* and *heart* that did it. He didn't make it as a trilled sound, which is what you would expect to hear further into Wales. Rather, he curled the tip of his tongue back, producing a darker sound, more like a West Country or American *r* than anything else.

But it definitely wasn't a West Country accent. Several of his vowel sounds were Welsh, as was the general lilt of his voice. And when I asked him if people recognized where he came from when he went on holiday, he was quite clear about it. 'They always know I'm from Wales,' he said. 'But they think it's Cardiff.'

Did everyone in the town have this 'English *r*', I wondered. And almost as soon as I had formulated the question, I had it answered. A customer arrived, a schoolfriend of the market-man. He too had lived in Welshpool all his life. They were the same age. They seemed to have similar farming backgrounds. And yet he had no trace of an *r* after vowels in his speech.

That's one of the fascinating things about the way people speak along country borders. Because they are exposed to two ways of speaking, they make all kinds of different choices from the array of sounds that surround them. Even quite short distances can produce a noticeably different accent. I wasn't surprised to learn that the two friends lived on opposite sides of the town.

I asked them whether they could tell the difference in the speech of someone from Welshpool itself and someone from nearby. 'Of course,' they said. 'Someone from Llanfair Careinion sounds much more Welsh than we do,' the market-man added. 'I sometimes have difficulty understanding what they're saying, when they come into the market.' That village was just five miles to the west. 'And if you go that way across the border,' said his friend – gesturing vaguely towards England – 'they're even more different.' That was only three miles away.

Professor Henry Higgins came to mind, from Shaw's *Pygmalion*. He announces himself as a practitioner of phonetics: 'The science of speech. That's my profession, also my hobby. Anyone can spot an Irishman or a Yorkshireman by his brogue, but I can place a man within six miles. I can place him within two miles in London. Sometimes within two streets.' And presumably in Welshpool, also.

Two streets? In parts of Victorian London, this might not have been too far from the truth. Accents identify communities, and there would have been areas abutting each other which displayed major social differences, and thus different accents. Then as now, Mayfair and the East End are two hugely contrasting linguistic worlds.

Higgins would have had an even more enjoyable time today. There are over 350 language communities in present-day London, and when people from these ethnic backgrounds speak English their accents inevitably reflect features of their mother-tongues. Nor is it just their accents. Words and features of grammar from their mother-tongue enter their English as well, producing new hybrid dialects – Bengali English, Hindi English, Chinese English . . . It's all a natural process. Increased language variation is an inevitable consequence of an ethnically diverse society.

Phoneticians are having a great time trying to disentangle the multiple influences which operate on modern English accents, but it isn't easy. The situation has changed dramatically in the past century. Until relatively recently, most people lived their whole lives in one place, and rarely travelled. They would encounter only the occasional visitor with a different regional accent. As a consequence, their local speech would change little during their lifetimes.

Today, people are always on the move. Commuting over long distances is normal. And even if you don't commute, innumerable accents and dialects enter your home every day through radio and television, the telephone, and, these days, Internet telephony. People move house more than ever before. Formerly isolated villages now have their eye on attracting tourists. Second homes are everywhere. It is unusual to find a village which does not have some incomers. And incomers do not usually adopt the accent of their new hosts wholesale, as my Gaerwen shepherd illustrated.

But if incomers find themselves integrating well into their new community, they will inevitably pick up a few features of the local speech – new words, sentence patterns, sounds, tones of voice. They will still sound 'foreign' to the locals, and they may not notice that their speech has changed. But if after a while they pay a visit to where they lived before, it's a typical experience to hear their old friends say they sound different.

My wife comes from Hertfordshire, and people in Holyhead, where we now live, readily notice the southern accent in her voice. When she goes back to Hertfordshire, they say she sounds Welsh.

Mixed accents are the norm these days. My own accent is a mix of the places I have lived in – Wales, Liverpool, London, Berkshire. That means it isn't an entirely consistent accent. Sometimes I say *example*, with a short *a*, sometimes *exahmple*. I never know which it is going to be. It depends a lot on who I'm talking to.

Generational differences are an influence. My children all say *schedule* beginning with *sk–*, as Americans do. When I was their age, I always said *shedule*. Today, I say both. If I'm talking to them, I join their *skedule* community. Otherwise I say *shedule*. They swap about a bit too, depending on who they're talking to.

Mixed accents mean that it isn't so easy to identify where people come from any more, just by listening to their voices. Quite often, when I meet someone for the first time, and they learn I am a linguist and discover what linguists do, they say smugly: 'I bet you can't tell where I'm from.' I never take the bet.

Radio programmes sometimes include quizzes or games with such names as 'Where Are You From?'. A team listens to guests and tries to work out which part of the country they come from. It wasn't too difficult to get the right answer a few decades ago. It's much harder now. Impossible, with many speakers.

I left the fruit and veg market and drove to the edge of Welshpool, where I had an appointment with another accent. I was keen to explore the identity question again. Here were people who had no Welsh language ability and whose accent lacked some of the most distinctive features of the English accents people associate with Wales. Would they feel as Welsh as their compatriots from the Snowdon hillsides or the Rhondda valleys?

Indeed they would, and the lady I had come to see proved it in a most unorthodox style. Halfway through the interview she began to take her clothes off – Huw the cameraman couldn't believe his lens – and displayed a Welsh dragon tattooed below her shoulder. She waxed lyrical about Wales. She was pregnant, and was determined that her baby would be born in Wrexham hospital and not in Shrewsbury, even though Wrexham was twice the distance away. Her speech had the English *r* in it again. To my ears, she hardly sounded Welsh at all. Evidently there isn't always a correlation between the national recognizability of a person's accent and the strength of the speaker's feeling about national identity.

Henry Higgins would have loved all this. Or rather, Henry Sweet would. Or rather, Daniel Jones would. *Was* there a real-life model for Henry Higgins?

Henry Sweet was the leading English philologist and phonetician at Oxford in the late nineteenth century. Daniel Jones was Professor of Phonetics at University College London a generation later. Phonetics, as Higgins, said, is the science of speech – or, slightly more precisely, of human soundmaking. Phoneticians spend all their time happily analysing how people speak, how speech sounds are carried through the air, and what happens when people listen to them.

What phoneticians *don't* do is work with people like Eliza Doolittle in the way that Higgins did. No phonetician these days would dream of trying to change someone's natural pronunciation so that it sounds more like the upper-class accent of a country. Traditionally, the people who would do that sort of thing are called elocutionists. And even they value regional accents more these days than they used to. Audibility and clarity of speech are still important goals, but they can be achieved in any accent.

Shaw had had a great deal of correspondence with Sweet over the years, but he says quite plainly in the Preface to *Pygmalion* that 'Higgins is not a portrait of Sweet.' Yet he adds: 'still . . . there are touches of Sweet in the play'. Shaw was puzzled that Sweet had not achieved greater public recognition, given his scholarly achievements. 'With Higgins's physique and temperament,' he says, 'Sweet might have set the Thames on fire.' Shaw felt the reason was the way phonetics as a subject was being seriously underrated at Oxford, and he concludes: 'if the play makes the public aware that there are such people as phoneticians and that they are among the most important people in England at present, it will serve its turn'.

Phoneticians among the most important people in England? Could there be any doubt? But when non-phoneticians say so, it makes you think, well, maybe they are. And Shaw is not alone in his opinion. The novelist Anthony Burgess states just as firmly, in the epilogue to his language memoir *A Mouthful of Air*: 'Phonetics, phonetics, and again phonetics. There cannot be too much phonetics.'

It was probably Shaw's correspondence with Sweet, along with supposed similarities between the characters of Higgins and Sweet, who didn't suffer fools gladly, that led people to assume that the one was based on the other. In fact, if Shaw is making a bow in the direction of a real phonetician at all, it has to be Daniel Jones, who in his youth had worked with Sweet.

Jones helped Shaw in several ways. He gave him advice on phonetic detail, corresponded with him several times, and invited him to see his department at University College London. The technology used in Higgins' laboratory in the play is close to what would have been in a phonetics department of the day. After *Pygmalion* was completed, Shaw offered Jones an unlimited supply of complimentary tickets to see it.

Where did the name of Higgins come from? By all accounts, it was borrowed from a London shop sign. By whose accounts? Jones himself, via one of his students. It seems that Shaw was riding on the deck of a bus through South London, wondering what name he should give his character, and saw the shop name 'Jones and Higgins'. The student recalled Jones saying: 'he could not call me Jones, so he called me Higgins'.

If Shaw's bus route was through Peckham, he couldn't have missed the shop. Jones and Higgins was the largest and most prestigious department store in the area, in Rye Lane. It closed down in 1980, but the distinctive building is still there.

Why couldn't Shaw call his character Jones? It would have been very risky to portray a living character as a fictional one. Flattering as the idea might seem at first, we can immediately imagine the real-life source being unflattered by aspects of Higgins' character. The plot contained taboo language. Higgins, moreover – to put it in modern terms – has an affair with one of his students. Not the best set of associations for a career academic.

Furthermore, the play wasn't doing phonetics many favours. True, it brought the word *phonetics* to the attention of millions who might not otherwise have heard of it, but – as Jones himself remarked – 'In *Pygmalion* phonetics is represented as providing a key to social advancement,' and he adds, drily, 'a function which it may be hoped it will not be called upon to perform indefinitely.' His dryness, it seems, was replaced by fury when he saw the play on the first night. This was not how he wanted phonetics to be seen.

In *The Real Professor Higgins*, Jones's biographers conclude that he wanted to distance himself from the character and the play, and that Shaw agreed. Shaw then went further, writing a preface which made no reference to Jones but hinted at a portrayal of the now-deceased Sweet. The ruse was successful. Nobody publicly associated Jones with Higgins, and Sweet remained the link in the public mind.

And in mine. For many years I thought it was Sweet, and I say so in a book or two. I recant.

There is a lot of recanting to be done. Type 'Henry Sweet and Henry Higgins' into Google and you will get over 800,000 hits. Start scrolling down and you will see the Sweet claim asserted over and over.

Another of Jones's students was David Abercrombie, who later became Professor of Phonetics at Edinburgh. He passed his recollections of Jones on to one of *his* students, Peter Ladefoged. And this brings the story up to date. Because it was Ladefoged who acted as the phonetics consultant for *My Fair Lady*, the screen adaptation of *Pygmalion*, designing Higgins' laboratory and sounding out the vowels that Eliza hears there on her first visit.

At the very beginning of the film, Higgins shows Eliza his notebook, in which he has been transcribing her speech in Sweet's Revised Romic phonetic script, and the camera shows us what he has written. In the upper paragraph of the right-hand page, there is a transcription of her utterance 'I say, captain . . .'. It is the lower paragraph that is interesting, for it is nothing to do with the film at all. It is a greeting to David Abercrombie from Ladefoged. I wonder if director George Cukor knew?

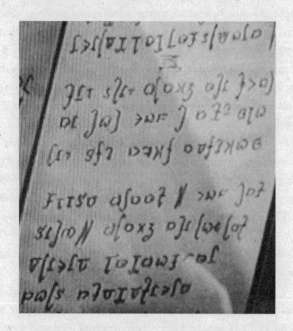

If you have a DVD of the film, pause it at that point and look at the third line up from the bottom. It says:

Peter Ladefoged died in London in January 2006, on his way back from a field trip working on the Toda language in India, just as I began writing this book. It was a tremendous loss to the world of phonetics.

One of his many interests was a concern to establish just how many vowels and consonants the human vocal tract is capable of producing in the languages of the world. The answer is more than people think. He estimated that there were over eight hundred different consonants and some two hundred different vowels.

First impressions count, so I have good cause to remember David Abercrombie. I first met him when I was an external examiner for his department in Edinburgh, back in the 1970s. Or rather, I met an aspect of his character before I actually met him. I had arrived a little early at the university, so I made my way to his office, where, the departmental secretary had told me, there were some examination scripts waiting for me to read.

I knocked at the door. No reply, but it was unlocked so I went in. There in the middle of the room was a fridge, and on top of the fridge a piece of cardboard with a large green arrow on it, pointing towards the door of the fridge. I opened the door. Inside were the examination scripts. And on top of the scripts were a bottle of French wine, a glass, and a corkscrew. No examiner ever had such a pleasant introduction to the dull routine of marking.

We had dinner at the Old Howgate Inn in Penicuik, just south of Edinburgh, where I learned that David had a house in France and was one of the Confrérie des Chevaliers du Tastevin, the elite wine-tasting society in Burgundy. The restaurant-owner knew him well, and when it came to choosing a wine, there was nothing as mundane as a wine list to read. Instead, we were ushered down into the wine cellar, and the bottle was chosen straight from the racks. I learned more about wine from that one meal than I have ever done since. I just wish I could remember half of it.

Henry Higgins wasn't the first fictional language expert. Four hundred years earlier, Shakespeare had given us the caricature of the pedantic schoolteacher Holofernes in *Love's Labour's Lost*. Holofernes is very much concerned with correct Latin and with English spelling. He insists on having words pronounced as they are spelled. People (he is thinking of Don Armado in particular) should pronounce the *b* in *doubt* and *debt*, he says, and the *l* in *calf* and *half*. And as for leaving out the *h* in *abhominable* ... Those who do so are 'rackers of orthography', he says – torturers of spelling – and they 'insinuateth me of insanie'. They drive him mad!

There were several linguistic pedants around in Shakespeare's day, most of them interested in ways of reforming English spelling. Any of them might have been the model for Holofernes. One of them was Richard Mulcaster, the first headmaster of Merchant Taylors' School in North London, and the teacher of Edmund Spenser, who would become the leading Elizabethan poet. Another was the humanist scholar Roger Ascham, the young Princess Elizabeth's Greek and Latin tutor, famous for his 1570 treatise on the best way of teaching Latin, *The Scholemaster*.

Shakespeare would certainly have been aware of Mulcaster, as the boy actors of Merchant Taylors' were a well-known theatre company. They may even have been the ones chiefly in mind when Hamlet and Rosencrantz pour scorn on the 'eyrie of children' who were so fashionable that they were putting real actors out of work.

Or, of course, they may not. Neither Mulcaster nor Ascham, nor anyone else, may have been in Shakespeare's mind when he was writing his play. Still, it's a tempting thought. Mulcaster didn't die until 1611. *Love's Labour's Lost* was written in the mid-1590s. Both Mulcaster and Shakespeare had their companies play at Hampton Court. Depending on which biographical temperament you choose, they possibly, probably, definitely met.

Searching for sources of characters is always a dangerous occupation, unless you have the author there to ask. And even then, when you do meet the author, you don't always get a clear answer. Or, sometimes, any answer at all.

At an event in Paris, back in the 1980s, I met William Golding. We had both been at the Paris Salon du Livre – the annual book fair. He was signing his books and I was signing mine. My queue was a few yards long. His stretched outside the building.

Golding arrived late from the hospitality room, expressed surprise at the length of the queue, and reluctantly sat down at his table. He signed half a dozen books, then decided he'd had enough. He got up abruptly and walked off the stand, heading back for the hospitality room. I saw raised eyebrows, shoulders and rounded vowels through-out the queue, in that unmistakeably French body language which simultaneously expresses puzzlement, disgust, and amusement. The queue disintegrated, with people talking animatedly. They did not seem especially surprised. Evidently this is what famous literary authors were permitted to do, at least in France. Expected behaviour, almost.

I did invite people to join my queue instead. Nobody took up the offer.

I don't know whether Golding came back to the signing area. He hadn't by the time I left.

As I walked away from the Salon I passed hundreds of visitors arriving for a day out. Several were whole families. I saw a man (carry-ing a picnic basket), his wife, and their three children, aged between about five and twelve. They were chattering excitedly about where they would go first. A day out. A picnic. At a book fair. It seemed so typically French. And so typically not English.

Try the following dialogue out in virtually any English accent, and it doesn't really convince. ''Ave a good weekend, Arthur?' 'Yeah, lovely, thanks. 'Ad a nice day out on Sunday. Took the kids to the Book Fair.'

It works perfectly in a French accent.

That was in the 1980s, mind. Today, you will see such sights regularly at the Hay Literary Festival. Times have changed.

Later that day my wife and I went to a soirée at the British Embassy, and after a while we met Golding and his wife. He was taciturn, so I searched for a conversational topic. What do you say to a Nobel Prize-winner?

Coincidentally, the week before I had given an evening of readings back home in support of a local parish community trying to raise money to renovate its church spire. One of the readings was, I thought, particularly appropriate: the climactic scene from Golding's *The Spire*, where the masterbuilder, Roger Mason, realizes that the weight of the new spire being added to the cathedral is causing the building to be in danger of collapse. I had no idea then that I would be meeting the author a week later.

So that was my conversation opener.

'This is a nice coincidence,' I said. 'Just last week I was doing a reading from one of your books.'

He showed a spark of interest: 'Oh, which one?'

'*The Spire*,' I said, and I explained the reason.

'Which bit did you read?' he asked.

'The bit where everyone looks down into the pit and they see the ground moving.'

There was a silence.

'"The earth's creeping!"' I quoted, lamely.

His eyes seemed to glaze over. There was a pause.

'I don't recollect that,' he said. He turned to his wife. 'Did I write that?'

'Yes, William,' said his wife, 'You remember . . .'

She went on to provide a bit more context. He still seemed uncertain.

It was a pretty important moment in the novel, so I was a bit taken aback. But then, I reflected afterwards, why should he be able to bring it to mind, years later, just because someone randomly presents him with a moment from what is, after all, a pretty extensive *œuvre*? Readers tend to think that authors know their books better than they do. That doesn't follow at all.

One forgets. I remember once someone asking me whether I had read a certain book. I said I hadn't. Later, I came across a reference in my files. Not only had I read it; I had reviewed it.

Authors are human. They forget, like everyone else.

'So, Mr Shakespeare, I loved that bit in *Hamlet* where the prince meets Ophelia and he tells her about going to a nunnery.'

'Excuse me?'

'*Hamlet*, you know, where . . .'

'Oh, yes, *Hamlet*, *Hamlet* . . .'

'Going to a nunnery?'

'Did I write that?'

'Yes, William, don't you remember . . .'

Well, why not?

Authors sometimes turn up quite unexpectedly. A few years ago I was giving a talk at the Hay Festival about English accents, and describing the mixed London accent often called 'estuary English', which was receiving some media publicity at the time. To fix it in the minds of my audience, I thought I would refer to some well-known personalities who spoke with it, and mentioned Pauline Quirke and Linda Robson, the two actresses in the television sitcom *Birds of a Feather*.

After the talk there was time for questions. A man in a middle row put his hand up. He was delighted to hear me talk about *Birds of a Feather*, he said, and he went on to say how the actresses had needed to modify their originally broader London accents to ensure that they would be readily understood on national television. I didn't know any of that, but I was glad to hear it, because it was an excellent example of the kind of social factor that fosters the spread of new accents.

'You seem to know a lot about it,' I said.

'I ought to,' he replied. 'I wrote it.'

It was Laurence Marks, half of the writing partnership of Marks and (Maurice) Gran. They were the ones who also created the acclaimed *The New Statesman*, with the larger-than-life politician Alan B'stard, played by Rik Mayall.

That's the kind of thing that happens at the Hay Festival. You never know who's going to be there. And you'd better not make careless literary allusions to modern writers, as it would be just your bad luck to find one of them sitting in your audience.

It turned out that Laurence was staying at the same hotel as I was, The Swan at Hay, so we had other chances to talk. A year later we were both at The Swan again, and so it has been most years ever since. From time to time I would give him one of my linguistics books, and he would give me one of his scripts. We talked a lot about the overlap between our two professions. We were both fascinated by English usage, but had come at it from totally different directions.

I would get emails from him with questions about slang, related to the latest characters Marks and Gran were creating. Where does *by hook or by crook* come from? Why do people say *on the wagon*? (Or earlier British *waggon*?) Not all of them had answers.

In fact, the American spelling is the appropriate one, for earlier versions of the phrase can be traced back to the early 1900s in the USA. There we find 'on the water cart', and later, 'on the water wagon'.

Horse-drawn water carts were used in late-nineteenth-century America to damp down dusty roads in summertime, and they seem to have provided an appropriate metaphor for the temperance movements of the time. You would hear men who had pledged to stop drinking say that they would rather drink the water from a water-cart than break their promise.

The earliest reference found so far is in Chapter 9 of Alice Caldwell Rice's social novelette *Mrs Wiggs of the Cabbage Patch*, published in 1901. She comments on poor consumptive Mr Dick that 'he had a orful spell while I was there. I wanted to git him some whisky, but he shuck his head, "I'm on the water-cart," sez he.'

Going on the wagon came along soon after, and was quickly supplemented — to the gloom of the temperance supporters — by *falling off the wagon*. Both idioms stayed virtually unchanged throughout most of the century. And then, surprisingly, people started extending the phrase to other areas than drink.

Abstaining from virtually any vice can be seen as being on a 'wagon', these days. I've heard someone say that she was 'on the wagon', when all she meant was that she had started a diet. I've also heard someone referring to coming 'off the wagon', meaning she had stopped her aerobics course. And one of the slang historians reports that it was used in a US newspaper in 2000 to refer to the times in which a serial killer failed to murder anyone. 'He didn't murder at all for two long periods . . . before falling off the wagon each time.'

In 2002, Marks and Gran went on the wagon again, and wrote *Believe Nothing*, a futuristic satirical comedy introducing an eccentric academic, Adonis Cnut, played by Rik Mayall. This is not a Caernarfon malapropism: it was pronounced 'Canute'.

Cnut is known to be the cleverest man in the world, a quadruple professor at Queen Edward College, Oxford, and a Nobel Prize-winner. But he is bored by his own brilliance, and is looking for fresh challenges. He therefore accepts an invitation to join the Council for International Progress, a secret underground organization which controls all the governments and corporations in the world. The series presented Cnut with challenges to be solved, such as getting the whole world to use genetically modified food. He usually succeeds, aided by his faithful manservant Albumen, played by Michael Maloney. However, he fails to make much headway with the beautiful (and palindromic) Dr Awkward, first name Hannah, the college's Professor of Pedantics.

Laurence invited me to the recording of one of the episodes, at Teddington Studios on the River Thames. I was introduced to the cast as 'the real professor of semantics'. I sometimes wonder which bit of me had lodged in Marks and Gran's subconscious, and transmuted into the characters. I'd like to think it was an aspect of Adonis Cnut. More likely it was Albumen.

Believe Nothing had one of the best pieces of word-play ever. In one episode, Albumen is under the weather and looks awful. Cnut asks Hannah to check up on him, then asks her: 'How green is my valet?'

Of course, if you had never come across the 1939 novel about South Wales by Richard Llewellyn, *How Green Was My Valley*, you wouldn't get it. But judging by the audience reaction, most people did. The novel won a National Book Award, and it was made into a very successful film, winning an Oscar for John Ford as best director in 1941. It also became a televised mini-series in the 1970s. The name is almost a catch-phrase.

Audience laughter is a curious linguistic phenomenon, though, as I learned at the recording in Teddington. There were about a hundred people watching the show, seated in tiered rows facing the studio set. It's a bit like watching a play on stage, but there are some crucial differences.

The warm-up man, for a start. He comes on about ten minutes or so before the recording begins, and gets everyone into the right comic mood. He tells a few funny stories, asks where people are from, makes a few cracks at their expense, and generally gets everyone feeling at home. He also tells them a bit about what's going to happen as the recording proceeds. It's an important role if the audience is to sound relaxed and natural when the show begins.

I wonder what would happen if theatre went in for warm-ups? 'Hey, everyone, welcome to Stratford, and to this evening's performance of *Othello*. Hope you've all got your hankies ready? Well, the actors will all be here in a few minutes, and – oh I see we have a late arrival in the front row. Travel by swan, did we? . . .'

The television warm-up man has a second important role: filling the gaps between retakes. Every scene will be shot several times, because something invariably goes wrong. Props out of place. Actors forgetting a line. Camera angles not quite right. Or just a hoped-for better performance. There's a television fashion these days to show some of the worst disasters as 'out-takes' in special compilations.

So what does the audience do, if there's a long gap while waiting for a scene to be shot again? Enter warm-up man, with a fresh supply of gags. And a reminder to the audience: 'Yes, you've seen it before and laughed at the joke already; but pretend you're watching it for the first time. Force out some really spontaneous laughter.' Even the best of jokes palls after you've heard it three or four times. The audience does its best, but often it's not good enough, and another piece of laughter has to be inserted when the show is finally edited. That's why the audience reaction in some programmes doesn't sound as natural as it should.

The Welshpool lady with the dragon on her shoulder put her clothes back on, and we left, the BBC producer chuckling over what she knew would make excellent television. 'That's what you need to make phonetics popular,' I reflected. 'Nothing like a bit of sex to raise the profile of an academic subject.' Maybe elocution *is* a sexier subject than phonetics. After all, Higgins married Eliza in the end.

5

Good Evening, Each

BIRMINGHAM

Welshpool might be linguistically more interesting, but Builth Wells was more direct if I was to be in Hay by the evening, so I carried on along the A470. It's the most direct route between North and South Wales, but it has few straight stretches, and you don't get any serious dual carriageway until you're almost in Cardiff. People who have to make the journey regularly often drive across North Wales along the A55 into England and then follow the motorways south until they reach the M4, which takes them back into Wales again. That's not very patriotic, and I'm not convinced it's any quicker. Farm tractors permitting, you can get from Holyhead to Cardiff via the A470 – two hundred miles – in less than five hours. The motorway traveller has to negotiate the regular traffic jams to the west of Birmingham.

If you do stay on the A470 you are rewarded with spectacular scenery. Just south of Dolgellau the road ascends to pass the mountain called Cader Idris – 'the Chair of Idris' – which rises to just under three thousand feet. There's a huge depression beneath the summit. It really does look like a place where some giant once sat.

Nobody knows exactly who Idris was. Some think he was indeed a giant, who used the top of the mountain as an observatory. Some think he was a Welsh hero killed in battle against the Saxons in the seventh century. Of course, some are sure he was a vassal of King Arthur.

Local people will tell you that the mountain is haunted. They say that if you spend the night on the top of Cader Idris, you will wake up as either a madman or a poet.

As you pass the mountain there's a fine view along the river valley, with wooded hills on either side all the way down. On a clear day, you may find the occasional Hawk jet from RAF Valley noisily overtaking you in some low-flying mountain practice. The road is higher than the pilots in places.

As if on cue, a Hawk roared past me just as I was negotiating a bend, and scared the living daylights out of me. It seemed to be heading straight for a mountain, then without warning suddenly turned sharp left and went down a valley. I don't know . . . some drivers . . . Didn't even signal!

The living daylights . . . The plural of *daylight* is known from the eighteenth century. Henry Fielding is the first recorded user, in Chapter 10 of his novel *Amelia*. During a lively piece of prison table-talk we hear one woman say of another, who has called her a 'good woman': 'Good woman! I don't use to be so treated. If the lady says such another word to me, d—n me, I will darken her daylights.' 'Black her eyes', we would say these days. *Daylights* was slang for 'eyes'.

Even mild swear-words didn't get printed in full in those days.

During the next few decades, the usage became more varied. 'Blast your daylights' or 'toplights' was a nautical curse in the early nineteenth century. And the meaning widened to refer to other vital organs of the body, apart from the eyes. If you 'had the daylights knocked out of you', you were thoroughly beaten up.

The living daylights seems to have arisen in the late nineteenth century. It became popular about fifty years later – so much so that Ian Fleming used it as the title of a James Bond short story in 1962. It was adapted into a film in 1987, with Timothy Dalton making his debut as the hero. Idioms have really made it when they achieve movie stardom.

As I passed through Corris, on the A487, I met Arthur again. King Arthur's Labyrinth. It was set up inside the workings of an old slate mine. When it's open, during the summer months, you can float through underground caverns and hear sound-and-light tales of ancient times.

It's twenty-three miles from Trawsfynydd to Corris. If the situation I found in Welshpool was replicated here, I would have passed through about six accents in thirty minutes. I was travelling at twelve accents an hour.

At least the attitudes expressed by the Welshpool people towards the local accent were universally positive. That doesn't always happen. City accents, in particular, often get a strongly negative reaction, even from the city-dwellers themselves. 'They're ugly,' people say. And nowhere more so than in Birmingham.

Most people in England would have no difficulty recognizing a Birmingham (or 'Brummy') accent. It's one of those that stand out, like Glaswegian or Scouse. Often we associate accents with radio or television personalities. Jasper Carrott for Birmingham. Billy Connolly for Glasgow. A Beatle for Liverpool. This association can be enough to moderate the negative feelings. The Beatles did more to make the Scouse accent popular than an army of Higginses could ever have done.

But this never happened in Birmingham, where the accent in recent decades has attracted some particularly unpleasant associations. It isn't just that people have said it's ugly. They've gone further, and said that it makes the speakers sound lazy, bolshy, and stupid.

There is of course no correlation whatsoever between the sound of a language or dialect and the level of intelligence or sociability of its speakers. The only reason we might think otherwise is because for generations people were told so by their − for want of a better word − 'betters'. Traditionally, the English aristocracy looked down on provincial speech, considering it harsh and rough. Nobles who had received a good education would naturally think of provincials as ignorant and lazy, and would associate their lack of knowledge with the way they talked. It is then a short step from saying that people are ignorant to saying that they are unintelligent.

Today, in a more egalitarian age, crude stereotypes about social class and intelligence are no longer in fashion. Media personalities have helped the process. Billy Connolly, with his acerbic and highly intelligent humour, has driven a coach and horses through any residual belief that people who speak with a Glasgow accent are stupid. The clever dialogue of Alan Bleasdale's television plays helped to do the same for Liverpool. But the Birmingham stereotype has remained.

It's difficult to say why. If you play a set of English accents to foreigners, and ask them to rate the accents in terms of their beauty or ugliness, you would be surprised at some of the results. Birmingham actually comes out top of the beauty scale for many listeners. When I played some tapes to a group of foreigners at a summer school, they described it as melodious and musical. This suggests that what people are reacting to is not so much the acoustic qualities of the accent as the psychological associations that it has accreted over the years.

Where did these associations come from? The outcome of the BBC's 'Voices' project was a whole week of national and local programmes in August 2005. One, made by West Midlands Radio and called *Was it Something We Said?*, investigated the local linguistic situation. The contributors were quite clear about the origins of the negative stereotype. Birmingham was the prime example of the nineteenth-century dirty and sprawling city, and it was inevitable that the association of 'ugly city' would carry over into 'ugly speech'.

There is a story that Queen Victoria pulled down the blinds on the windows of the royal train as she travelled from Birmingham to Wolverhampton. It is probably only a legend, but truth is seldom a factor in the creation of stereotypes. And the name of the region to the north of Birmingham, 'the Black Country', doesn't help. The adjective probably derives from the huge thirty-foot coal seam that underlies the area, the richest in Britain; but it is the black smoke and soot of the industrial chimneys that people think of when they hear it.

Today the area is far more green than black. The bright and spacious regenerated Birmingham city centre has begun to eat away at the old stereotype, and other major things have happened. The city has hosted a G8 summit and over thirty world or international sporting championships. It contains the National Exhibition Centre. I had been to Birmingham just a couple of months before, because the 'Voices' project had held its major planning meeting at a conference venue there. I must have visited the city twenty or thirty times over the years. You can see the progress at every visit.

But it is much easier to regenerate a city than an accent, especially one like Birmingham's, which – if you are so inclined – is so easy to mock. It is an interesting accent, a blend of northern and southern features, slightly nasal, strongly velar (towards the back of the mouth), with lengthened vowels. It has a slow rate of articulation and a somewhat singsong intonation. A slow delivery is much easier to exaggerate than a fast one, so it is not surprising to hear it often caricatured on radio and television.

Needless to say, the exaggerated versions you hear from comedians bear little relationship to the accents that are actually used on the streets. And note – *accents*. There are huge differences between the way they speak in different parts of the Black Country. Locals can tell where people are from within just a few miles, exactly as in Welshpool. Birmingham speech is not at all like the speech of Dudley or Wolverhampton. But to the media comic who wants a cheap laugh, they are all the same.

The industrial history of the city might explain the sense of ugliness, but why the stupidity and the bolshiness of its inhabitants? Here we have to look for individuals. Ask older people who they associate with the Birmingham accent and they will usually remember the comedienne Beryl Reid, who invented the character of Marlene, the Pride of the

Midlands, in the radio show *Educating Archie* in the 1950s. She was known for her enormous earrings, her catch-phrase 'Good evening, each,' and her hugely exaggerated Brummy accent. Marlene wasn't the brightest of individuals. The whole nation heard it, believed it, and generalized it to the entire Birmingham community.

The myth of stupidity was reinforced by other characters from other series, such as the half-witted Benny from the ITV television soap *Crossroads* and the dopey electrician Barry Taylor from the BBC's *Auf Wiedersehen, Pet*. The myth of bolshiness was reinforced by the British Leyland strikes at Longbridge during the 1970s, when shop steward Derek Robinson ('Red Robbo', as the media called him) and his associates were regularly heard on television calling for strikes.

It only takes one voice to foster a national stereotype about an accent. In a totally different connection, the voice of Ian Paisley has added an association of intransigent fundamentalism to one of the accents of Northern Ireland.

All the Birmingham voices were duly satirized on radio and television. Comedians sensed the comic power of having an accent that could, it appeared, express special stupidity. There's nothing unique about this. Most nations have a part of the country where the people are thought to be mentally slower than everywhere else. Usually it's in a remote corner of the land, well away from the capital. It's a bit unusual to encounter it in the centre of a country, as with Birmingham, and unique, I think, to see it in relation to a country's second-largest city.

The stereotype has carried over into the theatre. In Stratford in 2005 there was a splendid production of *A Midsummer Night's Dream* by the Royal Shakespeare Company, directed by Gregory Doran. Bottom and the other rustics presented us with some side-splitting moments. But they had all adopted Brummy accents. This gave the opportunity for a number of cheap laughs, but not from me. Theatre companies above all should be trying to break down stereotypes, not fostering them.

The presenter of the BBC radio programme for the 'Voices' project concluded that London was frightened of Birmingham, and that there has been a long-standing southern prejudice against the wealth-creators of the Midlands. Londoners have a vested interest, so the argument went, in keeping Birmingham down. And what better way to do that than to foster stereotypes that the people of Birmingham are lazy and thick, and to use their accent as a means to that end?

It will take another national character, with a totally positive image, to reverse the situation for Birmingham. It hasn't happened yet. People from the city are still scared of the accent, and go out of their way to change it as they plan their careers. I can think of hardly any media or theatre personalities from the Midlands who have kept their home accent. Some have even taken elocution lessons to eliminate it.

We don't think of Birmingham when we hear comedian Tony Hancock, broadcaster Sue Lawley, novelist Barbara Cartland, CBI director-general Digby Jones, actress Julie Walters, or politician Clare Short.

We do with comedian Jasper Carrott. He is a noble exception.

Things will change, but only if more positive role models become known through radio and television. The media have the primary responsibility. And slowly, attitudes are indeed changing, helped by an evolving cultural climate which attacks negative stereotypes about social groups. The 'Voices' project gave fresh impetus to these new attitudes in 2005. But I had seen this myself a few years earlier.

In 1998 I was invited to appear on *Esther*, a new chat show for BBC2 fronted by Esther Rantzen. For the first week of the show, the programme researchers had been working flat out to find the sexiest topics that would attract maximum viewer interest.

'Sexy' does not mean what you may think it means. When a broadcasting person says a programme is 'sexy', it simply means it's likely to get high audience ratings.

The producers had decided that two topics were sexiest of all. The first programme was to be about domestic violence. The second was to be on regional accents. I spent some time pondering whether there was any relationship between the two, but reached no firm conclusion.

They were recording both programmes on the same day, the domestic violence one first. So I watched that while waiting my turn. The studio audience arrived, and then the warm-up man – or, in this case, woman. Esther herself.

She explained the kind of programme it was, and stressed that she wanted as much audience reaction as possible. She didn't want a quiet show. If the audience liked what they heard, they could clap and cheer, as the spirit moved them. And if they didn't like something, they could hiss or boo. 'Now, let's practise,' she said.

She made a comment about how a famous politician of the day was doing a grand job. Happy applause from those who agreed; catcalls from those who didn't. The audience was indeed prepared to be noisy, and were proving it. Esther was happy.

Then the recordings began. I cannot be accurate about the details now, as I have no copy of what went on that day, but I remember something like this. The domestic violence programme was a positive and very moving debate about the issues, in which women who had been at the wrong end of violence gave brave testimonies. But it took the studio audience a good ten minutes before they achieved the levels of loud involvement that Esther had wanted.

With the accents programme, it took them about ten seconds.

This is how she did it. As the opening titles finished, Esther talked to camera. 'Everyone knows,' she said, 'that people from Birmingham sound thick.'

The oxygen seemed to go out of the room. Everybody in the audience was taken by surprise. Some half-laughed, in an embarrassed way. Some shouted 'No' or made booing noises. 'You can't say things like that,' was the general tone of the reaction. I had the impression that one gentleman was saying 'Quite right, Esther.' Probably a member of the Queen's English Society.

Esther knew what she was doing. She took her microphone and walked over to someone sitting in the front row. 'What do you think about that, sir?' she asked.

'I don't agree with it, Esther,' came the reply, in the strongest possible Brummy accent. The audience laughed. 'And why not?' 'Because I'm a professor at Birmingham University, and I don't think I'm thick.'

The oxygen went out of the room again. The entire audience did a double-take, and stared disbelievingly at him. The same audience that, just seconds before, had expressed principled disapproval of Esther's remark could not actually take on board the fact that you could be a university professor and nevertheless have such a strong Birmingham accent.

The speaker was proud of his accent, and defended it robustly. When he had finished, he was cheered, and rightly so. He must have been under a lot of pressure to change to a southern accent when he was on his way up the career ladder, and somehow he had resisted it. He was one of a very small number of people I knew who had reached the top of their profession yet retained the accent of their roots. This was in the late 1990s. There are more of them around now – though few, still, from Birmingham.

Why do accents arouse such emotions? Perhaps for the same reason that fashions do. The easy answer is to say that accents express our identity – which part of the country we come from, or where we belong socially or professionally. But there are lots of ways of expressing identity. We can don special clothes or wave a flag or wear a badge which tells the rest of the world who we are ... Why are accents so special?

I think part of the answer is to do with the naturalness of accents. We have to go out of our way to find clothes, flags, and badges. Also, they cost money. Accents, on the other hand, grew up with us. And they cost nothing at all.

Clothes, flags, and badges have some serious limitations as markers of identity. They cannot be seen around corners, or in the dark. The human voice doesn't have these problems. Corners and darkness are irrelevant. It is the only all-inclusive means of expressing identity that we have.

Perceiving identities in the dark would have been a critical factor in the early development of the human race, as speech was emerging, perhaps fifty thousand or more years ago. Imagine you are in a cave, and you hear voices outside. Are they friends or enemies? You call out. A voice replies. If the voice has the same accent as yours, it is probably safe to go outside. If it does not, you can still go outside, but you had better take your club with you.

Come to think of it, things haven't changed much. There are doubtless streets in several cities where survival is a matter of listening to accents round corners in exactly this way. That is one way of thinking about accents – as a linguistic dimension to the survival of the fittest.

Are accents dying out? The popular impression is that they are, because people notice the disappearance of old ways of life, especially in the countryside, and miss the regional accents associated with them. But the old ways of speaking are being replaced by new ones. The many mixed accents and new urban accents are proof of that.

People regret the passing of old ways of speech. That is why there are so many local dialect societies. We talk about 'dialect societies', and not 'accent societies', because the notion of dialect is much broader than that of accent. *Accent* refers only to a person's distinctive pronunciation. *Dialect* refers also to the distinctive vocabulary and grammar of a way of speaking.

Usually, when people talk about dialects, they mean 'regional dialects' – ways of speaking that tell us where someone is from geographically. The term is also often used to refer to 'social dialects' – ways of speaking that tell us about a person's class or educational background. And 'occupational dialects' can tell us what job a person does. Listen to a lawyer addressing the judge in court, or a football commentator describing a game, and you're hearing an occupational dialect.

Whatever types of dialect we have in mind, it's well worthwhile trying to document their linguistic character before they die out. That was one of the things that made the BBC 'Voices' project so appealing. It was the first nationwide attempt to take, as it were, an 'auditory snapshot' of the way people were using accents and dialects in 2005. In twenty years' time, it will be an invaluable auditory record of the present age.

If only we had such a record from times past – from the 1940s, say, or the 1930s. The few radio recordings we have from those decades are only the tiniest tip of the linguistic iceberg. We shall never know how the mass of ordinary people spoke across the whole country in the 1930s.

Even fragments of audio recordings from earlier times are a source of fascination. How far back can we go? Well, in theory as far back as 1877, when Thomas Alva Edison invented a means of recording sound. In the British Museum there is a phonographic cylinder recorded on 30 July 1890. On it you can hear the voice of Florence Nightingale.

In May 1890 it was reported in the press that many veterans of the Charge of the Light Brigade in the Crimean War were living in appalling poverty. Despite public outrage, the government failed to act, so the St James's Gazette set up the Light Brigade Relief Fund. Edison's representative in Britain arranged for three recordings to be made to support the fund. One was of a veteran trumpeter sounding the charge as heard at Balaclava. Another was of Lord Tennyson reading his poem on the Charge. And the third was a message from Miss Nightingale to the veterans, recorded at her home at 10 South Street, off Park Lane in London.

She says her name and the date, and then: 'When I am no longer even a memory, just a name, I hope my voice may perpetuate the great work of my life. God bless my dear old comrades of Balaclava and bring them safe to shore. Florence Nightingale.'

Her accent is reminiscent of the voices heard in early BBC recordings of the 1920s. She says *thirtieth* with the first vowel close to the one in modern *car*. *Ninety* ends with a short open vowel, rhyming more with modern *say* than *see*. If only there were more of it recorded. The fragment we have of this century-old accent is tantalizing.

We need to document the character of disappearing accents and dialects as we do disappearing languages. The world is a mosaic of linguistic visions, providing evidence of the ability of the race to adapt its way of thinking to varying geographical and cultural circumstances. Language diversity demonstrates the intellectual health of the planet on a grand scale. Dialect diversity is not so dramatic, but it is just as important.

Nothing can match dialects for expressing local detail, and it is always fascinating to see how words can change even over quite short distances. For instance, there was a survey of bird-names done in Yorkshire in the 1950s. It turned out that the local word for 'starling' was *cheppy* in the extreme north-west of the county, but *jibby* in the coastal areas of the North and East Ridings. If you went into the Wolds, the Vale of Pickering or the North Riding moors, it was called *jippy*. In the upper valleys of the Wharfe, Aire, and Calder it was *shebby*. It was *sheppy* in Middle Wharfedale and Airedale. And in the Vale of York, Hambleton, Ampleforth, and the Cleveland Hills it was *shippy*.

There's a nice gradual shift in pronunciation as you move from the coast inland: *jibby* – *jippy* – *shippy* – *sheppy* – *shebby* – *cheppy*. The last two are heard over the border into Lancashire too.

The standard name, *starling*, itself gets into some strange places. It is from Old English, *steor* + *ling*, 'spotted'. In the eighteenth century, two men who slept with the same woman were said to be *brother-starlings*. In the nineteenth century, the police used to refer to someone under surveillance as a *starling* – a person who had been 'spotted', a 'marked man'.

I passed through Builth Wells, and soon after turned left towards Hay and into the Golden Valley, which runs out of Wales into Herefordshire.

In the west the two Brecon Beacons stand out like a pair of giant doorsteps. The valley takes its name from the River Dore. But how do you get from *Dore* to *Golden*? The answer is nothing to do with French *d'or*, 'of gold'.

Dore is an old Celtic name. It has the same origins as *Dover*. Both come from the early British word *dubra*s, which meant 'waters'. There was a river at Dover, called the Dour. The one in the Golden Valley is found in Welsh from the twelfth century. It is spelled variously as *Estrateur*, *Istratour*, and *Stratdour*. The name is a combination of Welsh *ystrad* ('valley') and *Dore*. It meant 'Dore valley' – that is, the valley with a stream in it.

But then popular imagination took over. In Old Welsh, *our* meant 'gold'. It is *aur* in Modern Welsh. So it was an easy step from *ystrad* + *dore* to *ystrad* + *our*, dropping the second *d* – giving 'valley of gold'. And where would you prefer to live? In a valley with a stream in it? Or in a golden valley? No contest.

On a high ridge overlooking the valley there is a dolmen, a Neolithic burial chamber from around 3000 BC. The roof has partly collapsed, and many of the original stones have disappeared – presumably now forming a part of some nearby Victorian farmer's stone walls. Despite its date, the site has long been known as Arthur's Stone. One legend says this was the site of one of his battles. Another that it was his last resting place.

There is a real resting place nearby, in Bredwardine. The Victorian country parson and diarist Francis Kilvert is buried in St Andrew's churchyard.

Bredwardine, Leintwardine, Lugwardine, Wrockwardine, Stanwardine, Shrawardine, Pedwardine. The names toll like bells along the marches of the western Midlands, especially in the south-west. The distinctive *–wardine* ending comes from Old English *worþign* – pronounced 'war-theen', meaning 'enclosure' or 'homestead'. *Worthing* is related, as are all the places in the south-west ending in *–worthy*.

The first part of the name is usually some local natural feature: *bred*–
a bank, ridge; *leint*– a river name; *lug*– another river name; *wrock*–
near Wrekin hill; *stan*– stone; *shra*– a hollow.

Pedwardine is different. That is the homestead belonging to Peoda.
Pedeurde, as recorded in Domesday Book. Nobody knows who Peoda
was, but his name lives on in that Herefordshire village, and also in
Burton Pedwardine in Lincolnshire, named after a family that moved
there from Herefordshire in the thirteenth century. It has even achieved
aristocratic standing: in the peerage of Scotland, a subsidiary title for
the Earl of Kinnoull was created in 1711: Baron Hay of Pedwardine.

Peoda has crossed the Atlantic, too. In the early 1970s a Clun Forest
ram from Pedwardine was imported into Nova Scotia as part of a new
breeding programme. So now we have sheep with a possible Canadian
accent. Baa, eh?

And who was Beornmund, who set up a *ham* (pronounced 'hahm'),
a 'village' or 'homestead', for his people in the Midlands? The name
was *Beormundingaham* in Old English – the village of Beornmund's
people. It is *Birmingham* today.

A parrot used to frequent the bar and lounge of the Lion Hotel in
Leintwardine, but it left with its owner when the hotel changed hands.
There's another one in the White Lion at Ross-on-Wye.

There's no reason why parrots shouldn't help in the task of docu-
menting dying dialects. After all, they have already done sterling work
for dying languages. Or at least, two of them did.

This is a story that began in South America. In lands around the
Orinoco River, in what is today Venezuela, there lived an Indian tribe
called the Maypure (pronounced 'my-puh-ray'), but towards the end of
the eighteenth century the entire community was wiped out by a rival
group of Indians. The victors returned to their village carrying the
spoils of war – including some talkative pet parrots.

In 1799 the German naturalist and explorer Alexander von Humboldt
visited the village, and realized that the language spoken by the parrots

was not that of their new owners. The parrots were continuing to repeat the fragments of now-extinct Maypure, just as they had been taught. Von Humboldt brought one of the birds back to Europe, and made a phonetic transcription of the words.

Fast-forward now two hundred years. Rachel Berwick, Professor of Sculpture at Yale University, fascinated by the story, decided to construct a living sculpture as a way of focusing on notions of loss and extinction. She spent nearly two years researching von Humboldt's transcriptions, finding two Amazonian parrots, and teaching them the Maypure words. Then she built a cage, put in sound and light, and some vegetation to support the parrots, and exhibited them in 1997 – first in New York, and later at the Serpentine Gallery in London.

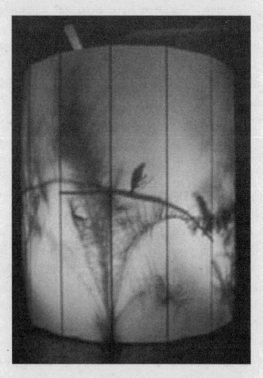

It was a brilliant way of focusing public attention on the concept of language death. People would walk up to the cage, wondering what on earth was going on. They would walk round it, metaphorically scratching their heads. They would say 'Pretty Polly' to the uncomprehending parrots. Then they would read the explanation posted nearby. And then they would walk back to the cage and look again at the parrots, in silent wonder.

Every now and then one of the birds would say something. It was utterly spine-tingling. Even though the listeners knew that the original sounds of Maypure would have been distorted in their parrotted reincarnation, the experience still put a lump in their throats. A language from beyond the grave. Nobody said 'Pretty Polly' any more.

Today, many once-flourishing languages, now dead, have been recorded. Linguists have tracked down several last speakers and got them to talk in and about their language. A 'last speaker' is the only person able to speak a language formerly used by a whole people. All the other speakers have died or forgotten their language through assimilation into another linguistic community. There are probably about a hundred last speakers around the globe, as I write. Their memories occupy lonely, unsharable linguistic worlds. Without the recordings and transcriptions made by field linguists, we wouldn't even know that their language had ever existed.

There are last dialect speakers, too. I met one once, a man in his nineties. He had been a coal miner in Durham, and he could remember many of the words that were used in his pit. As he talked about his working years, out came terms that described the tools he used and the types of coal: small coals were called *beans*; a rubbish tub was a *kibble*; a tool chest was a *kist*; a winch was a *jack-roll*. If the floor of a seam started to creep because of the pressure upon it, the faint crackling noise was called *fissling* or *nattling*.

The barrowmen wore *hoggers*, stockings without feet. The word must have derived from the resemblance to the *hogger*, a wide leather pipe that delivered water into a cistern. My informant told me he would get his *addlings* ('pay') every two weeks; the week in between was known as a *baff-week*. When it was time to stop work, the call *kenner* would be shouted down the pit and passed among the men from mouth to mouth.

In his account he used several general words from the local dialect, such as *grathely* ('tidy') and *ettle* ('arrange'), both Old Norse words that came into English in the Middle Ages. There was *crible* ('curry favour'), *lippen* ('reckon'), and *toom* ('empty'). And he used *mavies* to mean 'perhaps' – presumably a version of *may be*.

I asked him whether any of his old workmates were still alive. He didn't know of any. The pit he used to work in was closed in the 1960s. 'Some moved away,' he said, 'but all the ones that stayed here have gone.'

So has he, now. And with him, the last direct contact with a fascinating occupational dialect.

It was early evening when I finally reached the bridge over the River Wye, one of the entrances into Hay. Two hundred years ago barges used to carry coal from the South Wales mines along this river to Hereford. I parked my car for a moment and looked down at the placid waters. In Hay, Hertford, Hereford, and Hampshire, hurricanes hardly ever happen. But there is regular flooding here, and all along the Wye, which has one of the highest rises and falls of any English river.

Hay is as much a marcher town as anywhere could be. The national boundary between Wales and England runs right through it, along the Dulais brook, which flows into the Wye to the east of the town. It is technically part of Wales, at the edge of Powys, but in one of those anomalies which make us so love the British Post Office, the postal code is HR3 – Hereford. An excellent place to study mixed accents, you would think.

But in the first week of June, anything can happen. Large numbers of visitors were arriving for the evening performance at the circus which had set up its tent in the fields alongside the river. A family passed by, the kids shouting excitedly. No question: they were from Birmingham. Welcome to the Hay Literary Festival.

6

Book-Browser Syndrome

HAY

If you are searching for something that has been written in a book, you will probably find it in the second-hand and antiquarian bookshops of Hay. All you need is time, stamina, and a strong constitution. It is usually the lack of the last that lets you down. The symptoms of HBBS (Hay book-browser syndrome) are well known: sore eyes from too much title-gazing, torn fingers from too much page-turning, wobbly legs from too much haunch-sitting, and an inability to raise the head from a right-leaning neck-angle of forty-five degrees. It is fortunately a temporary condition, which for many people manifests its symptoms only during a visit to the ten-day Hay Literary Festival around the end of May and the beginning of June. I was expecting the worst, for the Festival was in full swing when I arrived.

I never know what I am going to find at Hay. All I know is that it will take me 2.7 days of paced browsing and neck exercises to pay due attention to all the sections which contain books on English in all the town's thirty-eight (at my last count) bookshops. I never go with any specific idea in mind, though sometimes I am exploring a theme, related to whatever book I happen to be researching at the time.

Doubtless I am experiencing huge duplication of effort, year by year. I wouldn't be surprised if 90 per cent of the books I look at this year are those I also looked at last year . . . and the year before. There can't be a huge turnover in English language books. But it's that elusive 10 per cent that are the attraction. And new acquisitions are sometimes flagged, or are given a prominent place in a bookshop window, so that helps.

That's where I found my copy of Shakespeare's First Folio of 1623. Geoffrey Aspin had it in the front window of his shop on Castle Street, a fine edition, the large thick pages with their rough edges crying out to be stroked, and turning with a sound that was more a rasp than a rustle. The whole thing smelled mustily of the past. It was heavy and awkward to manage – and absolutely gorgeous. And it was going cheap at £95.

Oh, did I forget to mention? It was only a facsimile. Printed in 1910 by Methuen. But still, it was a find. They don't make facsimiles like that any more.

Real First Folios do still turn up unexpectedly. In 2004 a Stockport housewife received a letter out of the blue from her solicitor telling her that she had inherited a copy from a distant relative who had left no will. She thought it was a facsimile, but it turned out to be the real thing. It wasn't in perfect condition: it lacked forty leaves from the front, including the famous engraving of Shakespeare and most of *The Tempest*. But 96 per cent of a genuine First Folio is still pretty impressive.

The owner put it up for auction, and it went for a miserable £176,750. Miserable when you consider that at another auction sale in 2001 a copy had gone for over $6 million; and another would go under the hammer at Sotheby's in 2006 for £2.5 million.

Maybe I'll get an unexpected letter from my solicitor one day.

It was Shakespeare who had brought me to Hay, in fact. My actor son Ben and I had prepared a performance talk based on our new anthology, *The Shakespeare Miscellany*, which had come out earlier in the year, and we were presenting it the next day. We met up in the back garden of The Swan at Hay for a rehearsal. There's something rather appropriate about rehearsing Shakespeariana in the open air with an inn sign above your head.

Perhaps unsurprisingly, given the way swans placidly populate the River Avon, there is a *White Swan* in Stratford, in a building dating from the mid-fifteenth century. However, Shakespeare would not have been able to drink there. In his day it was a large family house. It didn't become an inn until the 1790s. The modern name dates only from the 1830s.

Pub names change so much. There was a *Swan & Maidenhead* in Stratford, but it was first called *The Maidenhead*, and later *The Swan*, before the two names were joined together. Any visitor to Stratford will certainly have gazed at the site where it used to be, because it was actually a part of Shakespeare's birthplace in Henley Street. There were originally two adjacent houses. When William bought New Place, a more spacious home in Chapel Lane, he didn't need the others. His sister, Joan Hart, lived in the smaller one, and the larger building was leased to become an inn.

There are a goodly number of bird inn-signs in England, and *The Swan* is probably the commonest of all. There were no fewer than nineteen taverns, inns, or public houses in London called *The Swan* in an 1864 survey. Only *The Cock* came near, with twelve.

*White Swan*s turn up all over the place. There used to be one in Monmouth, down the road from Hay. No placid image there. The sign showed the bird standing with outstretched neck and open bill hissing fiercely at passers-by. White Swan Court is still there today – another television location. In the 2005 *Dr Who* episode called *The Unquiet Dead*, in which the Doctor visits Charles Dickens and Victorian England in 1869, the Court played the part of a snowy Cardiff square.

There have been some strange Swan combinations over the years. Over the centuries a Swan has been seen cohabiting on signs with all sorts of other animals, such as an Antelope, a Falcon, a White Hart, and a Salmon. Among its object accompaniments have been a Bottle, a Harp, a Helmet, a Hoop, a Horseshoe, and a Lyre. That's just a small selection.

The Swan & Hoop in Moorfields, London, was the birthplace in 1795 of John Keats. It later came to be called *The Moorgate*, and is now, appropriately enough, *The John Keats at Moorgate*. It is right next to the Underground station.

The Swan at Lechlade is the oldest pub in the Gloucestershire town of Lechlade, on the edge of the Cotswolds. Shelley passed through in 1815, and wrote 'Stanza in Lechlade Churchyard'. The path by the church is now called Shelley's Walk.

Then there are the pubs called *The Swan with Two Necks*, or *The Swan with Three Necks*. Two necks . . . three necks? The most widely held theory is that *neck* is an alteration of *nick*. There is an annual census of the swan population on parts of the River Thames called 'Swan Upping' – 'upping' because the birds are picked 'up' out of the water. It dates from the twelfth century and takes place during the third week of July. Traditionally a swan would be marked for identification by nicking its mandible, or some other part of its body. The swans belonging to the Worshipful Company of Dyers would be marked with one nick. Those belonging to the Company of Vintners would be marked with two nicks. In the past there were hundreds of marks granted by the monarch's Swan Master. Royal swans from the time of George III were marked with three nicks. It was Queen Alexandra who reduced the marking practice, concerned that it might be hurting the birds.

Not everyone accepts the 'nick' theory. Old inn signs didn't have inscriptions. The nick mark would have been very tiny, and a swan with such a mark would hardly have been identifiable from the road. Also, it is argued, if there were so many nick combinations, why aren't there inns called *The Swan with Four Necks*, and so on? A heraldic origin – swans encircled by a coronet, for example – has been suggested as an alternative.

However, in Worcester there is actually a pub called *The Swan with Two Nicks*. And there are others – in Sharnbrook, north of Bedford, for instance, and in Altrincham in Cheshire. But these are all recent names, and may have been copied from other 'nick' names. The one in Worcester, for instance, used to be called simply *The Swan*.

The different slants and variants go on and on. *The Swan Inn* at Stoford, near Salisbury in Wiltshire, has a restaurant called *The Cygnet*.

'Nick names' has nothing to do with nicknames. *Nickname* comes from an Old English expression, *an eke name*. *Eke* meant 'also'. It was your 'other' name. Over time, the *n* of *an* got transferred to the beginning of *eke*. *An eke* became *a neke*. The pronunciation changed, and the spelling, and eventually we get the modern word.

With *adder*, the '*n*-swapping' went the other way round. Old English *a nadder* became *an adder*.

Why *was* a swan so popular as an inn sign? There have been both downmarket and upmarket explanations. The downmarket one associates the swan with liquid, thereby uniting the two domains – liquid that you can float on and liquid that makes you feel as if you're floating. There are several traditional rhymes which actually make the connection, such as this one from Ireland:

> This is the Swan that dips her neck in water,
> Why not we as well as she, drink plenty of Crawford's porter.

The upmarket theory associates the swan with heraldic emblems. The swan is one of the many animals used in heraldry, expressing such desirable associations as poetry, harmony, learning, love, grace, innocence, sincerity, and perfection. Many families have used the swan as part of their coat of arms. If you're called Swan (obviously), Brough, Crispell, Hedges, Dawes, or Baker, for example, your arms could well contain a swan or two – and often three.

Four is an uncommon number on an inn sign, but there was a *Four Swans* in London's Bishopsgate, with a fine galleried courtyard where theatre companies probably played in Shakespeare's day. And there used to be another at Waltham Cross in Hertfordshire. It was an old post-house inn, which was demolished in the 1960s to make way for a shopping centre and a car park. But a memorial of the sign is still there, in an unusual place. Four swans nestle together on a gantry across the High Street. They are referred to in local literature as the *Four Swannes*.

When I visited them in 2006, two of them were headless, thanks to vandalism. The Council plan to replace the gantry with a free-standing timber structure and to recast the swans.

The coat of arms for Buckinghamshire County Council features a swan in chains. That's a tradition that goes back to Anglo-Saxon times, when swans were bred in the county for the king's pleasure. They're still a protected species, of course.

Or the queen's pleasure. Which means that Her Majesty must have been in a quandary in March 2005 when the Master of the Queen's Music, Sir Peter Maxwell Davies, was cautioned by police after they found the body of a swan at his home on Orkney. The bird had died after hitting a power line – a fairly regular occurrence – and he had hung it up as part of the process of preparing it for the kitchen. Evidently that's what people do in the islands when they encounter a dead swan. Waste not, want not.

The police had been in the islands on other business, and had seen the swan as they passed by. So they accused Sir Peter of being in illegal possession of the corpse of a protected species, and called at his home to take a statement. The nice part is that when they arrived, he offered them coffee, and then asked them if they would like to try some swan terrine. 'That,' he said afterwards, 'was a mistake.'

Sir Peter had reported the incident, as he always does when such things happen, to the Royal Society for the Protection of Birds. But would this be enough to stop the steamroller of the law? If not, given his position with the Queen, he thought Inverness Prison would not suffice. It would, he said, at least mean a ball and chain in the Tower of London.

Possibly the powers-that-be took note of an ancient Norse system called Udal Law, which gave Orkney and Shetland certain rights not found in the rest of Britain. One of these rights made swans the property of the people. Whether they did or not, I am glad to say that the Master of the Queen's Music remained a free man.

In the garden of The Swan at Hay, Ben and I finished our rehearsal and went inside for dinner. If we ate fast, I thought, we should be through by nine, but that wouldn't stop the book-obsessed at Hay. The Cinema Bookshop stays open late in Festival week, and it would still be an hour to closing. Just enough time to work through the English language section.

I might find something on Norse personal names. *Swan* as a person's name derives from *Swein*, common in the north-east of England in Anglo-Saxon times where the Danes had settled, because it came from the Norse name *Sveinn*. It was a very common appellation in medieval Britain, and has numerous variants today. Telephone directories will show *Swan*, *Swann*, *Swanner*, *Swayne*, *Sweing*, *Sweyn*, *Swein*, and more.

Whenever I eat in The Swan at Hay I think of Samuel Pepys and another *Swan*. This is the entry in his diary for 27 June 1660:

> Dined with my Lord and all the officers of his regiment, who
> invited my Lord and his friends, as many as he would bring,
> to dinner, at the Swan, at Dowgate, a poor house and ill'
> dressed, but very good fish and plenty.

The tavern was on the west side of Dowgate Hill, a few doors away from the church of St John, as you go south out of Cannon Street towards Upper Thames Street. A twelve-hearth establishment, it was kept by vintner Thomas Cox. It burned down in the Great Fire of London in 1666.

Perhaps it was the wine, or the 'good fish and plenty', but I never got to the bookshop that night. Still, I had three days before having to move on to interview more accents. Lots of time.

The next morning I made up for my bibliophilic dilatoriness of the night before, and had four bookshops under my belt by lunchtime. With pub-names on my mind, I noted the Hay animals as I passed them by. *The Blue Boar*. *The Old Black Lion*. And the not-animals, when I saw *The Three Tuns*, with its windows sadly boarded up, at the junction of Broad Street and Bridge Street.

A *tun* was a large cask for holding wine. As early as the twelfth century there are records of tables being set up at banquets by placing oak planks onto three such casks. In due course they became a symbol of vintners and brewers. There was a *Three Tuns* in Seething Lane in London. Pepys knew it well, for it was close to where he lived. A rowdy place, by all accounts. He reports in his diary entry for 9 May 1667:

> in our street at the Three Tuns tavern door find a great hub-bub, and what was it but two brothers have fallen out and one killed the other; and who should they be but the two Fieldings, one whereof, Bazill, was page to my Lady Sandwich; and he hath killed the other, himself being very drunk, and so is sent to Newgate.

Pepys got it wrong. It was in fact Christopher who had killed Basil.

The London *Three Tuns* survived the Great Fire. Not so *The Three Tuns* in Hay. It burned down in February 2005, to the great distress of local people.

Hay's *Three Tuns* had its share of famous visitors over the years, especially in Festival week. But it had some interesting guests at other times too. The former landlady Lucy Powell tells a story about the day five of the Great Train Robbers arrived. 'They came in and had a drink,' she said. 'They seemed quite normal people, just having a chat.' I suppose robbers do look like everyone else.

I wonder what the Great Train Robbers were doing in Hay? Perhaps that's why they stole the money. They were hard-up book-enthusiasts. Maybe they were looking for a First Folio.

You never quite know who you're going to meet in the bookshops of Hay. Turn the corner of one of the stacks, and you might bump into a familiar face or voice. They are usually not in the section you might expect them to be. Jools Holland was not looking at music books. Nor was Barry Norman looking at film. Part of the charm of Hay is that people wander around informally, and they don't usually mind if you approach them.

I, on the other hand, am much more predictable. You will find me in the English language section. Or if not there, in the section on foreign languages and linguistics. Or if not there, in the English literature section.

Now I start to think about it, I'm not predictable at all. If you are searching for interesting uses of English, you can find relevant material anywhere. There will very likely be good stuff in the humour section, or in general reference, or in folklore, or history, or travel. Some of the best material on personal and place-names turns up in those huge volumes encapsulating the history of a town or county.

Several of the examples in this chapter came from a book on the history of inn-signs that I found in Hay a few years ago. It is *English Inn Signs*, written by John Larwood and John Camden Hotton, a revision of their original book, *History of Signboards*, which was published in 1866. I wasn't looking for it, nor was it in a classified section. It was resting in Addyman's window. It called out my name as I passed by.

Hotton was also the publisher of the book. That's not a name we associate with publishing today, but there is a connection with well-known modern firms. Hotton founded his publishing house in 1853, and at his death in 1874 it was acquired by Andrew Chatto. He renamed the firm Chatto and Windus. It acquired Virginia and Leonard Woolf's Hogarth Press in 1946, then merged with Jonathan Cape some twenty years later. It became an imprint of Random House in 1987.

Humour books are a great source of language material because they often display some new and unexpected feature of language play. Everyone plays with language, and enjoys language play – puns, riddles, limericks, crosswords, poetry . . . Robert Graves once said that 'A poet has to master the rules of grammar before he attempts to bend or break them.' That is what language-players do. They bend and break the rules of the language – or, in the case of crossword-puzzle solvers, try to work out the way in which some linguistic torturer has bent or broken them.

Torturer? You only have to look at the pseudonyms that some famous crossword compilers have chosen. The *Observer* set the tone in

1926, with *Torquemada* (Edward Powys Mather), then *Ximenes* (Derrick Macnutt) in 1939, and then *Azed* (Jonathan Crowther) in 1972. All Spanish Grand Inquisitors.

Azed? It is *Deza* backwards. Diego de Deza.

Even inn-signs play with language. Why is that pub called *The Sheep and Anchor*? It was a play on *Ship and Anchor*. And that one over there? *The Coach and Dogs*? A play on *Coach and Horses*. More obscurely, *The Billy Ruffian* is a twisting of the name of the good ship *Bellerophon*. *The Cat and Wheel* is a Protestant avoidance of *Catherine Wheel*.

Nor is the elegant Swan exempt. The actors' pub across the road from the Swan Theatre in Stratford is called *The Black Swan*. Or, at least, it was. It is now also called *The Dirty Duck* – shortened by locals to *The Duck*. It is not the only one. There are dozens of *Mucky Ducks* around the country.

A murder mystery by the American crime writer Martha Grimes is set in Stratford. It is called *The Dirty Duck*.

Several large books could be written on the meaning of inn-signs. Once you leave the common names behind, each one invites exploration, and often they present real puzzles of interpretation. There's nothing new about this. In the early 1600s, Ben Jonson was so intrigued that he penned some lines about them:

> It even puts Apollo
> To all his strength of art to follow
> The flights, and to divine
> What is meant by every sign.

I crossed the road from the Swan and went into the Cinema Bookshop. Yes, the shop was indeed once the town cinema, the Plaza, but it became a bookshop in 1965. That's the charm of Hay. If you don't know what to do with an old building, turn it into a bookshop. Nor does ancestral status make any difference. Hay Castle is a fricassee of bookshops.

Upstairs in the Cinema Bookshop is Francis Edwards – the firm, I mean, not the person. It is a long-established antiquarian bookshop. It started in London in 1855 – and still has a branch there, in Great Newport Street off Charing Cross Road – but its main collection is in Hay. I enjoy reading their catalogues during the year, with their accounts of the comings and goings of old books. But there is nothing to beat a Francis Edwards browse. I always find something quirky to do with English there.

One year I found the amazing two-volume effort by Irish-American lawyer and politician – though 'enthusiast' or 'obsessive' would be better descriptions – Ignatius Donnelly, written in 1888 to prove that the plays of Shakespeare are a complex code revealing that their real author was Francis Bacon. It is called *The Great Cryptogram*. The subtitle is *Francis Bacon's Cipher in the So-called Shakespeare Plays*.

Donnelly is chiefly remembered for the extraordinary amount of research he put into a book five years earlier arguing that the lost civilization of Atlantis was in the middle of the Atlantic Ocean. *Atlantis: The Antediluvian World* was followed in 1883 by another investigation, *Ragnarok, the Age of Fire and Gravel*, which argued that a comet hit the earth in prehistoric times, wiping out a great civilization. Then he turned his attention to Shakespeare.

He devised a complex system of recurring numbers, roots, and arithmetical operations which demonstrated – to his own satisfaction – the existence of hidden messages in his facsimile of the First Folio which gave clues to the 'real' author. Here's an example of the sort of reasoning he used.

On page 53 of the Histories he finds the line 'I have a gammon of Bacon and two razes of ginger.' He calculates that *Bacon* is the 371st word on the page, divides this by the page number, and gets seven. This then becomes the cypher number for Bacon.

Applying this method to hundreds of words, he was able to find such messages hidden within the text as:

Francis Bacon Nicholas Bacon's Son.

And he works out a single root-number, 327, to obtain the message:

More low [Marlowe] or Shak'st spur never writ a word of them.

The detail shown in the book is remarkable, including several Folio pages dotted with tiny numerical annotations in red ink. It was a lovely piece of book-design by the publisher; but an extraordinary feat of misdirected energy by the author. When you look at the detail, you find thousands of arbitrary and inconsistent decisions. A hyphenated word at one place is counted as a single word; at another place as two words – just to make the calculations work.

It wasn't difficult to turn the method against its author. Indeed, in the same year, someone used Donnelly's exact procedure to show that hidden within the plays is the following coded statement by Shakespeare himself:

Master Will i a Jack Spur writ this play and was engaged at the Curtain.

Another time in Francis Edwards' shop I found, on a bottom shelf, one of my own books. I am used to seeing them on the shelves of second-hand bookshops. But in an antiquarian house? I mean, how old do they think I am!

Later that year Francis Edwards' catalogue 1423 arrived in the post. There was my book, solemnly described in the clinical elliptical jargon of the antiquarian bookseller – but with an unusual coda:

> *1st Ed. 4to. 489pp. Numerous cold. and b/w ills. and photos, etc. D/w. £25. Hello David!!*

I was much amused. I had never been greeted by name in a bookseller's catalogue before. Nor, I suspect, has anyone else. But you never know. Maybe hidden within the pages of a long-lost catalogue produced by the Elizabethan publisher Richard Field is a greeting: 'Hello, William!!'

4to is 'quarto', *cold* 'coloured', *b/w* 'black-and-white', *ills* 'illustrations', *D/w* 'Dust-wrapper'. I was let off lightly. The book next to mine had its 'spine slightly faded'. At my age, I know how it felt.

My copy of Donnelly had two book-plates at the front. One looked Victorian: it said 'Ex Libris G. Gregor Grant', and showed a medieval scholar poring over books. The other said 'John Cannon: His Book'. It showed a medieval soldier lighting a cannon. Nice visual pun.

I often wonder who were the previous owners of an antiquarian book. But how could one ever find out? Most owners would not be public figures. In today's terms, they have left no Google trace. So one is left to romantic imaginings, based on the handwriting of a signature or what can be deduced about the personality from the image displayed on a book-plate.

There is a world of difference, I imagine, between the personalities

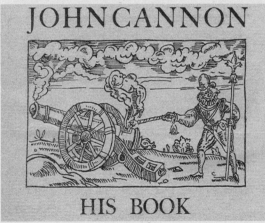

of someone who has a book-plate saying 'Ex Libris' and someone whose book-plate says bluntly 'His Book'. Try it out on your own name. 'Ex Libris David Crystal'. 'David Crystal: His Book'. The former is redolent of scholarship and musty shelves. The latter is more, well, Winnie-the-Pooh.

What sort of person would buy a book on Shakespearian cryptography, apart from eccentric linguists? In a stroke of good fortune, I found out about one of them. Tucked away between pages 662 and 663 in Volume 2 was a sheet of blank headed notepaper, presumably used as a bookmark. Top right was the address: 'New Wing, Somerset House, London W.C.2'. Top left was the sender: 'Memo from J.T. Cannon'. And underneath it gave his profession: 'Senior Principal Inspector of Taxes'.

I have to say my romantic imaginings had not extended as far as the Office of Inland Revenue. Nor, until then, had I associated tax inspectors with puns.

In another Francis Edwards catalogue, in the travel section, I encountered one of the best travel titles ever. The book was called *Because I Haven't Been There Before*. It might have been the title of this book too, for most of my stories are the result of travelling down linguistic side-roads that I've never previously explored.

I left Francis Edwards a few book-pounds heavier and a few bank-pounds lighter. The wonderful thing about staying at the Swan is that you can dump your purchases in your room before going out browsing again. Carrier-bag hand is another symptom of HBBS, but it can be avoided if you choose your accommodation well.

I was on my way to the bibliocathedral in Lion Street, in an absent-minded, book-induced stupor, when I remembered why I was in Hay. The Literary Festival. I was due on with Ben shortly. I turned on my heel and headed for the Festival site. Lion Street would have to wait. And indeed, what with the talk and the book-signing and the ensuing chats and the close encounters with old friends, it was the next day before I got my chance to worship there.

At 44 Lion Street is Richard Booth's main shop. It is a cathedral worthy of William Golding treatment, except that here the foundations are as solid as you would expect from a building that was once an agricultural hall, built in 1886 for a manufacturer of farm machinery and tools. That business was the first in the town to become a limited company, so it became known as 'the Limited'.

You can't miss the shop. Ornate picture tiles on the front of the building show rural and farming designs. In the front gable there is a shield held by a lion, inscribed 'R.W.&S. 1886', the initials of the manufacturing firm, 'Robert Williams & Sons'. Inside there are timber pillars supporting two floors, and there is a huge sprawling basement. In the old days, the upper floor was used for banquets, balls, and other public functions.

To find the English language section you have to go downstairs and wind your way through theology and foreign languages, minding your head against the low beams, until, round a corner at the end of a passageway, you are in a corner of the basement as far away from the entrance as it is possible to get. It reminds me irresistibly of one of those European cathedrals which has a crypt full of skulls and relics, except that here it is only old linguistics books that are sleeping the sleep of the just, side by side on dusty shelves. Others are piled randomly in cardboard boxes, awaiting their assignment to a resting place. You feel as if you are in the bowels of book-earth. Every now and then you catch the shuffle of footsteps along the stone basement floor. But few souls venture this far underground in search of books. It could be very dangerous down there, Mr Frodo, sir.

The shop in Lion Street is the largest bookshop in Hay. For that matter, it is the largest in Europe. Its turnover in used books is claimed to be the largest in the world.

Having said that, some books I know have been there for years. It is like recognizing old friends. If somebody does ever buy them I shall be quite upset.

Richard Booth was the founder of the Hay book-trade. A local man with a grand vision and energy to match, he planned his first book ventures in 1961. He bought the fire station, and put books in it. He bought the decaying Hay Castle, and put books in it. He bought the cinema, and put books in it. His idea was very simple, but breathtaking in its cheeky vision: buy books from all over the world, and get customers to come from all over the world. Fill the town with both. By the end of the 1970s there were at least a million books in Hay, and the customers were coming.

His flair for publicity helped enormously. On 1 April 1977 he declared 'Home Rule' for Hay, appointing himself King and his horse Prime Minister. This Unilateral Declaration of Independence was consolidated on 1 April 2000, when, in the State Room of Hay Castle, he held an investiture of the Hay House of Lords, creating twenty-one new hereditary peers. Dukedoms, earldoms, baronies, and knighthoods – or, for that matter, a foreign peerage of your choice – can still be conveniently and cheaply arranged during your visit to Hay.

The town's reputation grew enormously in 1988, with the establishment of the first Literary Festival. When Bill Clinton appeared there in 2002 he likened it to 'the Woodstock of the mind'.

It is the variety of the bookshops in Hay that is so striking. You might think that with thirty-eight bookshops there would be a huge overlap in their contents. There is some, of course, but it is the specialisms that are so intriguing. Boz Books, specializing in Dickens. C. Arden, specializing in natural history. Murder and Mayhem, specializing in – well, murder and mayhem. The Children's Bookshop. The Poetry Bookshop.

And the linguist's heaven: Marijana Dworski Books. You will find her in Backfold, the alleyway that runs behind Castle Street below the castle mound. Over 350 languages will typically be on her shelves, from every continent – books *in* the languages, books *about* the languages, dictionaries, phrase books, travel books too. Then there are books about language in general, books about analysing language, books on phonetics, books on grammar, semantics, and sociolinguistics, books on language teaching and learning, more books on phonetics. You cannot have too much phonetics.

Another dangerous place, Sam Gamgee. Beware. You can lose a day quite happily in Marijana's bookshop. It is the linguistic equivalent of a westward crossing of the International Dateline.

Fortunately for living authors, and especially for those attending the Festival, there is also a shop in Hay which specializes in non-used books: Pembertons, in High Town. Diana Blunt from that shop runs the Festival book tent, holds the stock for each literary event, and hosts the book-signings. It is the most remarkable operation. Think about it. You have to arrange enough copies to accompany each event so that authors have plenty to sign, but you never know which books are going to 'go'. There are usually three events taking place at the same time, so there are three book-signing queues to prepare for. There are three ego-sensitive authors (or more, for some are collaborations) to look after, and who knows if they are not going to do a Golding or worse? And there are the odd few thousand punters to be managed as they mill around, some browsing, some buying, some just wanting to chat.

Every year I look with admiration at Diana and her staff, and reflect that there must be easier jobs than bookselling. Like nuclear physics. Or brain surgery.

One year I was allowed to peep round the back of the book tent, where all the boxes of books await their turn to go public. Each is labelled with the number of the event in the Festival programme. We are talking about over three hundred events. The bookscape resembles the aftermath of a battle. Or beforemath, perhaps, for most of the boxes are awaiting their moment of glory.

Things can go wrong. In 2004 Penguin Books decided to open a new automated warehouse, but encountered major problems, so that there were huge delays in getting books out to booksellers. Around the Festival site were Penguin authors spitting blood, because their latest books weren't there. I was in the same boat. My *Stories of English* had just come out, but you would never have known. Of course, it's the bookseller who gets the flak from the punters – and often from the author too.

In my case, I was saved by the publishing equivalent of John Wayne. My commissioning editor at Penguin, Martin Toseland, arrived at the site just in time, struggling under the weight of a huge box of *Stories of English*. He had picked them up personally. If there is a medal for bookselling beyond the call of duty, he deserved it that day.

The next year, Martin left Penguin and joined HarperCollins. One day he suggested I read W.G. Sebald's *The Rings of Saturn*, and lent me his copy. 'I wonder if it would be possible to write a narrative like that on a linguistic theme?' he mused. I thought it might be possible, but if I were to do it the paragraphs would have to be shorter – less German. I promised to think about it . . .

Martin's copy was falling to pieces. The glue had gone on the spine. I needed one of my own. So I kept an eye out for it during my Hay trawl. Not a sign. 'We had one the other week,' became a mantra. There is only one thing more frustrating than hearing that from booksellers. It is when they say: 'I *think* we've got one downstairs/upstairs/in the back room/on the shelves outside' . . . when they haven't. Or, at least, as far as you can tell after an hour, they haven't.

But persistence pays, and I found one in the end, deep within Hay Castle. I crammed it into a bag already full of other purchases. My delight was tempered only by a severe recurrence of HBBS. It was time to move on.

7

Now Godiva was a Lady

LEOMINSTER

I left Hay after three days, the car boot a lot heavier, and crossed the river to join the road to Leominster in Herefordshire, where I had an appointment. I must also have crossed the line of Offa's Dyke, but there is no dyke to see here. The earthwork disappears where it reaches the Wye.

I looked back at Hay Castle. The main building you can see today is the Jacobean mansion, built on to the remaining medieval walls in the seventeenth century. The tall clustered red-brick Jacobean chimneys are highly distinctive.

What a chequered history that castle has. The fire in the Three Tuns had some illustrious ancestors. The castle was burned by King John in 1211, and again in 1231 by the Welsh prince Llywelyn ap Iorwerth. Rebuilt by Henry III, it was often attacked during the turmoil in the reign of Henry IV.

Throughout most of 1404 it was commanded by Sir John Oldcastle of Herefordshire. His name is familiar to Shakespeare buffs. It was used for Prince Hal's fat, bibulous companion in *Henry IV*. Shakespeare later changed the name to Falstaff – probably to avoid complaints from some of Oldcastle's descendants.

The burning didn't stop once the relations between England and

Wales settled down. The eastern part of the castle was devastated by a fire in 1939; and the western part forty years later. Renovation slowly continues. It is expensive. Visitors can help by buying a Hay peerage.

The name of the town is from Norman French *La Haie*, meaning 'an enclosure surrounded by a fence or hedge'. The same sense is found in the Welsh name, *Y Gelli*, meaning 'grove' or 'wood'. It's not clear what the original enclosure was. There are actually two castle sites in Hay. You have to know where to look to find the other one, in the car park behind the Swan. All you can see now is a broad mound with a flat top.

Also behind the Swan is the parish church of St Mary. The Catholic church in Broad Street is St Joseph's. There is an early medieval building in the town centre called St John's Chapel – or Eglwys Ifan ('Church Evan') in Welsh – which over the years has had many functions, including school, prison, and hairdressing salon. When I first saw the name, I thought 'very appropriate' – until I realized that it was the wrong St John. It would have been the Evangelist or the Baptist, and not St John of God.

St John of God is the patron saint of the book trade; and if he should have a presence anywhere, it should be in Hay.

John was a fifteenth-century Spanish soldier who turned to helping the poor, the sick, and the disadvantaged. His work led to the establishment of the Hospitaller Order, an international Catholic community of brothers who provide health, social care, and pastoral services to people in need.

He could be a role model for many in Hay. An avid reader, he left his job to become a travelling bookman, selling religious cards and books. Then he set up a small bookshop in Granada, Spain.

When the local hospital caught fire, he distinguished himself by leading the patients to safety and saving some of the contents. He even saved part of the building itself. The authorities had brought in a cannon to destroy the burning part of the hospital in order to preserve the rest. John stopped them, climbed up to the roof, and used an axe to chop away the burning section. He managed it, but then fell through the disintegrating roof. Everyone thought he had been killed, until he miraculously appeared out of the smoke on the ground floor.

He is therefore also the patron saint of firefighters. Richard Booth started his first bookshop in the old fire station. St John of God should definitely be in Hay.

I turned right onto the A438 to Leominster. It was one of those days when the Black Mountains, with their clusters of dark green woodland, really did seem black. The Golden Valley runs close by. Prominent in the distance was the elegant and distinctive fourteenth-century tower of Weobley church. It looks different from the usual church tower, and so it is. It is thought to be the only spire in the country to be supported by small flying buttresses connected to a pinnacle rising from each of the tower's four corners.

Weobley is pronounced 'web-lee'. It is spelled *Wibelai* in Domesday Book. It was originally the 'leah', or pastureland, of *Wibba*. Nobody knows who Wibba – or, in an alternative old spelling, *Weobba* – was.

The place contains echoes of Shakespeare. It was the centre of the rebellion by Henry Duke of Buckingham against King Richard III in 1483. Buckingham was executed in Salisbury, and his wife captured in Weobley.

And, three kings earlier, in 1402, we encounter part of the tale told during the opening scene of Shakespeare's *Henry IV Part I*. Westmoreland tells the court that last night there came

> A post from Wales, loaden with heavy news,
> Whose worst was that the noble Mortimer,
> Leading the men of Herefordshire to fight
> Against the irregular and wild Glendower,
> Was by the rude hands of that Welshman taken,
> A thousand of his people butchered . . .

This was the Battle of Bryn Glâs. It took place on a hill above the village of Pilleth, near Knighton, just west of Offa's Dyke. Bryn Glâs is only thirteen miles from Weobley.

A couple of miles further along the road, I passed another noticeable church at Dilwyn – St Mary's, with a thirteenth-century tower topped by an eighteenth-century spire. In 1733, six bells were placed in the tower. I would not expect to find first-person pronouns in a bell, but there they are. Inside each one is an inscribed message.

Prosperity to all my benefactors, A.R., 1733

Peace and good neighbourhood, 1733

A.R. Rudhall, of Gloucester, cast us all, 1733

A.R., 1733

Richard Bradford and Thomas Sherward, Ch. wardens

I to the church the living call, And to the grave do summons all

The paternal tones ring out across the centuries.

Villages such as Weobley and Dilwyn are part of the Black and White Trail. The name relates to the large number of timbered and half-timbered houses that are found throughout the area. The forty-mile circular trail starts and ends at Leominster.

Leominster is one of those place-names that make foreign learners of English despair. It is not pronounced 'Leo + minster', but 'lemster'. As with dozens of other towns, a local colloquial pronunciation has emerged which today bears only a rough approximation to the spelling.

One of the swans with two nicks was at *Altrincham*, where the *nch* is pronounced *ng*. If I'd travelled to Leominster from Holyhead via the A55, I'd have passed *Hawarden* near Chester, which sounds like 'harden'. Wherever you go you will find oddities. *Mousehole* in Cornwall is 'muzzle'. *Lympne* in Kent is 'lim'. *Woolfardisworthy* in Devon is 'woolzy' or 'woolzery'. *Happisburgh* in Norfolk is 'haysbruh'.

The unpredictabilities are by no means restricted to the UK. You have to learn that *Kansas* and *Arkansas* don't rhyme. Nor do *Athens* in Greece and *Athens* in Georgia (it's *a* as in *say* for the latter). *Tucson* in Arizona is 'toosawn'. *Natchitoches* in California is 'nakuhtush'. And *Leominster* in Massachusetts is 'leminster'.

The Herefordshire Leominster presents another question. Who or what was Leo? It looks as if the name means 'Leo's church'. But with place-names you should never trust what you see. And *Leominster* has several plausible sources.

Leo is Latin for 'lion'. It seems unlikely that a lion would have anything to do with a town in England, but one interpretation of the name does rely upon it. In the seventh century, a Northumbrian missionary, Ealfred, arrived at the court of Merewald, a subordinate ruler to Penda, King of all Mercia. According to legend, a ravenous lion appeared and terrified everyone; but when offered bread by the monk it ate quietly from his hands. Christianity was soon adopted, and Leominster Priory was founded.

The Anglo-Saxon priory was closed down by Edward the Confessor in the eleventh century. The remains we see today date from early Norman times, and there is evidence of a leonine tradition on the inside by the west door. There you will see a small carving of a man and a lion. But is it Ealfred's lion? According to some authorities, it is more likely to be a representation of the biblical story of Samson and the lion, and that is how it is described in the Priory literature. After all, what would a lion be doing in Herefordshire?

But place-names are no respecters of the distinction between fact and fiction. You can call your town after a legend if you want to. And in the great account of Wales written by Giraldus Cambriensis ('Gerald of Wales') in the twelfth century, we see Leominster referred to as *Leonis Monasterium* – 'monastery of the lion'. The resonance of *Leo* 'lion' also carries through from Welsh. 'Lion' is *llew* in Welsh.

Most accounts of Leominster opt for other theories. The original Welsh name was *Llanllieni*, meaning 'church on the streams'. The town is on the River Lugg. Leominster could have been a translation of that.

Then again, in Welsh *lleian* is 'nun', and there is a recorded form *Leanminster*. So it could have meant 'church of the nuns'. There were definitely nuns there, under an abbess, in the eleventh century. In fact, the reason why the pre-Norman abbey was dissolved by Edward the Confessor was because of a scandal involving the abbess. One of the new English earls, Swein, Edward's brother-in-law, abducted Abbess Edgiva and – as the Anglo-Saxon Abingdon Chronicle demurely puts it for the year 1046 – 'kept her as long as he pleased, and then let her go home'. He was exiled soon after. The twelfth-century chronicler Florence of Worcester adds that Swein wanted to marry her 'whom he had corrupted'.

Earl was a new title in late Anglo-Saxon England, introduced by the Danish King Cnut (Canute), who came to the throne in 1016. Previously, senior noblemen had been called *ealdormen* – 'aldermen', as we would say today. And one of the most powerful men in the kingdom was Leofric, Earl of Mercia. This is another possible source for *Leominster*. The town is actually spelled *Leofministre* in Domesday Book.

Domesday, or *Doomsday*, as it is more popularly known. The idea that it would last until doomsday is a twelfth-century development. Richard Fits Nigel, the treasurer of Henry II, wrote that 'this book is metaphorically called by the native English Domesdai, the Day of Judgement', because, he says, 'when this book is appealed to on those matters which it contains, its sentence cannot be quashed or set aside with impunity'.

Leofric is made up out of two elements: *leof* 'dear' + *ric* 'kingdom, ruler'. *Leof* is the origin of modern *love*, or *beloved*. It was Leofric who funded the nunnery, so it could legitimately be called Leofric's church. Or perhaps he and his wife Geodgifu endowed it together. *Geodgifu* means 'gift of God'. English legend knows her better by her Latin name, *Godiva* – Lady Godiva.

The story of Lady Godiva has become part of English folklore. As first recounted by the chronicler Roger of Wendover in the thirteenth century, her husband promised to withdraw some heavy taxes from the people of Coventry if she dared to ride around the town naked. This she duly did, and the taxes were stopped. In the post-Puritan account of the story that is generally told in children's books, she had conveniently long hair. Also, the townspeople are told to stay indoors. Only one man dared to look – 'peeping Tom' – and, in another account, was struck blind for his foolishness. But that part of the story was added many centuries later.

The event, if it happened, must have taken place before 1057, when Leofric died. Godiva is thought to have married Leofric around 1035. She lived until after the Conquest. Most sources say she died in 1067, but she is named in Domesday Book – the only woman mentioned as a landholder.

The ride is usually dismissed as a romantic legend. But something *might* have happened, for some records of early Coventry show, un-usually, no taxes being levied except on horses. And the ride lives on in folklore: a Godiva procession takes place in Coventry at the end of May every year. It also lives on in business: the Godiva Awards recognize excellence in tourism and leisure in the Midlands region. And it lives on in sport: there is a Lady Godiva Half Marathon.

It would be strange to meet a woman called Godiva today. As a personal name it never became fashionable. Most first-name books don't even mention it as a possibility. But its legendary status has made it surprisingly popular as an event name. In clinical psychology, *Lady Godiva syndrome* is one of the names given to exhibitionism. An asteroid discovered in the Main Asteroid Belt in 1982 is called *3018 Godiva*. A popular brand of European chocolate is called *Godiva*. You will often see the name at airports.

And Lady Godiva rules in some parts of the academic world. The University of Toronto, for example, has a student social event in January: they call it *Godiva Week*. In several schools of military engineering, especially in North America, she has almost divine status. *Godiva's Hymn* can be heard sung by engineers across campuses, in many versions, several verses of which are unrepeatable in respectable company. The first verse of one of them will give you a hint of the tone:

> Godiva was a lady that through Coventry did ride,
> To show to all the villagers her fine and lily-white hide.
> The most observant villager, an Engineer of course,
> Was the only one to notice that Godiva rode a horse.

The others I leave to your imagination.

Surprisingly, Leofric has a modern following too. There is a Leofric Hotel in Coventry, and a film and video production company based there has also chosen it as its name. The local Liberal Democrats in Leominster decided to call their area branch *Leofric* in 2002. Work to maintain Leominster Priory is called *Operation Leofric*. You will even sometimes encounter it as a person's first name. The full name of Lord Alexander of Tunis was *Harold Rupert Leofric George Alexander*.

The address of Operation Leofric is, appropriately enough, in Godiva Road. But there is nothing ancient about the road. It winds, rather incongruously, through an area of new housing.

Between 1965 and 1970 a Sealink boat plied between Holyhead and the Irish port of Dun Laoghaire ('done lair-ee'). It was called, in a hugely imaginative feat of name creation, *Holyhead Ferry 1*. The 1970 Britannia Bridge fire sent it elsewhere, then in 1974 it went for a refit at the Swan Hunter yard in Newcastle before being transferred to Dover. They changed her name for the Dover crossings. Sealink did rather better the second time. She was renamed the *Earl Leofric*. The *Earl Leofric* no longer exists. She was sent for scrap in Spain in 1981.

As I neared Leominster I passed through Monkland. The *land* is misleading. It doesn't mean 'land of monks'. The form comes from the Old English word *hlynn*, later *lene*, meaning 'torrent' or 'stream'. A *lene* was an area filled with streams. There are several names with this ending around here. *Kingsland*. *Eardisland*. There is a White Swan at Eardisland, another village on the Black and White Trail.

Eardisland was simply called *Lene* in Domesday Book. So was Kingsland. And Monkland was *Leine*. By 1170 it had developed into

Monecheslene – the part of the 'lene' belonging to the monks. In this case, they were a small cell of monks sent over from the Benedictine abbey at Conches in Normandy.

Leofric of Mercia is not the only famous personality so named in Anglo-Saxon times. There is another Leofric, who was the first Bishop of Exeter in the eleventh century. He is much more significant for the history of English, because he owned a tenth-century book which he left to the library of Exeter Cathedral upon his death in 1072. His will talks about a *mycel englisc boc* – 'a great book in English' – *be gehwilcum þingum on leoðwisan geworht* – 'concerning various matters written in verse'. It contains a sixth of all the surviving material we have in the Old English language. Without it, we would never have known some of the best Old English poems, such as 'The Wanderer' and 'The Seafarer', as well as dozens of poem-riddles, among the most intriguing poetic works of the Anglo-Saxon period.

Here is a translation of one of the Anglo-Saxon riddles from the *Exeter Book*, as it came to be called. What is being referred to?

> My garments fall silent when I tread the earth or inhabit my
> dwelling or stir the water. Sometimes my trappings and the lofty
> air raise me high above the homes of men, and the power of
> clouds then bears me far and wide over the people. My adorn-
> ments resound loudly and melodiously. They sing clearly when
> I am not resting on the flood and the earth – a soaring spirit.

The answer is: a swan.

It was a 'great book' indeed, for its time. The 131 parchment leaves measure 12.5 inches by 8.6 inches. The first eight pages are not original, the last few pages have been damaged by fire, and some pages from the middle are missing. There are signs of it having been used as a chopping board and a mug-rest. You can see the knife marks and the liquid stains.

It is surprising how few Anglo-Saxon personal names have come down to us. Most Old English names went out of use within a couple of generations after the Norman Conquest. Even royal names didn't survive. *Alfred* is an exception, presumably because of his special status as 'Great'. *Edward* is another, doubtless because of King Edward the Confessor, whose sainthood was recognized by the French. Other Anglo-Saxon saintly names which lasted include *Edmund*, *Edgar*, *Cuthbert*, *Edwin*, *Hilda*, *Audrey* and *Mildred*.

In the Victorian period, these Anglo-Saxon names came back into fashion. It's interesting that they tend to have an old-fashioned ring about them today.

Anglo-Saxon names followed the Germanic pattern of name-creation. Most names contained two elements, each of which had a meaning – though why they were combined in the way they were is by no means clear. Thus, *Alfred* is 'elf' + *ræd* 'advice'. *Edward* is 'fortunate' + 'guard'. Royal names often began with *athel* 'noble' – such as *Athelstan* + 'stone', *Athelwulf* + 'wolf', and *Athelbert* + 'bold'.

You can see the contrast between modern and Anglo-Saxon names if you look at a *Liber Vitae* – a 'Book of Life'. This was a book in which a religious house would record the names of its members, friends, and associates. Some people might find a long litany of names rather boring. I find them endlessly fascinating. If you read them aloud, you can hear the phonetic character of Old English. It is name-poetry.

> . . . *Herding, Aligua, Friubet, Hiuddi, Aldceorl, Cuthelm, Betuini, Pecthaeth* . . .

These are some of the monks listed in the Durham *Liber Vitae*. It is a complex manuscript which originated in the mid-ninth century as a list of several hundred names of people associated with a Northumbrian church, probably Lindisfarne, but possibly Jarrow or Monkwearmouth.

> . . . *Friodumund, Theodric, Cynibercht, Herebald, Osmund, Tilf-rith, Ælfsig* . . .

Around 1100 the list was extended, chiefly by adding the names of monks from Durham Cathedral Priory. The practice continued until the sixteenth century. And throughout the Middle Ages, thousands of names of lay people were added.

Alongside the names of abbots and monks are lists of abbesses and nuns.

> ... *Raegnmaeld, Eaufled, Iurminburg, Pendgith, Badugyth, Æstorhild, Ricfolcyn, Berchtae* ...

The names are written alternately in gold and either silver or ordinary black ink. Sometimes a series of names appears in gold.

> ... *Eardgyth, Siguaru, Hleoburg, Tidhild, Æbbino, Uilcumae, Ecgsuith* ...

Many letters are so worn that the names are now hardly legible.

Hleoburg, Beorngyth, Osgeofu ... The *eo* spelling turns up quite often in Old English, representing a spoken diphthong that would have sounded a bit like the one in *fair* today. It is unusual to see it in Modern English. I am always struck by the *eo* spellings in Herefordshire place-names: *Weobley, Leominster, Cleobury Mortimer* ...

An *eo* spelling representing a single vowel sound is an unusual one in English words generally. We find it in just a few loan-words – *jeopardy, dungeon, yeoman, luncheon, truncheon, puncheon* (a large cask), *leopard, people*. And it turns up in *George*, of course. Only *people* is very common – one of the most frequently occurring words in English, in the top hundred.

The *o* shouldn't be in *people* at all, really. In Middle English the word had a variety of spellings, such as *peple, pepule, pepille*, and *pepyll*. Forms with *o* occasionally appeared, presumably influenced by the Old French *poeple*, such as *pople*. Then, in the late fifteenth century, and increasingly in the sixteenth, the word appears as *people*. Why?

It was a time when a movement in favour of spelling reform was emerging. Several influential scholars were getting increasingly worried about the chaotic state of English spelling. They had good cause. Once upon a time, English spelling was in a quite respectable state, with letters reflecting sounds in a reasonably orderly way. That was in Anglo-Saxon times. The Irish missionary monks did a good job when they devised a system to write English down for the first time.

But the trouble with a writing system which reflects sounds accurately is that word-spellings begin to vary around the country, because local people write their local accent in their own way. In Old English, the word for 'old' appeared as *eald* in the southern dialects, but as *ald* in the Midlands and North. Hundreds of words show differences of this kind.

Then, after the Norman Conquest, the English writing system was largely put in the hands of French-trained scribes, who immediately began to introduce the spellings with which they were most familiar. They brought in the *qu* spelling for words which in Old English had been spelled *cw* – such as *queen* for *cwen*. They introduced *ch* for *c* in such words as *church* – *cyrice* in Old English. It is thanks to them that we now have an *ou* instead of a *u* in *house*, and a *gh* instead of an *h* in *might* and *enough*.

They noticed that when the letter *u* turns up in a manuscript next to such letters as *v*, *i*, *n*, or *m*, it was difficult to read the word, because all you could see was a sequence of identical downward strokes. They therefore replaced the *u* with *o*. That is why we have *come*, *love*, *one*, and *son*. The practice certainly helped legibility, but it added a new set of complications to spelling.

By the end of the Middle Ages, English spelling was already difficult, and scholars were beginning to think of ways in which they could improve the situation. The proposals ranged from jettisoning the whole system and starting again, to the moderate tweaking of individual words.

A large number of tweaks came from reformers who felt that it would be helpful if the history of a word could be reflected in its spelling. Many English words came from Latin, and in the original languages there were consonants and vowels which no longer existed in the modern spelling. So, the argument went, let's put them back in. All educated people had been taught Latin. They would be reminded of a word's Latin origin, and this would help enormously.

As a result, a *b* was inserted into the word *det*, because the Latin source was *debitum*, to give *debt*. An *s* was added to *iland*, from Latin *insula*, to give *island*. And the *o* in *people* was seized upon, because it was a reminder of Latin *populum*. Each of these spellings, and many more besides, as we now know, caught on, and eventually became the standard.

Did these changes help us to spell better? Most of us would say that actually they made orthographic life much more complicated. We have far more 'silent letters' to cope with now. And one of the commonest proposals in modern suggestions for spelling reform is to leave the silent letters out.

The traffic had been very light along the road from Hay, but as I approached Leominster I found myself in a queue. In the distance I could see red flashing lights and a barrier. A railway line and a level crossing.

Will spelling reform ever happen in English? A few years ago I would have said a definite 'no'. Now I'm not so sure. There are signs of it happening, but in a manner that spelling reformers never predicted.

Reformers have always had a problem getting their ideas accepted, because they try to introduce their system 'top down'. An enthusiast can spend hundreds of hours working on a proposal, and then hundreds more trying to get other people to accept it. There is immediate resistance, for obvious reasons. The new system looks very strange. And people who have learned traditional spelling are naturally reluctant to change their ways.

There is also a less obvious reason. Dozens of reform proposals have been made in the past hundred years, and no two are the same. I get a new proposal from someone every few months, asking for comment. Some are extraordinarily detailed – hundreds of pages. I can never respond. You could spend your whole life reading proposals for spelling reform, simplified English, artificial languages, or new systems of universal communication that will guarantee peace on earth. It seems to be a favourite pastime of retired civil servants. I wonder if J.T. Cannon ever invented one?

If there were an obvious front-runner for spelling reform, things might be different. George Bernard Shaw was convinced that his 'Shavian' system was the solution. It was roundly criticized by other reformers. And each reformer, in turn, has his (it is almost always a 'he') system eventually panned by others. There has always been division within the kingdom of spelling reform.

Only one set of proposals has ever succeeded in being taken up nationally. That was the system introduced by Noah Webster in the late 1700s for American English. Most of the simplified spellings that distinguish American from British English were proposed by him. *Color* for *colour*. *Program* for *programme*. *Traveling* for *travelling*. *Ax* for *axe*. Not all of his suggestions were accepted. *Definit* for *definite*, for example, never caught on.

Webster's spelling reform worked because it was a very special time in English linguistic – as well as cultural – history. He was in on the birth of a 'new nation', anxious to establish its identity. British English, he argued, could not be a model for American people. As he said in his *Dissertations on the English Language*, written in 1789, it was a matter of honour 'as an independent nation . . . to have a system of our own, in language as well as government'. And he asked the question:

> ought the Americans to retain these faults which produce innumerable inconveniencies in the acquisition and use of the language, or ought they at once to reform these abuses, and introduce order and regularity into the orthography of the AMERICAN TONGUE?

They ought indeed, was the universal reply. And in due course Webster's spelling became the norm for American English.

But it didn't solve the spelling difficulty. The 2002 film *Spellbound* illustrates that. This was a documentary about the annual school spelling competition in the USA. Who would ever have thought that spelling would make good drama? But it had you sitting on the edge of your seat. People got terribly involved. As the children on screen got a spelling wrong, you would hear the correct version shouted out around the cinema – if the adults knew it, of course. Some of the challenges were horrendous.

Spell *ptarmigan*, *zygote*, *diarrhoea*. It's usually just one place in the word which is the crux. Everybody starts off confidently enough with *diarrhoea*. It's what comes after the *r*s that causes the problem. It's slightly less effortful in American English, which drops the *o*.

The film is also an indictment. There would be no scope for spelling competitions at all if English orthography wasn't still so irregular. Webster's tweaks didn't solve the problem.

We mustn't overstate the irregularity. When you examine all the words in a college dictionary, you will find that over three-quarters of them are spelled on perfectly regular principles. There is nothing problematical about *cat*, obviously, but nor is there about *catatonic* or *catapult*. That is why a phonic approach to the teaching of reading in English is so essential. Most words can be 'sounded out' and related to spellings in a reasonably orderly way.

The problem with English is that many of the non-phonic words are among the most frequently used in the language. Words like *the* and *of*, *one* and *two*, *could* and *shall*, *might* and *ought*, *woman* and *women*, *write* and *people*. Some words just have to be learned as wholes. You will never solve the spelling of *could* by trying to relate its letters to its sounds.

But it isn't just a matter of sounding out letters or learning whole words. If you really want to get to grips with English spelling, you have to know the principles. There are dozens of principles governing the way we spell words, and some of them explain a great deal.

A train whooshed past and the barrier rose. I began to move forward very slowly. The warning notice came into view. I wasn't really reading it, but it looked oddly unfamiliar. I couldn't put my finger on why for a moment. Then it leapt out at me.

The sign said: *ANOTHER TRAIN COMMING* *if lights continue to show*.

I did an emergency stop, and pulled off the road onto some gravel. I got an angry toot from the driver behind me. 'I'm sorry!' I shouted. 'Emergency! Linguist on call.' I had to take a photograph. No one would believe the story without the evidence.

In fact there are some famous photographs of public spelling errors. One shows a group of men painting the word *STOP* on a road in large white letters. Only it says *SOTP*. Another road-painting one says *SHCOOL*.

I don't know how long the railway sign had been there. Or how long it stayed before it was changed. Last time I went past the spot it had been replaced.

Actually, I'm surprised we don't see things like that more often. The signwriter was only following a basic principle of English spelling. Whoever it was had obviously learned the different way in which short and long spoken vowels are typically represented. But not the exceptions to the rule.

This is the difference between such pairs as *batting* and *bating*, *hopping* and *hoping*, and *sitting* and *siting*. The first of each pair has a short vowel; the second has a long one (actually, a vowel with two phonetic qualities – a diphthong). How do you know which is short and which is long? The spelling tells you. If it is a short vowel, you will see it followed by a double consonant. If it is a long vowel, there is only one consonant.

You can test this out by using nonsense words. The words *latting* and *lating* don't exist in any dialect of English that I know; but if they do enter the language one day, you will deduce from the spelling that the first has a short vowel, rhyming with *pat*, and the second a long one, rhyming with *pate*.

However, no spelling principle in English works all the time. And even this basic principle has exceptions. Words like *having* and *coming* have just one consonant, but the vowel is short. If the system were perfect, they would be *havving* and *comming*. Not surprisingly, children and foreigners and uneducated characters in literature sometimes get confused, and fail to pay attention to irregular spellings. But not – we would hope – signwriters and printers.

I had the sign in view longer than I was expecting. Just as I was about to move off, the barrier came down again. A train from the other direction. That's the problem with linguistics. It can cause unexpected delays to your journey.

I reflected that the railway warning sign would have looked perfectly normal if Orm had had his way. He was an English Augustinian monk who lived around the turn of the thirteenth century. We know next to nothing about him, apart from his writing. He calls himself both *Orrm* and *Orrmin*, suggesting he was of Scandinavian origin. The name means 'serpent, worm' in Old Norse. We see the word used again in the headland in North Wales called the Great Orme – the Great Worm.

Orm (it usually has just one *r* in modern spelling) was a common name in the Danish-influenced part of England. The dedication to his book tells us that he had a brother, Walter, who was a canon of the same order of monks. The evidence of the text suggests a dialect from the East Midlands, so a possible location for them would have been at Elsham Priory, near Brigg, in North Lincolnshire.

Orm's idea was to provide a collection of homilies intended for church reading, based on the Gospel readings used in church throughout the year. He has a table of contents listing Latin texts for 243 homilies, but only about an eighth of these have survived – if indeed they were all completed. It was an immensely ambitious undertaking: the surviving English text is 10,220 full poetic lines. If he did complete it along the lines of what remains, the whole work would have been three-quarters of a million words.

Orm could claim to be the first English spelling reformer, and he had a simple and foolproof way of showing the difference between short and long vowels. If the vowel in a stressed syllable is short, double the following consonant. So he recommended *sitt*, *sett*, *satt*, *annd*, *unnder*, *forr*, and so on. The use of doubling in such words as *and* seems a trifle obsessive, but Orm certainly gets ten out of ten for consistency. Doubtless preachers were greatly helped in reading aloud, at a time when the language had been undergoing a period of rapid change.

He calls his book the *Orrmulum*, adding the charming explanation, *forrþi þatt Orrm itt wrohhte* 'because it was Orm who wrote it'.

His system was never adopted, nor – apart from Webster's – has any other idiosyncratic approach. So is spelling simplification dead in the water? Perhaps not. Mass usage governs all things. And on the Internet we are beginning to see signs of people voting about English spelling with their hands.

A few years ago it would hardly ever have been possible to see mis-spelling in a public printed context. The copy-editors and proof-readers would have seen to that. The occasional 'typo' would slip through, but would usually be corrected at the fisrt opportunity.

But the Internet has changed all that. Most of the writing we see in emails, chatrooms, instant messaging, texting, and blogging has received no moderation from editors. It is written English in its most naked form. And it is there that we see such simplified forms as *rubarb*, *autum*, and *zylophone*. These are not isolated cases. Type *peple* into Google and you will get 655,000 hits. A few are proper names, but most aren't. 'Did you mean to search for *people*?' asks the Google software, wistfully.

These new spellings have little influence at the moment. But think ahead fifty or a hundred years. Might some of them come to be universally adopted? I think so.

The barrier finally lifted and I left my mis-spelled sign behind. The town of the streams, the nuns, the lion, and Leofric was just around the corner, and I had an appointment with a dead poet just outside it.

8

The Robot's not Working

Everywhere you look in Marcher country you find battles. Welsh against Welsh. Welsh against English. English against English. Most towns and villages have a battle not far away.

The early history of the English language is reflected in the battle-fields. The Old English dialect forms we see in surviving texts reflect the changing power relations between local rulers in England and Wales, or between the English and the Danes – and, later, between the English and the Normans. If your kingdom becomes powerful, more texts come to be written by your people and are more likely to survive. One of the things you do if you win is burn the other side's books.

Leominster was the location of the Battle of Llanllieni in 1052, the first major encounter between the Welsh and a mixed army of Saxons and Normans. Gruffydd ap ('son of') Llywelyn led the Welsh to victory.

Gruffydd's rise was meteoric. The story goes that he was a lazy youth who, one New Year's Eve early in the eleventh century, was sent out of his house by his angry family. As he stood by a neighbour's kitchen, he overheard a cook complain about the pieces of beef he was boiling in a cauldron. Apparently one piece of beef kept coming to the top of the pot, regardless of how often it was pushed down. Gruffydd took this as a message telling him to do something with his life.

He certainly did. He was king of Gwynedd and Powys by 1039. He then defeated a Mercian army near Welshpool, killing Edwin, the brother of Earl Leofric. After Llanllieni, he joined forces with Ælfgar, Leofric's son, and defeated another army at Hereford. A further victory over the English followed at Glasbury in 1056. Along with other gains in South Wales, this made him undisputed King of the Welsh – a claim recognized even by Edward the Confessor. But the unity didn't last. Gruffydd's enemies forced him to retreat to Snowdonia, and his own men killed him in 1063. Wales was divided once again into separate kingdoms.

To get from Leominster to my appointment in Risbury I had a choice of roads – towards Worcester along the A44, or the slightly longer route towards Hereford along the A49. Most travellers choose their routes on the basis of the shortest distance or the shortest time. Those are the alternatives offered by the Internet route-finders. Linguists tend to be influenced by the presence of intriguing place-names. There is as yet no Internet place-name route-finder.

It was definitely the A49, then. For beckoning genially two miles down the road was Hope-under-Dinmore. What romantic tales someone might weave around that name. A lovelorn lady sighing for an impossible love? A father waiting for news of his son from the Crusades?

The truth is more prosaic. *Hope* is from Old English *hop* (pronounced 'hohp'), and it means a small valley. The form appears quite often in place-names. In Herefordshire we also find *Fownhope*, *Woolhope*, and *Hope Mansell*.

This particular *hop* was beneath Dinmore Hill. *Dinmore* is from Old Welsh *din* 'fortified hill' + *mawr* 'great'. It is a fine hill with a fine house at the top – Dinmore Manor – in private ownership now, and no longer open to the public. To the south there is a great view of the Malvern Hills.

Malvern, another Welsh name. From *moel* 'hill' + *bryn* 'bare'. For most people the name is associated with Edward Elgar, who loved the

Malverns so much. He is buried in St Wulfstan's churchyard in Malvern Wells. The grave is much frequented by music pilgrims.

Linguists would be more drawn to a different grave in the Malvern Hills, in St James's Church in West Malvern. For there lies Peter Mark Roget, 1779–1869, doctor, scientist, and polymath, the compiler of *Roget's Thesaurus*. He is the Henry Higgins of semantics.

A thesaurus is not a dictionary. In a dictionary, you begin by having a word in mind and you want to find its meaning. In a thesaurus, you begin by having a meaning in mind and you want to find its word. Or, having thought of a word, you want to find other words of related meaning. A very important feature of the type of thesaurus introduced by Roget is the index at the back, which takes up nearly half the book. It helps you find your way quickly to the area of meaning you are interested in. *Hook* in the sense of 'coupling'? Go to section 47. *Hook* meaning 'hanger'? Section 217.

Roget had the idea for a classification of English words and phrases early on in life, compiling what he called a 'classed catalogue of words on a small scale' in 1805, but he did not have an opportunity to work on the project until his retirement. It took him four years, and was finally published in 1852. A hundred and fifty years and innumerable editions and imitations later, it graces more shelves than any other single-authored reference work. I wouldn't be without it.

Nor would J.M. Barrie, the author of *Peter Pan*. Why did he locate the Darling family in Bloomsbury? Because, he tells us, 'Mr Roget once lived there.' And he adds:

> So did we [live there] in the days when his *Thesaurus* was our only companion in London; and we whom he has helped to wend our way through life have always wanted to pay him a little compliment.

Dinmore Manor. Look up *manor* in *Roget* and (the exact words depend on the edition) you will find it under 'Abode: place of habitation or resort'. It is listed along with *grange*, *lodge*, *mansion*, *hall*, *stately home*, *seat*, *place*, and several hundred more words for places where you can live. If you are looking for the right word to express your thought, you will very likely find it.

There is another *Dinmore Manor*. Steam locomotive Manor Class 4–6–0 No. 7820, to be precise. A familiar sight on the West Somerset Railway, in 2006 it was in a siding at Minehead awaiting an overhaul.

The formula 4–6–0 is part of a system of classifying steam locomotives based on their wheel arrangement. It was devised by an American engineer, Frederick Methvan Whyte, in 1900. He counted the number of leading wheels, then the number of driving wheels, and then the number of trailing wheels. *Dinmore Manor* had four of the first (two on each side), six of the second (three on each side), and none of the third.

I turned off the A49 onto the A417. Hampton Court is just on the right. Or perhaps I should say, the *other* Hampton Court.

Hampton – a *tun* 'homestead' in a *ham* 'meadow'. There were originally two manors – Hampton Richard and Hampton Mappenor, which merged to form this Hampton Court. It was granted by King Henry IV to Sir Rowland Lenthall, upon his marriage to one of the king's cousins. He completed the manor house in 1427. He could afford to do so. Twelve years earlier he had distinguished himself as a commander at the Battle of Agincourt, and took so many prisoners that he was able to finish the building with their ransom money.

There was a steam locomotive named *Hampton Court*, too. Great Western Railway Saint Class, No. 2943, another 4–6–0, built in 1912. It was withdrawn in 1951, but you can still go for a ride on it, in a reduced reincarnation, at Stapleford Miniature Railway near Melton Mowbray in Leicestershire.

That must be a challenging job, thinking up locomotive names. It sounds easy enough when we think of the famous locomotives such as *Rocket* and *The Flying Scotsman*, or trains like *The Irish Mail* and *The*

Welsh Dragon. But put yourself in the position of having to think up seventy-four names beginning with *Western* for the Class 52 first-generation diesel locos, all built at Swindon or Crewe in the early 1960s.

> *Enterprise, Pathfinder, Explorer, Pioneer, Crusader, Venturer . . .*

Keep going. (You may need a *Roget*.)

> *. . . Stalwart, Talisman, Harrier, Invader, Campaigner, Thunderer . . .*

Keep going.

> *. . . Firebrand, Ranger, Leviathan, Champion, Gladiator, Warrior, Buccaneer, Challenger, Hero, Cavalier, Sentinel, Fusilier, Huntsman, Guardsman, Centurion, Lancer, Hussar, Legionnaire, Musketeer, Rifleman, Marksman, Trooper, Dragoon, Yeoman . . .*

Then someone must have noticed a slight bias.

> *. . . Emperor, Empress, Sovereign, King, Queen, Prince, Princess, Duke, Duchess, Viscount, Marquis, Lord, Lady . . .*

But not for long.

> *. . . Monarch, Ruler, Ambassador, Viceroy, Patriarch, Governor, Advocate, Sultan, Chieftain, Nobleman, Empire, Dominion, Envoy, Courier, Monitor, Regent, Consort, Prefect, Druid, Reliance, Vanguard, Gauntlet, Renown, Glory, Bulwark.*

Not surprisingly, there is a huge amount of repetition in loco names, over the years and classes. Even female names are well represented, in an otherwise male-dominant era. In the name index of steam locomotives in the UK compiled by the Industrial Locomotive Society there have been twenty-one locos called *Alice*, twenty-two called *Annie*, and seventeen called *Daisy*.

Literary names don't do quite so well. There are two *Byron*s, but no

Wordsworths, *Shelleys*, or *Coleridges*. No *Shakespeares*. No *Dickenses*, but two *Walter Scotts*.

There is just one locomotive listed which begins with *X*: *XIT*. I presume they pronounced it 'exit'.

Actually, there is a *Shakespeare Express* nowadays. It runs between Birmingham Snow Hill and Stratford twice on Sundays during the summer months.

The turn to Risbury is a mile or so past Hampton Court. As I approached the village, I thought I would pay a quick visit to Risbury Camp, an iron-age hill fort, which I'd heard about but never seen. Another battle, possibly. The first-century British chief Caractacus is said to have made his unsuccessful last stand here, against the Romans in the West. However, other places claim this event, such as British Camp on the top of Herefordshire Beacon in the Malvern Hills, and there are hills named Caradoc (the Welsh version of Caractacus) in Shropshire. The problem is that a river is always missing.

Tacitus gives an account of the battle in his *Annals*. In Book XII he describes the way Caractacus chose a steep-sided hill-site for his defensive position:

> He selected a position for the engagement in which advance and retreat alike would be difficult for our men and comparatively easy for his own, and then on some high hills, wherever their sides could be approached by a gentle slope, he piled up stones to serve as a rampart.

That could be virtually any hill fort location. But then he says, 'A river too of varying depth was in his front, and his armed bands were drawn up before his defences.'

There is no river at any of the favoured locations. It's a puzzle. The River Severn is the obvious choice, but where exactly . . . ? So could it have been Risbury?

The Camp is an impressive site – once you find it. There are no signposts. You have to take the road out of the village in the direction of Leominster. As it bears right, at the bottom of a hill there is a wide entrance leading up to a house and a farm. An ancient, rusting fuel pump stands next to a gate. And beyond the gate is the fort. Broad grassy mounds top steep tree-covered sides. It's a fine defensive position.

And there *is* water at the foot. Two streams, Humber Brook and Holly Brook, meet at the bottom of the hill. They run under the road now. And an old water-mill is nearby. You would have to have a really strong imagination to see in them 'a river of varying depth'. But a lot can happen in two thousand years.

I was going to Risbury to meet Celia Brigstocke. She is secretary of the John Bradburne Memorial Society. Celia is John Bradburne's niece. And John Bradburne is probably the most prolific poet there has ever been in the English language. He is also a poet most people have never heard of.

I say 'probably', because of course who knows what vast stocks of poetry in English might have been amassed by obscure writers in India or Africa or America? But Bradburne's writing greatly exceeds in quantity the output of those well-known English-language poets who have produced the fattest collected works. Before I encountered him, I thought the title of 'most prolific English poet' would have been held by one of the Romantic poets – Wordsworth, very likely – or perhaps Chaucer. If we bring poetic dramatists into the count, then it has to be Shakespeare.

It's tricky, quantifying Shakespeare. The latest edition of the *Collected Works* contains poems (some uncertainly attributed) totalling 5,942 lines. If you count all the lines of poetry (as opposed to prose) in the plays, you get 81,726 – the total will vary a bit depending on which edition you use and which plays you include. (I used the Penguin edition, and included three plays not in the First Folio: *Pericles*, *Two Noble Kinsmen*, and *King Edward III*.)

That total of eighty-one thousand is just three-quarters of all the lines in the plays. There is a lot of variation among the texts. Three plays are entirely in poetry – *King John*, *Richard II*, and *King Edward III*. By contrast, *The Merry Wives of Windsor* is almost entirely in prose.

If we combine the totals for plays and poems, we get 87,668 Shakespearean poetic lines. That is undoubtedly a record. By comparison, Wordsworth wrote about fifty-four thousand lines of poetry, Chaucer about forty-five thousand and Milton about twenty thousand. I know. I counted them.

John Bradburne produced 170,000 lines – at least, for not everything he wrote has yet been found. His longest manuscript is over 10,800 lines. That's just a little longer than Milton's *Paradise Lost*.

Of course, quantity isn't everything. Someone might write thousands of lines of absolute rubbish. And certainly, from time to time, when Bradburne was feeling flippant or had had a drink or three, he wrote doggerel. Sometimes his writing is banal and clichéd. Sometimes he is verbose and repetitive. But most of his poems are none of these things. On the contrary. Wordsworth would have admired Bradburne's best nature poetry. Herbert would have envied his devotional intensity. And Byron would have adored his puns and word-play.

These claims cry out for examples. His work contains lines of great beauty and spiritual insight. Many of his images are original and vivid:

> Adhere to Truth as flies do to the ceiling . . .

> The Thought of God is written in the air . . .

He can produce romantic images of startling quality:

> Dreams are a chequered commentary made
> In sleep along the deeps of our desires
> Moving like riddles through a magic glade
> Lightly they touch the leap of hidden fires . . .

He looks at nature in ways that the Romantics would have been proud of, as in this image of bees:

> The night-sound of a hive is like the fall
> Of fairy raindrops on the tops of time . . .

And here is an atmospheric narrative opening:

> There's a long dark wood where the witches dwell
> By a marsh where the curlews call
> And above and beyond there is conned a Fell
> Whence a Wind doth the dales befall . . .

The trouble with country lanes is that if you start thinking of poetry, you can easily miss your turning. I had never visited Celia's house before, and there is an intriguing equilateral triangle of roads in downtown Risbury. A signpost suggested that I had turned left instead of right. A second signpost confirmed it. I was approaching a long dark wood. If I didn't do something about it soon, I was going to renew my linguistic love-affair with Leominster.

I reversed into a gap into a field. Bradburne was right. There is always a marsh by a long dark wood. The wheels of my car found it. And, thanks to the bootload of Hay books, the wheels looked very comfortable, settling down in the welcoming Herefordshire mud.

I needed some wood, or branches, to give the wheels some grip. Why is there never any loose wood around when you need it? There were plenty of low-branched trees about. Now, if I had a hook, or a crook . . .

The field was full of ravens, looking for an evening meal.

> Ravens are Yahweh's craftiness with wings . . .

They eyed me suspiciously, or perhaps it was hungrily.

The most striking thing about Bradburne's poetry is its gleeful exploitation of the traditional features of verse, such as onomatopoeia, verbal allusion, rhythm, and rhyme. He is a great formalist. He experiments with metres and rhyme schemes, explores phonetic patterns within lines, and gleefully neologizes:

> Take towers, turrets, copper-beeches, aisles
> And roses, rows of reverential yews
> And lilac and laburnum and the smiles
> Of Maytime married to the chiming views
> Of swallowdom and cuckomerry mews . . .

At nearby Hampton Court there is a maze of a thousand yews with a Gothic tower in the middle. I wonder if Bradburne ever saw it?

I opened my boot. Perhaps if I took the books out? They were in carrier bags, so they wouldn't be harmed on the ground. But one of the bags, thanks to the lately acquired Sebald, had too many books crammed into it. And that bag didn't like the experience of being hustled out of its nice warm boot. There was a tearing sound.

And that was how the farmhand found me. Crouched in a marsh, scraping mud off a copy of *The Rings of Saturn*, and glaring at the ravens. Sebald would probably have approved.

'Looks loike you be a bit stuck,' he said affably, as if this was a daily occurrence. Perhaps it was. I can't have been the first to have taken a wrong turning at Risbury. His accent didn't sound particularly Herefordshire. 'You be' . . . That's a form used in the south-west Midlands, certainly, but also across into Oxfordshire and Berkshire and down into Sussex. And 'loike' – that wasn't this bit of Herefordshire, where the first part of the vowel would have been more 'uh'-like. An 'oi' quality could be Birmingham, or more likely further south. Berkshire again, perhaps. His intonation certainly wasn't Brummy.

I desperately wanted to ask him where he was from, but there are times, as Henry Higgins also found, when phonetics must yield to more pressing priorities.

My face and frame exuded inadequacy. He pushed the car out of the mud with an ease that would have put a tractor to shame. We picked up the rest of the books together and put them in the boot along with the others. He whistled when he saw the contents. 'Ne'r seen so many books,' he said. There was a strong West Country 'r' at the end of *never*, but you hear that all the way across to Hampshire too.

I explained I'd just been to Hay, and was about to explain when he forestalled me. He knew all about Hay. 'Used to live near there,' he said. It seemed a bit rude to reply with 'No, that's impossible.' Instead I said, 'You don't sound as if you're from round that way.' 'True. It were just for a few month, on a job.' He pronounced it 'jawb'.

'So . . .'

He forestalled me again. 'Used to be on the farm in Oxfordshire.'

'Is that where you were brought up?'

'Ar. Near Wallingford.'

Wallingford is right on the border with Berkshire.

Footballers push their fists up in the air, rip off their shirts, and cuddle each other when they score. I did none of these things. Just thanked him, set a new course for Celia's house, and brought John Bradburne back to mind.

Forestall is a curious word, though. It means 'prevent by anticipation'. It originally meant, literally, 'before the stall' – that is, before the market stalls opened. In the Middle Ages, in many parts of the country, you were not allowed to sell goods on the roads before the bell was rung for the local market to begin. To do so was a crime. It robbed the lord of the manor of the taxes he levied on what was sold in the market.

The practice lasted until the eighteenth century. In the annals of Hay, there is a record of a Mary Higgins being fined ten shillings for 'buying fowl and eggs before time out of the market place'.

The most extraordinary thing about Bradburne's poetry is that most of the poems were written in a single decade, which ended with his murder near the leper settlement of Mutemwa in Southern Rhodesia (present-day Zimbabwe) in 1979. Mutemwa means, in the local language, 'you are cut off'. The name applied to the lepers, banished by society. In the end, it applied to Bradburne too.

He was born at Skirwith, in Cumbria, in 1921, the son of an Anglican clergyman. After secondary school in Norfolk he joined the army in 1939, and served in Malaya and Burma, before being invalided home. Something in Malaya – a Pauline experience, it is said – turned him from adventurer into pilgrim.

He became a Roman Catholic in 1947 when staying at Buckfast Abbey in Devon. After some months with the Carthusians he felt the urge to travel, and for sixteen years wandered around England, Italy, and the Middle East. Then he wrote to his friend Father John Dove in Southern Rhodesia, asking, 'Is there a cave in Africa where I can pray?' There was. And soon after his arrival, in 1962, he confided to a Franciscan priest that he had three wishes: to serve leprosy patients, to die a martyr, and to be buried in the habit of St Francis.

From 1964 he was caretaker of a mission centre near Harare. Then in 1969 he was appointed warden of Mutemwa. His first wish.

During the Rhodesian civil war, his efforts to prevent the exploitation of his patients brought local hostility and suspicion. Although threatened, he refused to leave them. He was abducted by guerrillas, and on 5 September 1979 they shot him. His second wish.

At Bradburne's Requiem Mass, eyewitnesses saw three drops of blood fall from the bottom of the coffin, forming a little pool on the ground. The coffin was reopened, but no sign of blood was found. However, it was noticed that he was wearing a shirt. It was replaced by the Franciscan habit. His third wish.

His hut at Mutemwa is now a place of pilgrimage, and there is a growing movement in support of his case for sainthood. Around fifteen thousand pilgrims visited Mutemwa for the twentieth anniversary of his death in 1999.

I had not expected any of this when I had my first close encounter with John Bradburne.

I had left the full-time university world in 1984, and come back to Holyhead – where I was brought up – to carry on a career as a home-based writer and editor. My wife and I bought a house near the centre of town from people we knew – parents of a lad, Kevin Jones, who had been in my year in primary school.

Eventually, we met Kevin once again: a professional cabaret musician now, widely known by his professional name of Casey Jones. Kevin would call in at the house from time to time, to renew his memories of his old family home, and one day he brought out of his pocket an airmail letter, and asked me, 'Have you ever seen anything like this?' It was a letter from John Bradburne to Kevin, about perfectly ordinary things, but it was written entirely in poetry.

It transpired that Kevin had worked as a teacher in missionary settings in East Africa during the late 1960s, and when he and his friends had some time off they would travel around the southern parts of the continent. On one of these trips, they all had their money and passports stolen, so they hitch-hiked back to their base, relying on the help of missionary centres along the way. At Archbishop's House in Salisbury Kevin first met John Bradburne and Father Dove. Some time later he was in the area again, but went down with a bout of malaria, and was looked after by – John Bradburne. They had a shared interest in music, and after Kevin left Africa they corresponded a few times.

I had never seen anything like the poem-letter that Kevin showed me. And then I asked the question which today seems rather naïve: 'Are there any more around like that?' Kevin put me in touch with Celia Brigstocke, and not long afterwards a very large case arrived, filled with manuscripts. If they were placed in a pile, they would have reached my waist.

How can anyone write so much poetry in such a short time? A few poems are from earlier years, but most date from 1968. He sometimes wrote a dozen in a day. And we know how long it could take him to write one, because he sometimes not only dates a poem but notes the time of day he finished it. For instance, in one year on 10 August he finished 'To Paddy Bidwell' at 3.55 a.m. The next poem on the page, 'Mattins', also ends with the time: 04.45 on the same night. There are thirty-six lines in the second poem – and they were written within fifty minutes. A line a minute, more or less.

Hundreds of the poems are in manuscript. Few of them have any corrections. Every bit of the paper is used up, even when he is typing. Well, paper was expensive and in short supply. Often he writes a couple of sonnets on a foolscap sheet and finds he has just an inch of space at the bottom. So he fills it with a two- or three-line poem.

He hated writing in prose, even to his family. On 20 April 1969 he begins a letter to his mother like this:

> Dearest Mother, many thanks for your three last letters: of the 9th, of the 12th and of the 15th. Writing in anything other than verse is to me a sterile, fruitless and abortive pain, so I am sure you will allow me the pleasure of replying in verse, and in verse of giving you what news and Paschal tidings I may have . . .

And he then launches exuberantly into a poem of over a hundred lines, in which joyful romanticism and domestic chat are obliviously intertwined:

> It makes me happy and augments my glees
> To read about the pleasure which you had
> In Paschal greetings on Masasa trees
> The sight of which in Spring makes many glad;
> Bless-ed be God that Allelulias leapt
> To Easter sunshine best of twenty years,
> Receded winter cold, no longer slept
> The daffodils but trumpeted their cheers!
> Hurrah for Mary gladdened in the way
> With Auriol on Easter holiday.
> Such marked improvement in the health of him
> Whose name is Charles (which rhymes with nothing well)

Is also Alleluliattic, swim
May he this Summer, sound as any bell . . .

You get the impression that he could go on like this indefinitely.

Its fluency reminds me a bit of modern rapping, but it would be hard to find in rap the complexity that we find in most of Bradburne's work. I'm not thinking here of the originality of the thought, or its theological content, which is intriguing enough, but of his literary facility. He is a stickler for metre and versification, taking great pains to work out a symmetrical structure for a poem. His rhyme schemes are intricate, his word-play even more so. And there is something else. Read this poem, 'Sonnet on Timu' (Timu was one of the Mutemwa lepers), written in September 1969:

Timu's no Timon, Athens were to him
Inseparable word from hens at hand,
Many a time I greet him daily, Tim
Ever is bright, dimness to him is banned;
Intent on converse and on getting round
Wondrously well on only hands and knees,
Enters he here and there, all's fairy ground
Native to happy Tim who's born to please;
The produce of his poultry he will beg
That I may purchase any time I pass
Only providing that it is an egg
But not a chicken cheeping 'Fresh is grass
Even as I am flesh!': three pence a time
Duly I pay and Timu's lay's sublime.

Did you notice anything? Look at it again, following the initial letters of each line. They make up words, forming a perfect acrostic.

So, think about it: write a poem like that, with an acrostic, making sure that each line has the right metre and that the sonnet rhyme-scheme is followed (*abab cdcd efef gg*). Don't forget to add alliteration in most lines, and a sprinkling of puns. The whole thing has to make good sense, of course. Oh, and do it a line a minute, with no corrections.

The opportunity to edit a new poet doesn't come one's way very often. The task has kept me busy, on and off, for the past decade, and it isn't over yet. But it has moved in a fresh direction.

The impossibility of getting such a huge œuvre produced by a conventional publishing house had been bothering me for some time. Enquiries about the poems were beginning to come in from all over the world from people who had heard about him. The Internet seemed the obvious solution. And after my visit to Risbury, and several more conversations with Celia, a website finally went live in 2006.

Biographers I know tell me that when you start to explore the life of a person in intimate detail, you end up wanting to visit the places where he or she lived. I was no biographer, but for intimacy there is nothing quite like editing someone's poetry. Very early on, I knew I wanted to visit Mutemwa, and I finally got there, but by an unusual route.

In 1998 I took up an invitation from the British Council to give some lectures in South Africa. Zimbabwe was next door. I added a few days to the end of the tour, and planned a visit.

It was my first trip to southern Africa, a region I knew well by linguistic repute. I had studied the evolution of South African English over the years. There is nothing quite like it in the English-speaking world.

The vocabulary is the really striking thing. It is hugely distinctive and diverse, thanks to the number of languages which feed it. There are eleven official languages in South Africa. Each one borrows wildly from the others. And English borrows most of all.

English has always been a vacuum-cleaner of a language, sucking in new words from whatever languages it happens to make contact with. Hundreds of Latin and Norse words arrived in English during the

Anglo-Saxon period. Thousands of French words arrived after the Conquest. Over the past 1,500 years, English has taken words from over 350 languages. Indeed, only 20 per cent of English vocabulary is Anglo-Saxon in character.

Words which come into one language from another are called *loan-words*. Linguists talk about languages *borrowing* words from each other. Both are strange usages, for the words are certainly not on loan, to be returned at some later date. A more accurate way of talking would be to say that languages *share* words in which they have a common interest. But *loan* is the conventional expression.

Actually, words do sometimes return to the language whence they came. A contemporary example is *computer*. This originated in Latin *computare* 'to reckon, sum up'. It can be found in sixteenth-century French as the verb *computer* ('com-pu-tay'). Its earliest record in English is 1631. The noun *computer* is recorded soon after, in 1646, meaning 'one who computes'. We don't get a mechanical use until 1897.

Today, the word *computer* is being used again in French and in many other languages. The odd thing is that the French haven't made it welcome. You might have expected at least a '*Merci beaucoup* for giving us the word back,' but no. French purists, curiously, hate it, and insist on an alternative, *ordinateur*. Some have gone out of their way to condemn *computer* as an unwanted, polluting Anglo-Saxon word. But it is as Anglo-Saxon as Camembert.

When I arrived in Johannesburg, I certainly needed my *Dictionary of South African English*. It has thousands of loan-words from Afrikaans, Xhosa, Zulu, and the other local languages. Most are unknown in English outside southern Africa. At the top of a newspaper column I saw:

Aandag! Massage and sauna . . .

I had to look it up. It means 'Attention!'. It is Afrikaans, from Dutch *aandacht*. There is a similar expression in German: *Achtung!*

I overheard a woman in the British Council office talk about going to meet her *mamazala*. I found out later this was a Zulu word for 'mother-in-law'.

And at various times, in South Africa or Zimbabwe, I was offered *mealie-meal*, *sadza*, *biltong*, and *bunny-chow* – respectively, fine maize-meal, a type of thick porridge, salted meat, and curry in a hollowed out half-loaf. It is an unusual experience, checking in a dictionary before you eat something.

Not all the distinctive South African words are from other languages. Several are familiar words from British English which have been given a new sense. I first noticed this when we were driving into Johannesburg from the airport. We passed a sign saying ROBOT AHEAD. I looked up at the sky. Had they landed?

Robot turned out to be the South African word for traffic lights. 'The robot's broken,' someone said. 'Turn right at the robot,' said another. It seems to have widespread currency in southern Africa. I heard people using it in Zimbabwe too, at least in Harare.

Mutemwa, or Mtemwa, is in north-east Zimbabwe, about a hundred miles north of the capital, Harare. The nearest town of any size is Mtoko. The road runs straight and empty through miles of dry dusty scrubland. Just the occasional tree, and granite outcrops in the distance. Every now and then, I passed piles of boulders shaped by the wind and storms into surreal faces.

I knew we were approaching Mutemwa, because I could see the rounded shape of Chigona Hill on the skyline, standing out like the Rio sugar-loaf. John Bradburne wrote dozens of poems about it. That was the hill he used to climb every day for a mixture of prayer and exercise. It is now a pilgrimage site.

This is Shona-speaking territory. The region is called Mashonaland. But as I approached the settlement, I could see signs only in English. First, *John Bradburne Memorial Site*, with a big red arrow. Then, as I reached the path entering the village, in crude white capital letters on a piece of brown board: *Mutemwa Leprosy*.

Beyond the entrance is a long avenue of jacaranda trees. Bradburne called it a 'triumph-arch' because of the way the trees on each side meet overhead. The huts of the villagers cluster close together, alongside a medical centre.

It is Shona-behaving territory too. I quickly learned to respond in like manner to the Shona greeting, a gentle clapping of the hands to show pleasure at the meeting.

John Bradburne's presence is strong in Mutemwa. Some members of the settlement still remember him. His 'tin hut' – actually galvanized iron – in which he wrote many of his poems, is there much as he left it, with an altar 'ark' against one wall, a statue of the Virgin Mary, and other devotional memorabilia. Across one corner of the hut are some of his favourite Latin expressions in his handwriting. *Per crucem ad lucem.* 'Through the cross to the light.' The pictures of animals and birds he used to hang on the walls have now been replaced by pictures of him, in life and death. A pile of pilgrim petitions lies in one corner.

Every year on 5 September, the anniversary of his death, there is a huge gathering in the village, and a procession up Chigona. The man is not (yet) a saint, but the place has already become a shrine.

I climbed Chigona. The view across the Mashonaland plains is breathtaking. You have to be careful not to lose the path, especially on the way down, for it is a sheer drop to the settlement below. Some thoughtful soul has painted white arrows on the ground every now and then. And the words 'FOR DOWN'.

Most of the Bradburne poems had already been sent to England, but I wanted to see if there was anything left behind. In one of the buildings near the compound I found a cupboard containing a number of his possessions, including some books from his library. I flicked through some of them. There were poem-fragments all over the place – inside the front covers, across the contents pages, in the margins . . . There was no time to go through everything. It is a job for a researcher, one day.

I do not know what the true size of the Bradburne corpus is. Because most of his letters home and to his friends were written in verse, there must be many more poems languishing forgotten in attics and drawers around the world. From time to time someone comes across a sheaf of letters in their home, or a collection of copies of poems, and sends them to the Memorial Society. They usually contain a few previously unknown items.

Much of the poetry has an ethnic resonance. It comes straight out of Africa. He writes poems about the landscape and the animals, as well as the people. He talks about *kopjes* and *vleis* – small hills, marshy depressions – about augur-buzzards and eagles. He explores the meaning and sound of Shona names and words, especially – as in the case of Timu – the names of the lepers in his care.

Literature is one of the best places to look if you want to find out about regional varieties of English around the world – in the intimacy of poetry, the dialogue of the short story or novel, and the conversations of plays and films. Authors more than anyone else hold a mirror up to linguistic nature. They hear how people are talking, and they reflect it in their writing. Linguists do this too, but more accurately, and thus less interestingly. There is nothing more boring than a detailed transcript of an everyday conversation.

I remember reading a review once which said that Harold Pinter had a tape-recorder for an ear. The reviewer intended it as a compliment. I thought it the greatest of insults. For if that is all it takes to make a great playwright, then I must publish the many conversational transcripts I have made over the years as quickly as possible. I must be the world's most neglected playwright. Fortunately, it is not so. Something inserts itself between the ear and the hand – call it 'insight', 'structure', 'art' . . .

I reached my Risbury destination and had my meeting with Celia. There's quite a lot to be done when you develop a poetry website. You want people to read it, but you want to protect it from unscrupulous use as well.

What an extraordinary opportunity the Internet has given to poets and lexicographers alike – indeed to anyone interested in language variation and use. If you want to publish your own poetry, you can easily do so now in the form of your personal blog. If you want to read some South African English, all you have to do is click a mouse. If you want to find people who share your interests in language-play, there are many websites and chatrooms waiting for you.

And we are only at the beginning. Speech is steadily increasing its presence on the Internet. In a generation's time there will be a huge corpus of regional accents and dialects of English out there, from all over the world.

I left Risbury and, my head full of poems and planning, turned the wrong way again – as I realized when I saw the road leading to my Leominster railway line comming into view. I needed to go north, and then east.

After a few miles I passed through Kingsland – the King's lene –

and Mortimer Cross. Another battle. In 1461 the Yorkists defeated the Lancastrians there. It was the decisive battle of the Wars of the Roses. An appropriate site to precede a visit to Stratford.

9

Who was Leonard Slye?

STRATFORD

I wasn't going to Stratford to look for accents. I was there to give a talk, visit The Dirty Duck, see a play, visit The Dirty Duck again, and then make my way back to North Wales.

Driving into Stratford is a curious experience for a playgoer. You see the titles and character-names from the plays right away, but out of context. *Cymbeline House. Twelfth Night. Hamlet House* ... They are all the names of guest-houses.

A B&B called *Hamlet*. I imagine that when you arrive you have to say, 'For this relief much thanks. 'Tis bitter cold.'

Alternatively you can go into town and stay at one of the hotels there. To B&B or not to B&B, I suppose, is the question.

I wonder what you'd get for dinner in a B&B called *Titus Andronicus*?

I bet there isn't one called *Macbeth*. Or if there is, only the most perverse of actors would ever stay in it.

It's amazing how the taboo status of that name has persisted in the theatre world. The superstition is that you should never say 'Macbeth', unless you're actually performing the play or rehearsing it. You have to replace it by 'The Scottish Play' or some such euphemism.

Taboo words in a language, and the euphemisms which replace them, are usually associated with sex, excretion, death, and the supernatural. We don't normally find words which are tainted with a vague general notion of 'bad luck'. It's actions that are supposed to do that – such as walking under ladders or opening an umbrella indoors.

I've come across a few 'unlucky words' over the years. It's bad luck to say the word *pig* while fishing at sea. I've never found a fisherman who could tell me why. And in the Royal Navy, the number *232* is avoided. If someone has to refer to it, you would hear a circumlocution such as '231 and a bit'. I know the origin of that one: if your ship is involved in a collision or a grounding, you have to fill in Form 232.

Sailors have strong feelings about it. In a famous instance, the Type 23 frigate HMS *Lancaster* was originally given the pennant number *F232*, but after protest it was changed to *F229*.

Verbal superstitions are understandable with dangerous professions, such as those to do with the sea. Even people who say they are not superstitious would never name their boat *Titanic*.

But is acting a dangerous profession? Well, it can be. On 2 April 1891, the *St James's Gazette* reported the death of the actor playing Mercutio, following his duel with Tybalt in *Romeo and Juliet*. The stage sword had penetrated his chest to a depth of seven inches. The jury returned a verdict of 'Death from loss of blood from a wound received while taking part in a dramatic performance.'

It is not especially surprising that accidents surround *Macbeth*. It contains a great deal of violent action. This often takes place in the dark, which makes it more likely that accidents will happen. And it is Shakespeare's shortest tragedy, which has led to the theory that companies in difficult financial circumstances find it easier to put on, and perhaps cut corners when it comes to rehearsals and safety.

It wouldn't have taken much to launch a superstition. The fact that the plot of *Macbeth* involves witchcraft would have been enough. And a coincidence would have fuelled it. There is a story that during the play's first performance, Hal Berridge, a boy actor thought to be playing Lady Macbeth, fell ill or maybe even died backstage, and

Shakespeare had to take over the part. If it happened, that would have started it.

Something must have started the superstition. Taboo words don't just happen.

The play has certainly had its share of deaths over the years. In a production in Amsterdam in 1672 the actor playing Macbeth used a real dagger and killed the actor playing Duncan. In New York in 1849 there was a riot following two performances of the play on the same night by actors who were bitter rivals, William Charles Macready and Edwin Forrest. Over twenty people died. Three actors died during John Gielgud's 1942 touring production. And after a performance of the play at Holyhead's Ucheldre Centre in 1995, the director twisted her ankle. Also, the actor playing Macduff had his car broken into and his stage weapons stolen.

The problem is, we don't know how many accidents, deaths, twisted ankles, or thefts happened during the productions of other plays. Nobody records them. *Romeo* is just one story that made the headlines. There are hundreds of others. Early in the production of *Pericles* at Shakespeare's Globe in London in 2005, Corin Redgrave suffered a stroke and had to withdraw. Nobody says that *Romeo and Juliet* or *Pericles* are unlucky plays because of these events. Imagine what would have been said if Corin had been playing Macbeth.

Whatever the origins of the taboo, it is now a self-fulfilling prophecy. Actors expect something to go wrong, and may unwittingly make it happen.

It takes a brave director to combat the curse. Gregory Doran was one. On the first day of rehearsals for his 1999 production at Stratford he was quite explicit:

> We're calling it *Macbeth* . . . Not *Mackers*, not *The Scottish Play*, none of the euphemisms. *Macbeth*, *Macbeth*, *Macbeth*. There, I've said it and I haven't been struck down. There's supposed

to be a curse on this play. Bollocks! The only curse is that it's
so hard to do.

If none of this convinces, and you do say 'Macbeth' outside of performance or rehearsal, there are a number of stratagems that you
can perform to 'remove the curse'. A widely practised one is to leave
the room or the space you are in, close the door behind you, turn
around three times, swear, knock on the door, and ask to be let back
in. The swearing is important. Words can only be defeated by other
words.

Alternatively, quoting Hamlet's 'Angels and ministers of grace
defend us' will do it.

I gingerly made my way to my B&B – the Carlton, where I had
stayed several times before. I can't remember why we went there
originally. Perhaps because it *didn't* have a Shakespearean name? A
more mundane reason, very likely. A handy car-parking space always
helps in Stratford.

You have to drive gingerly in Stratford town centre. There are
tourists everywhere, from all over the world, many of them evidently
acting on the belief that cars have not yet been invented. Along
Southern Lane, next to the River Avon, I once encountered some
ducks waddling purposefully along the middle of the road, presumably
operating on the same principle.

Maybe they were going to The Dirty Duck, which is also on Southern
Lane. If so, they would have recognized it by the unique signboard. I
don't know of another pub sign which has different names on its two
sides. On one side is *The Black Swan*, floating serenely. On the other is
The Dirty Duck, holding a beer glass and plastered.

My gingerliness paid off. As I drove along Chapel Street I saw a
group of Japanese tourists standing outside the Falcon Hotel, waiting
to be photographed. There was no sign of the photographer.

Yes there was. He was in the middle of the street, oblivious to all

but his viewfinder. I stopped a few inches from him. He took his photograph, and with supreme aplomb bowed to the group, and then to me. I bowed back.

It must be something in the pre- or post-performance atmosphere. I have done the same myself, walking down the middle of Chapel Lane towards the Swan Theatre, absent-mindedly reflecting on the play seen or about to be seen, and forgetting that City Sightseeing Tour buses also use this street. Because they're travelling slowly past New Place gardens, they have a habit of creeping up on you. If you're lucky, you hear the loudspeaker commentary first. Otherwise it is an admonition from the driver in Elizabethan English.

You can encounter absent-mindedness anywhere, of course, but it turns up especially in academic settings. The image of the 'absent-minded professor' persists. I have met several.

There was a professor at Bangor who used to wander along the main A5 road through the town. Every now and then he would wave down a lorry and ask the bemused driver what the time was, in case he was due to give a lecture.

Another, at Reading, drove to a conference some miles away. When the event was over he forgot he had come by car and took the train back to Reading. The next day he went to his garage to drive to the university, saw his car was missing, thought it had been stolen, and called the police. His wife sorted everything out.

But probably the title of most absent-minded professor of all time must go to Norbert Wiener, the Professor of Mathematics at the Massachusetts Institute of Technology, and the creator of cybernetics, the science of communication and control. Dozens of stories have been told of him – including, as it happens, a car story like the Reading one.

The corridors and rooms of his university used to have wainscoting along the walls – a continuous strip of protective wood with a central moulded groove. Wiener had the habit of sticking his finger into this groove and closing his eyes, while he thought out some problem, allowing it to guide him along the corridor. If a lecturer had not closed the classroom door, while Wiener walked along, the class would be treated to the sight of him entering the room, his finger following the wainscoting through the doorway and around the walls of the classroom until he reached the door again.

The most famous story of all may well be apocryphal, but I hope it isn't. It seems that one day the Wieners moved house. Knowing her husband, Mrs Wiener wrote the address of the new house on a piece of paper, which he put into his shirt pocket. During the day, needing a piece of paper on which to scribble down some new thought, he used the piece in his shirt pocket. Then he found a flaw in his calculations, and crossly threw the paper away.

At the end of the day he realized he had thrown away the address and had no idea where his new house was. He therefore decided to go to his old home, and wait there for someone to rescue him. When he arrived at the house, a young girl was standing in front of it. 'Excuse me, little girl,' he said, 'can you tell me where the Wieners live now, please?' 'It's OK, Daddy,' the girl replied, 'Mommy sent me to wait for you.'

Years later, the daughter was tracked down and asked whether it was true that he had failed to recognize her. She said it wasn't. But I wonder.

They don't make 'em like that any more. Wiener died in 1969. Crater Wiener on the far side of the moon was named after him.

After I had checked in at the Carlton, I wandered round the town for a bit. I had a couple of hours to kill before my talk. There is always something new to see in Stratford.

Stratford. The name comes from the Old English word *stræt*, 'road, highway', + *ford*, 'water crossing'. *Stratford-upon-Avon* was thus 'the place where a road crossed the River Avon by means of a ford'. The location has been settled at least since the Bronze Age. In Anglo-Saxon times the area contained a monastery called *Stretforde*. The name is recorded in Domesday Book as a manor owned by Wulfstan, Bishop of Worcester.

I walked down to the river through Bancroft Gardens, past the bronze statue of the seated Shakespeare surrounded by four of his creations – Prince Hal, Hamlet, Falstaff, and, er, the Lady from the Scottish Play. It is called the Gower Memorial. The name is nothing to do with the medieval poet who acts as the narrator in *Pericles*. It is that of Lord Ronald Sutherland Gower, who completed the work in 1888. Oscar Wilde was present at the unveiling.

Gower chose the characters to represent – respectively – history, philosophy, comedy, and tragedy. The whole complex was moved to its present location when the Shakespeare Memorial Theatre was opened in 1933, after the original theatre had burnt down seven years before.

Now *there* was a first name! Sir Squire Bancroft. A great actor-manager of the Victorian theatre. He was originally Squire Bancroft White Butterfield, but he dropped the last two names when he became an actor. It's inconceivable now that anyone would call their son *Squire*. But it was quite a popular choice during the nineteenth century.

Everyone has the right to change their name, if they want to. Most people don't want to, but actors often don't have a choice. If you want to be an actor, and you find that some other actor is already out there with your name, you must, quite literally, make a name for yourself.

When my son Ben became an actor he was fortunate. No other actor was on Equity's books with the name Ben Crystal. Good thing we didn't call him Billy.

Quite a few actors have changed their names simply because they didn't like the one they already had. Or their agent didn't like it. Or their name didn't suit the kinds of character they wanted to portray. Would we be as scared of *William Henry Pratt* as we would of his horror-film stage-name, *Boris Karloff*? It's unlikely. And certainly children would be more impressed by cowboy *Roy Rogers* than by the name he was born with, *Leonard Slye*.

There is a tendency for men to avoid gentle continuant sounds, such as *m* and *l*, when looking for new names, and to go in for the hard-sounding 'plosive' consonants, such as *k* and *g*. *Maurice Micklewhite* became *Michael Caine*. *Marion Michael Morrison* became *John Wayne*. *Alexander Archibald Leach* became *Cary Grant*. *Julius Ullman* became *Douglas Fairbanks*.

Women tend to go the other way. *Dorothy Kaumeyer* became *Dorothy Lamour*. *Hedwig Kiesler* became *Hedy Lamarr*. *Norma Jean Baker* became *Marilyn Monroe*.

Actually, *Roy Rogers* is a bit weak, compared with most cowboy names. Cowboys tend to be full of plosives and short vowels – *Bill, Bob, Buck, Chuck, Clint, Jack, Jim, Luke, Tex, Tom. Billy the Kid. Buffalo Bill. Wild Bill Hickok. Kit Carson. Roy* doesn't quite explode from the lips in the same way. His horse, *Trigger*, actually does rather better.

These are only tendencies, of course. There are plenty of exceptions. Also, languages other than English would have different preferences. But there is something in the 'sound symbolism' of names which deserves study. It is a fact that some names sound prettier than others. Why is this so?

When you analyse all the patterns, you can show that the words which people find most beautiful in English have a high proportion of consonants like *m*, *n*, *l*, and *r*. Most have two or three syllables, with these consonants varying throughout. Conversely, words with such consonants as *p*, *k*, and *g*, and consisting of just a single syllable, tend to be rated much lower, unless their meaning forces them up the scale. A word like *peace* will always get votes, regardless of its sounds, because of what it means.

Every now and then, newspapers or radio programmes have a competition to find 'the most beautiful word in English'. It's remarkable how often the winning words reflect these tendencies. In a *Sunday Times* poll back in 1980, *melody* and *velvet* tied for first place. Third was a tie between *gossamer* and (!) *crystal*. Then came *autumn*, *peace*, *tranquil*, *twilight*, and *murmur*, with *caress*, *mellifluous*, and *whisper* tying for tenth place.

You can do linguistic thought-experiments to see whether these tendencies work. Imagine you are in a space-ship approaching a new planet, Xarg. All you know about Xarg is that it contains two races, one friendly towards Earth people, the other antagonistic. One race is called the *Lamonians*. The other is called the *Gataks*. Which do you think is the friendly race?

Or transfer the example to parts of London. If you don't know the city, which sounds the nicer place to visit? *Pimlico* or *Wapping*?

People whose mother-tongue is English usually choose the *m/l* names.

In real life it is always unwise to behave on the basis of sound symbolism. As the Lamonians charge at you with ray-guns, it is no use shouting, 'But your consonants say you're friendly!' And whether Pimlico is in fact more pleasant than Wapping depends on economics rather than linguistics. But in literature, the aesthetic properties of sounds do influence authors a lot when they are choosing names for their characters.

Including Shakespeare. If you collect all the personal names – first names and surnames – of his characters, they divide more or less into two types: the serious and the comic. There's nothing much to say about Shakespeare's linguistic creativity under the 'serious' heading. The names of these characters are usually simply taken from history (*Henry V*, *Gloucester*) or from the classics (*Chiron*, *Portia*) or are perfectly standard Romance or British first names (*Antonio, Juliet; Edward, Alice*) or surnames (*Montague, Aragon; Evans, Page*). Indeed, so ordinary are some of these names that you have to have quite a memory to recall who's who among the lay characters in a given play. What is the name of Antonio's chief friend in *The Merchant of Venice*? Brabantio? Stephano? Bassanio? None of these?

It doesn't particularly matter if you didn't choose Bassanio. There seems to be no especial linguistic reason for his name, nor can we easily see a difference between a Salanio and a Salerio in that play – or, for that matter, between a Rosencrantz and a Guildenstern in *Hamlet*, as both King Claudius (in Kenneth Branagh's 1996 film production) and Tom Stoppard have in their different ways observed. Such names seem to be arbitrarily chosen – or at least, they haven't been chosen in order to make an impact on their audience. If the name Antonio aroused any comment among regular theatre-goers as they left *The Tempest*, it could only have been, 'Is that the fourth or fifth time Will's called somebody *Antonio*?' (Fifth, in fact.)

I walked past the main Royal Shakespeare Company theatre. A huge poster was advertising *Twelfth Night*. That was the play I was going to see.

Sir Toby Belch. Sir Andrew Aguecheek. It's a different story with the names given to the English-nationality characters who are comic, ridiculous, or in some way inferior. Here Shakespeare found plenty of scope for word-play. There are some forty of these figures in the plays – almost all of them male. Most of their names do duty as common adjectives or nouns in the language, so they are really puns, yielding a double meaning which the audience would certainly appreciate as a character-note.

We find clergymen, schoolmasters, justices and their associates: *Martext, Pinch, Shallow, Silence*, and *Slender*. Dissolute or foolish gentle-men: *Falstaff, Aguecheek, Belch*, and *Froth*. Sergeants, constables, and other law-enforcers: *Dogberry, Verges, Snare, Fang, Dull*, and *Elbow*.

Rustics and other local characters: *Quince*, *Bottom*, *Flute*, *Snout*, *Snug*, *Mouldy*, *Shadow*, *Starveling*, *Wart*, *Feeble*, *Bullcalf*, *Nym*, and *Pistol*. Clowns, jesters, and other servants: *Mote*, *Touchstone*, *Costard*, *Simple*, *Speed*, *Lance*, *Gobbo*, *Thump*, and *Pompey* (also known as *Bum*). And a few ladies of the town: *Quickly*, *Tearsheet*, *Overdone*.

You have to work at some of Shakespeare's names to see their sharp edge. *Aguecheek* relies on the word *ague*, or 'fever'. *Starveling* was a common word at the time, meaning 'lean' or 'weak'. *Dogberry* is an old name for a kind of shrub (the wild cornel), and *Verges* is probably a dialect form of *verjuice*, meaning 'sour-faced'. *Costard* is a large apple, thus a word often applied to heads – in effect, 'bighead'.

Nym is from the Old English verb *niman*, meaning 'take'. *Niman* was replaced by *take* in standard English, but it stayed in regional dialects, developing the sense of 'steal'. I've never heard it used, but lexicographer Eric Partridge said he had encountered it with this meaning when he was exploring slang expressions in the mid-twentieth century. I wouldn't be surprised to find it in deepest Warwickshire still.

The sonic resonance of these names is very much part of their effect, and hasn't changed much between then and now. Nearly half are monosyllables which pack a sonic punch, heard at its best in *Fang*, *Pinch*, *Snug*, and *Thump*. All the names with two syllables have their strong stress on the first element – a contrast with most of the foreign names in the plays. And there are only three longer names in the above collection, all of them also initial-stressed – *Aguecheek*, *Dogberry*, and *Overdone*. The list provides a marked contrast with the typically multi-syllabic appellations of the serious characters who live in such realms as Italy, France, and Athens. No *Lodovico*s or *Andronici* here.

I turned the corner into Chapel Lane, walking against the traffic and therefore easily able to avoid the tour bus bearing down on me. A metallic voice told me, 'We are passing the gardens of New Place, the house that Shakespeare bought in 1597 and lived in from 1610 when he returned to Stratford from London as a wealthy man' – or words to that effect. It was an impressive building, judging by the earliest drawings – the second-largest house in Stratford at the time, we are told, and the only one made from brick. Only its foundations, and part of a well, are left now.

The house was demolished in 1759 by its owner, the clergyman Francis Gastrell, who had become increasingly infuriated by the growing number of Shakespeare tourists interfering with his peace and quiet. He first chopped down the mulberry tree in the garden, thought to have been planted by Shakespeare himself. Then, angered by local taxation demands, he pulled down the entire house. The outrage he provoked was so great that he was forced to leave town. There is a story still circulating that his surname was banned for ever from Stratford, but it is a myth.

I would love to do a linguistic experiment and check in to the Shakespeare Hotel in Chapel Street calling myself David Gastrell, just to see if there is any folk-memory of that surname, but I've never had the courage. Mind you, I'd probably get no reaction. The last time I stayed in a Stratford hotel, the receptionist was Polish (I asked), and she hadn't been there long. Still, you never know. Maybe it's like the airport security computers where if your name shows up in some central database you are immediately whisked away into a dark room and bound. A prisoner in some Shakespearean Village . . .

> SHAKESPEAREAN PRISONER: What do you want?
> STRATFORD NUMBER 2: Information.
> SHAKESPEAREAN PRISONER: Whose side are you on?
> STRATFORD NUMBER 2: That would be telling. We want information. Information. Information.
> SHAKESPEAREAN PRISONER: You won't get it.
> STRATFORD NUMBER 2: By hook or by crook, we will.

I wonder if there was anyone called Gastrell in town on 27 March 1926, the day the original Memorial Theatre burned down?

New Place had large gardens and orchards at the rear. Today the space is occupied by the Great Garden, tended by the Birthplace Trust. It is laid out in a formal Elizabethan style, with a big lawn and yew and box hedges. There is a large mulberry tree in the centre, by tradition thought to be a cutting from the original. And an evolving sculpture trail.

That was what I was aiming for. Dotted about the garden are bronze sculptures of some of the plays by the American artist Greg Wyatt, sculptor-in-residence at the cathedral church of St John the Divine in New York City. The series began in 1999 with *The Tempest*, followed by *Hamlet*, *King Lear*, and *Julius Caesar*. A new work, *A Midsummer Night's Dream*, had been unveiled by the Royal Shakespeare Company's associate director Gregory Doran earlier in the year, and I wanted to see it.

I visited that cathedral once. It's on Amsterdam Avenue at 112th Street. Three facts about it stay in my mind, two general, one linguistic. It is, firstly, either the largest cathedral in the world, or the co-largest, depending on the rival claim of Liverpool's Anglican Cathedral. Both are acknowledged by the *Guinness Book of Records*.

I must say this bothered me, until I realized that the much larger St Peter's in Rome is technically not a cathedral. Nor is the even larger Basilica of Our Lady of Peace of Yamoussoukro, in Côte d'Ivoire, modelled on St Peter's. That is a truly extraordinary size. It has a floor space of thirty thousand square metres – equivalent to half a dozen football pitches.

Each spring, St John's has a ceremony called the Blessing of the Bicycles. It's a colourful service, in which bike messengers, cycle commuters, racing cyclists, and people who ride just for fun – adults and children – gather to pray for a safe cycling year. The celebrant sprinkles holy water on the bikes while everyone rings their bells. There's a silence in memory of cyclists who have died during the year.

The linguistic fact about the cathedral is its nickname. The building work began in 1892, and is still ongoing. Some wag in the 1960s called it *St John the Unfinished*, and the name stuck. It's going to be unfinished for a bit longer than anticipated, too. There was a major setback in December 2001. A fire devastated the incomplete north transept, and left a huge amount of smoke damage.

St John's isn't as unfinished as the Sagrada Familia in Barcelona, though. That started in 1882 and has a tentative completion date of 2026, the centenary of the death of its architect, Antonio Gaudí. When I was last in the city I didn't meet a single Barcelonian who believed that target would be met.

On the other hand, Barcelona has a history of making things happen. I was there in 2004 when it held its huge cultural Forum. It mainly took place in a specially constructed site along the seafront in the north of the city. One of the pavilions contained an exhibition called simply

'Voices', devoted to the celebration of linguistic and cultural diversity. When you went in you were surrounded by the sounds of the languages of the world. It was mesmerizing. Along one wall was a long row of video screens. Each screen presented a language 'in action'. A map showed where the speakers were from, and a transcript told you what they were saying. And you just listened, and listened, and listened, to the variety of auditory tones and textures that make up the linguistic life of the planet.

That sort of experience ought to be available to everyone everywhere. Indeed, way back in 1997 I had proposed a World of Languages exhibition centre to be based in London. Cities routinely have museums or galleries devoted to science, or natural history, or the arts – but there has never been a public 'space' in which languages are celebrated. There ought to be one in every city.

Other people thought so too. Detailed plans were drawn up and costed. An available building was located, in a perfect spot on the South Bank, just opposite Shakespeare's Globe. The British Council took the idea on board, and planning meetings were held. It looked as if it was going ahead. I got quite excited about it. All it needed was a small amount of government support.

Then it fell through. The government had a better idea. It was called the Millennium Dome. The amount of money wasted on that project would have funded a dozen Worlds of Language.

But I never lost sight of the idea, and seven years later at the Forum in Barcelona, talking about the importance of preserving linguistic diversity, I mentioned that the world still lacked a 'house of languages'. It wasn't the first time I had reaffirmed the point. Anyone who had attended my talks on this theme more than once would have had a distinct sense of *déjà entendu*. I was used to nothing happening, and I was beginning to resign myself to the prospect that it wouldn't happen – at least, not in my lifetime.

This time, though, it was different. The President of Catalonia,

Pasqual Maragall, was in the audience. I remember noticing that he turned to his neighbour and talked animatedly. Afterwards I learned that he thought it would be an excellent post-Forum project for the city. I agreed, but didn't hold my breath. I figured that even if they did take up the idea, the Sagrada Familia would be finished sooner.

Well, I was wrong. A mere two years later, in July 2006, there was another meeting in Barcelona, this time at the government offices, to launch the 'House of Languages' – in Catalan, *Casa de les Llengües*. Its name is *Linguamón*. They have a building, located right in the centre of the new Innovation District, Can Ricart, in the north of the city, and funding is in place. They hope to have it ready by 2008. It will be a feast of languages, well worth a visit, and in the meantime you can follow its progress online.

'They have been at a great feast of languages and stolen the scraps.' In *Love's Labour's Lost*, Mote makes the remark rather cynically, having heard fragments of other languages as his master Don Armado greets the pedantic schoolteacher Holofernes. That's one of several vivid images to do with language that you find in Shakespeare. They deserve to be visualized.

As I admired the latest Greg Wyatt creation in the Great Garden, I wondered what a sculpture of a feast of languages would look like. I hope there will be some art works in the new House of Languages. Language is a subject which cries out to be represented in art forms, and yet it has had so little treatment. The Maypure-speaking parrots were one of the few exceptions. I know of no celebration of human linguistic diversity in dance. No painting. No novel. No jazz. No orchestral treatment. The subject deserves at least a symphony.

Or a blessing. Maybe St John's will celebrate languages one day, as well as bicycles, in multilingual New York. Or for that matter Westminster Cathedral, seeing as there are hundreds of languages spoken in London these days.

They put the finishing touches to the plans for Linguamón's staff and budget in April 2005. That year the bicycles event at St John's in New York City took place on 22 April. It was a Saturday, the same day that the annual Shakespeare procession was wending its way through the streets of Stratford. The celebrations always take place on the Saturday closest to 23 April, the date traditionally thought to be Shakespeare's birthday.

I left the Great Garden and followed the processional route to get to the Shakespeare Institute, where I was due to give my talk. I knew the route well, as I had been invited to take part in the procession a couple of years before. It starts in the Garden, wends its way up Bridge Street and along the High Street, and ends up at Holy Trinity Church. Everyone carries some flowers, which are solemnly laid around Shakespeare's tombstone. After the formal procession has passed through, you can lay your own flowers there, if you want.

It's a great procession, with bands, civic leaders, ambassadors from several countries, costumed actors, academics, morris dancers, local school staff, and pupils of all ages. Special events keep the celebrations going over the weekend. In 2006 there was a football match: Montagues *vs* Capulets.

The year I was involved, I had a flag-unfurling role to perform. Along Bridge Street, Henley Street, High Street, and Union Street is a series of flagpoles representing each of the plays, and during the birthday weekend the flags and banners are ceremonially unfurled. At 11.15 a.m. The signal would be a roll of drums followed by a fanfare. All it would take was a tug on a rope. There would be Boy Scouts on hand to help in case absent-minded professors pulled the wrong thing or forgot to pull anything at all.

It might have happened. I got to my assigned flagpole early, at 10.45, and with nothing else to do but wait for the unfurling moment, found myself engaging in a reverie about Shakespearean place-names.

Why are there no towns called *Shakespeare* in Britain? There are over 250 drives, avenues, roads and streets named after him, but no towns. Even the Americans, who go out of their way to name places after famous people, have avoided him. Jefferson City. Columbus City. No Shakespeare City.

Mind you, there are a few unusual locations named after Shakespeare in the USA. There is a *Shakespeare Canyon* in Magdalena, New Mexico, and a reservoir called *Shakespeare Tanks* in Fort Hancock, Texas. But the prize for the most unusual Shakespearean name in the world must surely go to *Shakespeare Ghost Town*.

It's a national historic site, on Interstate 10 near Lordsburg in the 'boot heel' of southern New Mexico. It started out in 1858 as a mail stagecoach station, on the route to California, and it grew rapidly when silver ore was discovered nearby. Few places can have had so many names in such a short period of time. Within twenty years it was called *Mexican Springs*, then *Pyramid Station*, then *Grant*, then *Ralston City*, and finally *Shakespeare*.

It attracted all the swindles and lawlessness typical of mining towns of the period. The supposed discovery of diamonds in the area turned out to be a hoax. Several gunfighters used it as a base. Curly Bill Brocius. Black Jack Ketchum. Names resounding with bullets and plosives.

In 1879, a Colonel William G. Boyle tried to give the town a fresh start, sorting out the good mining claims from the bad ones. To symbolize the new era he envisaged for the town, he decided to call it *Shakespeare*. He started the Shakespeare Gold and Silver Mining and Milling Company, and the town enjoyed a second boom. But the renaissance was short-lived. The railroad passed it by, and the depression of 1893 caused the mines to close. The town slowly faded, leaving only empty buildings and the cemetery.

Billy the Kid passed through, before he became (in)famous, looking for a job. He was too young and diminutive to be of much use for heavy work, so he ended up washing dishes in the town hotel. It's now called the Stratford Hotel. It's on Avon Avenue.

The site of the town became a ranch in the 1930s, and the new owners gradually developed it as a heritage location. The New Mexico Heritage Preservation Alliance has it on its list of most endangered places.

Endangered it certainly was in 1997. On 10 April the old blacksmith shop went up in flames, and strong winds sent the fire into the general merchandise building. Many records and old artefacts were destroyed before the Lordsburg brigade managed to put the fire out. But the place has survived, and remains a popular tourist destination.

10.55. The procession started to move out of Chapel Lane and along the Waterside. I could hear the first band in the distance. I saw a knot in my rope. Was that deliberate? Where's my Boy Scout? Isn't it always the way? There's never one around when you need one. I had visions of all flags being unfurled, except one.

I need not have panicked. Scouts and Guides were already marching up Bridge Street, and one duly took his place in front of my flagpole. The knot turned out to be insignificant. I relaxed. The Shakespeare vexillographic canon would be complete.

Interesting coinage, *vexillology*, 'the study of flags'. It dates only from the 1950s. The *vexillum* was a type of banner used by the Roman legions. It wasn't flown from the top of a pole, as modern flags are. Rather, its top side was fastened to a crossbar fixed across the top of a spear.

There's nothing remotely like Shakespeare Ghost Town in Britain. Shakespeare is conspicuous by his absence from the list of English place-names. So when you do come across one, it takes you aback.

I did once find a *Shakespeare Farm* in Buckinghamshire. It's in Grendon Underwood, nine miles west of Aylesbury. The farm goes back to the sixteenth century, when it was the Ship Inn. The local story goes that Shakespeare wrote *A Midsummer Night's Dream* there.

There is also a *Shakespeare Cliff* in Kent, west of Dover, and you can travel right through it, because it is the entrance to the Channel Tunnel. It was the main construction site on the British side of the Channel. They dug out some four million cubic metres of rock.

What on earth do you do with four million cubic metres of chalk waste? It's enough to build another cliff. And that's more or less what they did. They decided to enlarge the existing platform at the foot of the cliff by putting the spoil into the sea behind a new sea-wall. Then they landscaped it and turned it into a nature conservation area. It is now a popular venue for walks, picnics, and fishing. The UK increased in size by ninety acres as a result.

The cliff was earlier known as *Hay Cliff*, but the name was changed in honour of the action that takes place in *King Lear*. The play was first performed at court on 26 December 1606, and must have been written that year, or perhaps begun in late 1605.

On 4 October 1605 the 'King's Men', Shakespeare's theatre company, visited Dover, and it is quite likely that Shakespeare himself was with them. He certainly must have visited Dover at some time, given the vivid description of the view seen from the clifftop in Act IV Scene 1 of *Lear*. The blinded Earl of Gloucester asks Edgar – his son, but disguised as a mad beggar, Poor Tom – to lead him to Dover so that he can kill himself.

> GLOUCESTER: Dost thou know Dover?
> EDGAR: Ay, master.
> GLOUCESTER: There is a cliff whose high and bending head
>   Looks fearfully in the confined deep;
>   Bring me to the very brim of it,
>   And I'll repair the misery thou dost bear
>   With something rich about me. From that place
>   I shall no leading need.

When they reach the cliff, a few scenes later, this is how Edgar describes the place:

How fearful
And dizzy 'tis to cast one's eyes so low!
The crows and choughs that wing the midway air
Show scarce so gross as beetles. Halfway down
There's one that gathers sampire – dreadful trade!
Methinks he seems no bigger than his head.
The fishermen that walk upon the beach
Appear like mice, and yon tall anchoring bark
Diminished to her cock; her cock, a buoy
Almost too small for sight. The murmuring surge
That on th'unnumbered idle pebble chafes
Cannot be heard so high.

There are some who say that Shakespeare's vocabulary is so different from Modern English that it needs to be translated. What a load of samphire! Take those extracts I've just quoted. How many words in them are different from anything you might hear today?

'Tis looks odd, written down; but we say it like that all the time in colloquial speech. *Dost thou* and *methinks* are still used in some regional speech, and have a public presence in many a modern film on knights and damsels. They were heard at movie-Camelot in Trawsfynydd not so long ago. And *yon* for *yonder* is very common in dialects throughout the country.

Apart from that, we have *choughs* – members of the crow family. And *sampire* in its modern spelling is *samphire*. It is a rock herb which grows near the sea, and is eaten pickled or in salads. Both words are still used today. When the Chunnel was finished, they called the new nature conservation area Samphire Hoe.

Gross means 'large'. It isn't often used in that sense any more, but the word is still in English, referring to large things. A gross of potatoes. Teenage girls, especially, describe something that's hugely awful as *gross!*

And *dreadful* doesn't have the meaning we give it today. It doesn't mean 'disgusting'. It is literally *dread + full* – 'full of dread'. 'Terrifying', in a word.

Only two other words in the extracts are so Elizabethan that they need a gloss. A *cock* is a 'cock-boat', or dinghy, pulled behind a bigger ship, or *bark*.

If we include all these words under the heading of 'unfamiliar' we get a total of ten out of 135. Hardly enough to justify the demand for translation, it seems to me. And most of Shakespeare is like that.

If there is difficulty in reading the above extracts, it is because the images force us to use our imagination, instead of relying on a television screen to do it for us. A cliff with a 'high and bending head'. Unnumbered pebbles lying 'idle'. They also show a very economical use of language. Not 'the air that is midway down the cliff', but 'the midway air'. Not 'the deep that is confined by the cliff', but 'the confined deep'. The meaning is packed into the words like compressed air in a cylinder, flooding your mind when you release it.

It was 11.15. The drums rolled. I pulled my rope. My Scout stood to attention. All along the street the flags and banners waved in the breeze, including mine. The band played – not 'Happy Birthday to You' but the National Anthem.

A handbill blew against my feet. I looked down at it. It was advertising a local hotel mystery weekend called 'Macbeth Murders'. 'Macbeth Murders!' I said to my wife. 'What will they think of next!' A man standing next to me in the crowd looked at me in horror. I nodded at him. 'Angels and ministers of grace defend us,' I said affably. He nodded back. And then, with a seriousness that I found slightly unnerving, he thanked me.

10

Shall We Shog?

KOLKATA

I think you could spend your whole life going to a Shakespeare birthday celebration in a different place each year and still not attend them all. Nobody owns Shakespeare. Or rather, everybody owns him. And these days, that sense of ownership is worldwide.

The day after my talk/Duck/play/Duck evening, I took the Birmingham Road out of Stratford, heading for the M40. My next stop was Lichfield, via the old Forest of Arden.

Just as you join that road, on your right, you pass Shakespeare Street, round the corner at the top of Henley Street where the birthplace is. Given its name, it is a remarkably unprepossessing street, leading to nowhere in particular. A cul-de-sac, in fact.

But then, street names are often misleading. In Wolverhampton, if you walk up into the city centre from the railway station, you will pass Long Street on your left. It runs for about thirty yards.

It was my second encounter with a Shakespeare Street in six months. The first had been in India at the end of 2004.

I had been on a British Council tour of the main Indian cities, several of them now with new Indian names reflecting a linguistic shift away from colonial tradition. The tour included Chennai (formerly Madras), Mumbai (Bombay), and Kolkata (Calcutta), as well as Delhi. Within the cities, many of the previously English street names had also been replaced by names in the local languages. But in Kolkata there is a prominent exception. One of the main streets in the city centre is still called *Shakespeare Sarani* (Street).

I went along it several times, because it contains the British Council office. The International Club is there too, as well as several major businesses and dozens of small shops. It's an odd feeling, seeing *Shakespeare* on so many addresses and shop frontages. And in so many unusual contexts. For instance, No. 40 is the Shakespeare Parlour. It is a fast-food eatery.

For anyone interested in the English language, and the way it varies through place and time, a visit to India is like entering linguistic paradise. The country currently has a special place in the record books: it contains the largest English-speaking population in the world.

The population of India passed a billion a few years ago, and is increasing at the rate of nearly 2 per cent per annum. In 1997 an *India Today* survey suggested that about a third of the population had the ability to carry on a conversation in English. This was an amazing increase over the estimates of the 1980s, when only about 4 or 5 per cent of the population were thought to use the language. And given the steady increase in English-learning since 1997 in schools and among the upwardly mobile, we must today be talking about at least 350 million. This is far more than the combined English-speaking populations of Britain and the USA.

All of these speakers – bar a *lakh* (hundred thousand) or so – have learned English as a second language. English has special regional status in India, and is an important unifying medium between the Indo-European north and the Dravidian south. Special status means much more than having a place in the public institutions of the country – in Parliament, the law courts, broadcasting, the press, and the education system. It means that the language permeates daily life. You can't avoid it, especially in the cities.

As we drove into Kolkata from the airport, I found myself surrounded by English everywhere. It was the same in every Indian city I went to. Even the smallest shops and stalls had an English sign or poster nearby. Nor were the slums exempt: on the corrugated walls of one straggling complex was a series of ads for vitrified tiles, all in English.

Outside one of the main tourist spots, a teacher was marshalling a class of thirty teenagers, and giving them instructions about where to meet and when their bus would leave – but not in their mother-tongue. In English.

Outside another I met a group of children leaving their primary school at going-home time. They waved excitedly and came rushing over, shouting out 'Hello,' 'Hi,' 'How are you?'

'Fine thanks, how are you?' I replied.

'We're fine too,' they chorused.

They tumbled into their school bus. As it drove off they carried on calling through the open windows: 'Thank you . . . Bye bye . . .' Seven-year-olds, I marvelled, on a confident career-track towards English.

Towards Indian English, of course. India has had a longer exposure to English than any other country which uses it as a second language, and its distinctive words, idioms, grammar, rhetoric and rhythms are numerous and pervasive. Collections of Indian English vocabulary have been around for over a century, but none has yet catalogued the extraordinary stylistic range and regional diversity of Indian English.

I had a free day before having to give some talks, so my hosts showed me around. I encountered hundreds of distinctive English usages, and would have written them all down if I hadn't been gripping the side of the car with white-knuckle intensity as the drivers played traffic-chicken with one another. I managed to record several dozen in my notebook, but a number are illegible. The writing starts well enough, but then tails away into a wavering line as our car swerved to avoid the unpredictable turning of an auto-rickshaw immediately in front of us.

The worst emergency swerve was to avoid hitting a cow, wandering unconcernedly along a main road into the city, apparently fully aware of its privileged status as a sacred animal in Hinduism. It knew where it wanted to go, but my driver didn't. He acted like a goalkeeper facing a penalty kick. He anticipated that the cow would turn to the left, so started to overtake on the right. And, as with most goalkeepers, he got it wrong.

The road signs sometimes reflected the reality. At one pedestrian crossing there was a sign indicating right-of-way. It showed a man running like hell!

But, fair play, despite a thousand near-misses – more than I have ever had in the rest of my driving life – I passed only one accident.

The distinctiveness of written Indian English greets you wherever you go. I was especially struck by the way words are split in different ways from what we are used to in British English. Signs warn of an approaching ROUND ABOUT. Above a store I read SUPER MARKET. A housing ad offered PENT HOUSES. Outside a university building was the greeting WEL-COME. A roadside warning said LAND SLIDE PRONE AREA. Another said OVER-SIZE VEHICLES KEEP LEFT.

It is far more than just vocabulary. On just one stretch of motorway, between Mumbai and Pune, I saw dozens of unfamiliar expressions. This is a small sample:

OVERSPEEDING AND TYRE BURSTING CAUSE ACCIDENTS

DO NOT CRISSCROSS ON EXPRESSWAY

DO NOT LITTER ON YOUR EXPRESSWAY

SPEED BREAKER AHEAD

LANDSCAPING AND BEAUTIFICATION

DON'T FOLLOW TOO CLOSELY

ROAD IN CURVE AHEAD

PLEASE DRIVE SLOW

NO BULLOCK CARTS

NO 2-/3-WHEELERS

That last one was when approaching an expressway. *2-wheelers* is the generic term for motorbikes and scooters. *3-wheelers* are auto-rickshaws.

Some locutions turn up regularly. *Pay 'n' Park*, said a sign outside a car park. A food store advertised *Heat 'n' Serve*. A removals firm described itself as *Movers 'n' Packers*. A gift shop was called *Greet 'n' Gift*.

The historical background of India is never far away from everyday usage. 'What do you think you're doing? Cutting grass?' said a boss to a worker lazing about. How can cutting grass be equivalent to doing nothing? Because grass-cutting used to be done by servants.

But this history also promotes correspondences. In particular, there is a remarkable sharing of linguistic humour between India and Britain. Both countries have the same penchant for word-play. 'Austensibly, it's about Jane' was a review headline about a critical book on that author.

'Be Ecofriendly' said a sign in Delhi – but it spelled the second word *Ecofriendelhi*.

You have to be careful, though. There are 'false friends' – words or phrases which are the same as those used in other varieties of English, but which have a different meaning or range of application. In Kolkata I saw an ad for fashionable men's clothing under the banner headline *HOORAY HENRY*. British people have to forget the negative associations of the phrase in the UK if they are to interpret this correctly. There is no hint of the loud-mouthed ineffectual upper-class twit here.

I'm not surprised that *Hooray Henry* reached India. What is surprising is that it isn't more well-known in America, seeing that's where the phrase started. Damon Runyon used it in his 1936 short story 'Tight Shoes', when he described Calvin Colby, a rich layabout, as 'strictly a Hoorah Henry'. It then crossed the Atlantic, and turns up in British writing from the late 1950s. The Americans then seemed to lose track of it. It now appears in guides to British English for American readers, along with *hoo-ha* and *Horlicks*.

You also have to be careful not to generalize about Indian English. It is changing very fast. Regional dialects of Indian English are increasingly apparent – an inevitable consequence of this huge country's cultural and linguistic diversity. There are noticeable differences of accent and dialect, especially between north and south, and 'regional' jokes are common. I was told one which began: 'There was this man from Kerala . . .' Kerala is in the far south-west of the country, and receives the same kind of treatment as does County Kerry in Ireland. The joke-teller, of course, was from the north.

You can see change in the newspapers too – in the matrimonial columns, for instance, where families advertise for desirable brides or grooms. A generation ago these were full of such terms as 'wheatish' – meaning light-complexioned – as a desirable physical characteristic. Today these have largely gone, and we find such criteria as 'professionally qualified' instead – a linguistic reflection of an important social change.

Three generations on after independence, Indian English is still having trouble distancing itself from the weight of its British English past. Many people there still think of Indian English as inferior, and see British English as the only 'proper' English. It is an impression still fostered by the language examining boards which dominate teachers' mindsets. At the same time, a fresh confidence is plainly emerging among young people, and it is only a matter of time before attitudes change.

It could hardly be otherwise when we consider the way Indian writing is increasingly reflecting indigenous varieties of language use. Gone are the days when everyone in a novel, from sahib to servant, spoke standard British English. The same linguistic diversity is apparent in the films – over a thousand each year – produced by Bollywood and the other growing film studios. If I had to choose a single instance of this newfound assurance, I would cite *Bride and Prejudice*, in which Jane Austen's novel is relocated to modern India.

Bollywood has generated a small family of related names. There is now *Kollywood* in Chennai – the *K* stands for the suburb of Kodambakkamin, where the studios are located. There is also *Tollywood* in Andhra Pradesh – the *T* stands for Telugu.

The really interesting question, of course, is what status this rapidly growing English dialect will come to have in the eyes of the rest of the world. Linguistic status is always a reflection of power – political, technological, economic, cultural, religious . . . – so this is really a question relating to the future of India as a world player. If I were a betting man, I would place quite a large sum on India as an eventual cyber-technological superpower. The call-centre phenomenon has already stimulated a huge expansion of Internet-related activity. The amount of daily text-messaging (SMS) exceeds that in the UK and USA. The IT press is always speculating about where future Googles will come from. One day I think it will be India.

India has a unique position in the English-speaking world. I see it as a linguistic bridge between the major first-language dialects of the world, such as British and American English, and the major foreign-language varieties, such as those emerging in China and Japan. China is the closest competitor for the English-speaking record. Currently with some 250 million speakers of English, it plans to increase this total dramatically as the 2008 Olympics approach.

But China does not have the pervasive English linguistic environment encountered in India; nor does it have the strength of linguistic tradition which provides multiple continuities with the rest of the English-speaking world. When Indian operators answer your call about train times between Birmingham and Glasgow, they are far more likely to be aware of where you are travelling than would any equivalent operators in China. Apart from anything else, they probably have lots of relatives in Britain.

And it is the Indian presence in Britain which marks the other end of this linguistic continuity. British people are familiar with (British dialects of) Indian English as a result of several generations of immigration. When the spoof chat show *The Kumars at Number 42* became successful on television, I heard local English kids playfully using its catch-phrases and copying its speech rhythms, without a hint of racism, just as they did when *Crocodile Dundee* made them play with Australian English.

There are parallels in the literary world. Suhayl Saadi's 2004 novel *Psychoraag* is an amazing mixture of South Asian English (Urdu, in this case), Standard English, and Glaswegian. How's about this, for a new variety of British English?

> *Ahhh, thur's nuhin better, in the deeps ae the nicht, than a wee bit ae clean terror. Lang teeth. Gleamin eyes.* Bhookee annkh.

> *Annkh.* Saamnp. *Memphis on the Nile. Sleepy asps. Broken circularity.* Baat-chit, raat-*shit*. Saans. Saaz. *Snake charmer.*

This needs translating more than Shakespeare does. Saadi helpfully gives an Urdu glossary at the back of the book. Some people would want a Glaswegian one too. My translation reads:

> *Ahhh, there's nothing better, in the deep of the night, than a little bit of clean terror. Long teeth. Gleaming eyes. A glutton.*

> *An eye. A snake. Memphis on the Nile. Sleepy asps. Broken circularity. Small talk, night-shit. Breath. Music. Snake charmer.*

India is special in one other respect. Alongside the spread of English there is a powerful concern for the maintenance of indigenous languages. I repeatedly heard young students express the need for a balance between an outward-looking language of empowerment and an inward-looking language of identity. CHOOSE YOUR LANGUAGE FOR YOUR POWER BILL, says one of the Mumbai billboards, offering Marathi, Hindi, Gujarathi, and English. Many of the smaller tribal languages are seriously endangered, there is no denying it, but there is an enviable awareness of the problem, which is lacking in many Western countries. India, it seems, can teach the rest of the world some lessons not only about multidialectism but about multilingualism too.

And about Shakespeare. I have never met so many people of all ages able to quote so much, apparently at the drop of a hat. It was like a second language within a second language. At the university in Kolkata I met one old gentleman who told me he used to know all the plays off by heart. He was getting rusty now, he said, so I wasn't to test him, but he rattled off a speech from *All's Well That Ends Well* as if to prove his point. I believed him. No civilian knows speeches from *All's Well That Ends Well*.

I asked him how old he was. 'Ninety-two,' he said.

I met another man who said he had first learned his English entirely from studying Shakespeare. Again, I had to believe him. The evidence was in my ears. At times he lapsed quite naturally into iambic pentameter. And every now and then he would, quite unselfconsciously, drop a *verily* or a *forsooth* into his sentences.

A group of teenage schoolchildren showed me the scrapbook they had put together recording their Shakespeare birthday celebration earlier in the year. It was full of colourful photos of scenes from the plays. They asked me whether I had been to Stratford. I said I had. They wanted to know all about the procession. They had seen pictures of it on the Internet. I told them my stories.

This was all in English, remember.

They asked me whether I had been at the procession that year. I said no, because I'd been at the birthday weekend at Shakespeare's Globe on Bankside in London. 'What was *that* like?' they wanted to know. They hadn't found it on the Internet. I paused, not knowing quite how to sum it up.

It had been a glorious, riotous affair, very different from the formal ceremonial of Stratford, but much more in keeping with the London life one imagines Shakespeare would have had. No processions. No ambassadors. The company opened the theatre for a day. Visitors explored the stage, got a sense of what it was like to perform there. They could even recite something on it, if they wanted. Actors were around to talk to. There was period music and food. Outside there were street performers and sonnets read alongside the Thames. A green man paced about, his face adorned with leaves and flowers. When I saw him, he was eating an ice-cream. It was an exuberant, light-hearted occasion.

Around the corner, in the atmospheric foundations of the Rose Theatre, the performance artist Will Sutton was presenting his first sonnet marathon – the whole 154-poem sequence, by heart. It took him two hours and thirty-two minutes.

Will's website is called *iloveshakespeare.com*. His initials are W.S. What more can I say?

I told the students as much as I could about all this. I got the impression that they were a bit shocked by the informality of what happens at the Globe. They were used to seeing Shakespeare on a Stratfordian pedestal.

I'm glad it was the 2004 event that I was talking about, and not the one which took place the following year. I'm not sure what the effect would have been on their state of mind.

In 2005, in addition to the usual events, they put on an evening of improvisation called *Shall We Shog? Shog* is Elizabethan English: it means 'go away, move along'. Historically, it relates to such 'movement' words as *shock* and *shake*. The title is a line from *Henry V*. 'Shall we shog?' says Nym to Bardolph. And away they go.

The show was compiled by actor, writer, and director Ken Campbell. I have never seen anything like it for crazy, irreverent Shakespeare foolery. It was a cross between *Whose Line is it Anyway?* and *It's a Knock-Out*. Three comedy companies, from Liverpool, Newcastle, and London, competed for the maddest interpretations of famous scenes (The Suggestibles from Newcastle won). There were 'To be or not to be . . .' time trials, the fastest recitation winning. There were dancing dogs. During the interval you could talk to actors in the yard, but they were allowed to reply only in strict iambic pentameter.

Maybe I did see something crazier, once. At the Edinburgh Fringe in 2003 a company performed *Bill Shakespeare's Italian Job*, directed by Malachi Bogdanov. There were red, white, and blue Mini Coopers on stage. The number plates were *BARD 1*, 2 and 3. The whole thing was in pseudo-Elizabethan English, of course. 'Thou wert only supposed to blow the bloody doors off!'

And then of course there is the other RSC – the Reduced Shakespeare Company. In their *Complete Works of William Shakespeare (Abridged)* they perform thirty-seven plays in ninety-seven minutes. It is a show for everyone. As one reviewer put it: 'If you like Shakespeare, you'll like this show; if you hate Shakespeare, you'll love this show.' It was London's longest-running comedy: ten years at the Criterion Theatre.

Shakespeare madness is everywhere, it seems. And it is lucrative madness.

Shall We Shog? also had a demonstration of the rare art form of 'nubbing'. A *nub* is a passage of blank verse that Shakespearean actors have sometimes relied upon when they forget their lines. It doesn't have to make any sense, but it must sound plausible. To alert the other actors on stage that the speaker is in difficulty, the word *nub* is used in the first line. When the actor gets back to the script, the end of the nubbing passage is indicated by the words *Milford Haven*.

Milford turns up repeatedly in *Cymbeline*, and once in *Richard III*, but why this innocent place should have been chosen as an index of thespian absent-mindedness is a mystery.

The word *nub* is also an etymological puzzle. It could be a variant of *knub*, meaning 'protruberance, lump', which led to its being used as a slang term for 'neck'. An associated sense around 1700 was 'hanging' and 'gallows'. That line of thinking has led some people to think that *nub* was then taken over by theatre people to describe the effect of leaving other actors 'dangling in the air'.

I find that etymology a bit forced. Rather more obvious is the use of *nub* to mean the 'point, gist' of a story. The *Oxford English Dictionary* records it from the mid-nineteenth century in such phrases as 'the nub of the business' and 'the nub of the matter'. It is easy to see how a shift in meaning could have taken place to express the notion of 'losing the point'. Unfortunately, the *OED* doesn't (yet) record the theatre sense.

Whatever the etymology, the theatrical effect is well attested, at least in earlier days. This is one speech said to have come from the last great actor-manager, Donald Wolfit:

> List, I sense a nubbing in far glens, where minnows swoop the pikey deep which is unpiked less pikey be, cross-bolted in their crispy muffs and choose the trammelled way . . . Oh freeze my soul in fitful sleep lest wind-filled sprites bequim the air and

take us singly or in threes in mad agog or lumpsome nub, aghast to Milford Haven.

In *Shall we Shog?*, Globe artistic director Mark Rylance hilariously found himself having to nub the Quarto version of Hamlet's speech to the players.

As always at the Globe, the audience was well involved. In a radio interview with Ken Campbell earlier in the month, my son Ben – defending the proposition that Shakespeare's language wasn't as difficult as people make it out to be – had claimed that any speech could be acted in such a way that it would be possible to understand it. Ken bet him £50 that he could find one that would never be understood on stage. Ben took the bet. He had two days to learn the chosen speech before performing it in *Shall We Shog?* The audience would decide how much of the £50 he should get, on the basis of how much they understood. If he performed it badly, he would get nothing. If he did well, he'd get the lot.

That's good money for a couple of minutes on stage. It horrifies me when I hear what poor pay most actors get. In 2006 you could be on stage a whole week, doing eight performances, and get a measly £366.82 for your pains. That was the minimum Equity rate for a West End performance. It was less elsewhere. Then of course you have to allow a percentage for your agent. And tax. No wonder actors look so thin.

The chosen speech turned out to be one from Act V of *As You Like It*, where Touchstone reports on a quarrel with a courtier which grew through seven degrees of ferocity. Touchstone hadn't liked the cut of the man's beard. The courtier had responded mildly, with a 'Retort Courteous'. But Touchstone persisted in expressing his dislike, so the courtier got angrier, responding first with a 'Quip Modest', then moved to a more intense level with a 'Reply Churlish', then a 'Reproof Valiant', then a 'Countercheck Quarrelsome', and then a 'Lie with Circumstance', ending up with the ultimate reproof, a 'Lie Direct'.

Making those seven distinctions of increasing severity intelligible in a short speech is indeed a tricky task, but the laughter and cheers left Ken in no doubt that the audience had understood it well. A paper cashometer was brought out, graded at £10 intervals. Was that performance worth £10? 'No!' howled the crowd. £20? 'No!' £30? £40? £50? A great cheer erupted. Ben got his money.

People expect to be involved when they go to a Globe performance. The theatre can impress you for all kinds of reasons – the best-guess effort to replicate the original architecture, the original practices in movement, music, dress, or pronunciation – but for me it is the dynamic interaction between actors and audience. The response to the play is the thing.

When I first went to the Globe, soon after it opened in 1997, I have to admit that I wasn't expecting to be a regular attender. I was curious to see what it was like, and that was all. I had seen the building growing from outside, and once – when planning the ill-fated World of Language – I'd been taken around. I can't remember why, but I have a photo of me alongside a bust of Shakespeare, both of us with hard hats on.

The first play I saw there changed everything. The stage thrusts out into a courtyard, capable of taking up to seven hundred people, the 'groundlings'. Those at the front press up against the stage, or lean on it. They are inches away from the actors. Everyone in the yard feels close to the action, and they react to it. Sometimes, even, they are part of it, as the players often leave the stage and use the space. It dawned on me that I would be seeing Shakespeare's plays there as I had never seen them before, and would be involved in them as I had never been before. It would also be as close as I would ever get to how Shakespeare himself saw them.

All sorts of unusual things happen linguistically at the Globe. If a character asks a rhetorical question in a conventional theatre, the shrouded audience would never dream of shouting out an answer.

Indeed, if you responded aloud to what you saw on stage, you would be massively shushed, and if you did it regularly you would end up being escorted outside. Laughter is the only routinely permitted vocalization during a performance. Not so at the Globe. When Mark Rylance's Hamlet asked, 'Am I a coward?' he wanted an answer from the audience, and he waited until he got it. When, in one production of *The Tempest*, Caliban proudly proclaimed his new freedom with the rhyme, 'Ban, ban, Cacaliban, Has a new master – get a new man!' he invited the audience to shout it with him. The roaring chant which followed would have put the crowd at Manchester United to shame.

Any regular Globe attender could tell you dozens of such stories. I remember, in *The Winter's Tale*, the travelling pedlar Autolycus plucking at his guitar for his opening song, putting down his hat, as buskers do, and looking at the audience expectantly. Coins showered around him. I remember, in *Henry V*, the English king making his stirring speeches, and the audience cheering. When the French king came on, they booed – apart from a small group of French tourists, who shouted '*Vive la France!*' Agincourt was nearly re-enacted in the Globe yard.

It is truly remarkable how the 23 April birthday has captured the imagination around the world. The irony, of course, is that nobody knows the real date on which Shakespeare was born. The custom of celebrating the event on the twenty-third didn't begin until the eighteenth century, fostered probably by a natural desire to see England's greatest dramatic poet associated with the feast day of St George, England's patron saint.

The only relevant evidence is the baptismal register of Holy Trinity Church in Stratford, which records the baptism of *Gulielmus filius Johannes Shakspere*, 'William, son of John Shakespeare', on 26 April 1564.

If the birthday was the twenty-third, then there is a problem. The baptismal practice of Elizabethan England, as specified in the 1559 Book of Common Prayer, was this:

> The Pastors and Curates shall oft admonish the people, that they defer not the Baptism of Infants any longer than the Sunday, or other Holy day, next after the Child be born unless upon a great and reasonable cause, declared to the Curate, and by him approved.

Now, in 1564, the twenty-third was a Sunday, and the main holy day in April, St Mark's Day, followed soon after, on the twenty-fifth. If the parents were following the usual practice, a child born on the twenty-third would be baptized, at the latest, by the twenty-fifth. So why the twenty-sixth?

Maybe there was a 'great and reasonable cause' to delay things. Or maybe the Shakespeares were influenced by the widespread superstition of the time that St Mark's Day was unlucky. Without any evidence to the contrary, the tradition stands, and the birthday procession takes place each year as close to the twenty-third as it can.

Actually, if we want to be Holofernistic about it, early May would be more accurate. 23 April in 1564 was not the same as 23 April today. By the mid-sixteenth century the Julian calendar had fallen ten days behind the solar year, so in 1582 Pope Gregory XIII introduced the Gregorian calendar which we follow today. Most European countries immediately made the change, but the then anti-papal England rejected the idea (and didn't catch up until 1752, when 2 September was immediately followed by 14 September). This means that, in 1564 in England, the date referred to then as 23 April corresponds to what we would today call 3 May.

Somehow I don't think a proposal for change would go down well among the students and scholars of Kolkata, or for that matter, with Stratford District Council.

11

A Rash of Dermatologists

ARDEN

Echoes of Shakespeare continue to resound as you drive north out of Stratford, into the old Forest of Arden, for this is his ancestor territory. After a mile or so I passed a signpost pointing to Snitterfield, where William's grandfather, Richard, set up as a farmer in the mid-sixteenth century. The surname appears in the village church baptismal register, spelled *Saxper* and *Shaksper*.

There is nothing unusual in finding variations in the spelling of a person's name in Elizabethan times. Standardized spellings didn't become the norm for another two hundred years. Six signatures of William Shakespeare are thought to be authentic. They display five different spellings.

I made a short detour through the village. Farmland still surrounds Snitterfield church. There is a fine half-timbered farm building which would have been there in the Shakespeares' time. A much renovated property in Bell Lane camouflages the original farmhouse.

I wasn't expecting to find any literary reminders in the village. But on the way out, along The Green, I passed a learning centre, Prospero Barn.

Snitterfield. A full-blooded Anglo-Saxon name. The *field* element had a broader meaning then. Today we think of fields as relatively small enclosed areas. In Old English, *feld* was a treeless stretch of countryside, of indeterminate size, either natural or cleared by men, and used either as common pastureland or for crops.

And the area around the Sherborne Brook, which flows through the village, was evidently frequented by flocks of snipe – a species of wading birds. In Old English, the name was *snite* – pronounced 'snee-tuh'. It probably relates to such words as *snout* and *snitch*, as the snipe has a distinctive long bill, but the etymologies are obscure.

Snipe haven't been seen in the area for a long time, though one was reported flying over a nearby golf course a few years ago. No wisps, however.

An unusual collective noun, *wisps*. Wisps of snipe. It's the same word as in 'wisps of smoke', but here it means 'flocks'. Birds have attracted several such collective names, ranging from the common *gaggle of geese* to the obscure *muster of peacocks*. Most have fallen completely out of use, known only by wordsmiths, and receive a new lease of life only in wordgames and quizzes – *a paddling of ducks*, *a murder of crows*. Some are colourful and imaginative: *a pitying of turtledoves*, *a tidings of magpies*, *an unkindness of ravens*.

It's difficult to know just how widely used such expressions were. None has many recorded instances. There are just two fifteenth-century references to *an unkindness of ravens* in the *OED*. I have the feeling that a group of medieval monks sat around the fire one Christmas and thought most of them up.

And why not? Human nature doesn't change much, and collective-noun inventing is a game that continues today. The aim is to find a word which puns on the meaning of the plural entity. Here are twenty-one of the best from my own collection:

> An absence of waiters
> A rash of dermatologists
> A shoulder of agony aunts
> A crop of barbers
> A clutch of car mechanics

A vat of chancellors
A bout of estimates
An annoyance of mobile phones
A lot of auctioneers
A bumble of beekeepers
A flutter of gamblers
A body of pathologists
A complex of psychiatrists
A fidget of choirboys
A mass of priests
A sulk of teenagers
A whored of prostitutes
A crash of software
A depression of weather forecasters
An exces's of apostrophes
A muckingfuddle of spoonerisms

Everyone loves to play with language. The ways of doing so have no order and no end. Some people love to create new words and expressions. Some make puns. Some parody famous authors. Some put on silly voices. Others have a daily routine which involves solving a word puzzle. Or being tortured with a crossword. Or playing Scrabble.

Some direct their energy into making up new words – words that don't exist in the language but, the inventor thinks, ought to. I recall using *circumtreeviation* recently – the phenomenon where someone taking a dog for a walk on a lead finds the human going around one side of a tree or pole and the dog going round the other. I heard someone in an office say, *I'll de-bag the cups*, meaning 'take the tea-bags out'. And I know of a man who – being a regular visitor to, and a reluctant departer from, his friend's settee – is called a *sofa-limpet*.

None of these is (yet) in the *OED*, and perhaps they never will be.

Correction. *Debag* is in – but only in the sense of 'remove the trousers from (a person) as a punishment or for a joke'. Known from 1914. Oxford University, doubtless.

Radio programmes and newspapers often have word-creation competitions. In the *Washington Post* in 2005, the game was to invent a new word by adding, subtracting, or changing just one letter from an old one. The winners included:

> intaxication: euphoria at getting a tax refund, which lasts until
> you realize it was your money to start with
> reintarnation: coming back to life as a hillbilly
> glibido: all talk and no action

Some people direct their language energy into graffiti. Intrusive and disfiguring this may be, but it can also be extremely clever, testifying to the universal nature of the ludic linguistic impulse, where there are no boundaries, and the only rule is 'break the rules'. Or perhaps: 'Make something different from what it was before.'

As I rejoined the main road from Snitterfield, my eye was caught by a graffitied signpost. Some wag had elongated the first leg of the letter *n* upwards, turning it into an 'h'. I imagine it's a fairly regular occurrence. The poorer and more obvious linguistic jokes tend to be reinvented by each generation, each one thinking it has been mind-blowingly original.

The best linguistic jokes can last for years. The '. . . rules OK' graffiti genre probably began as a gang rivalry or soccer boast: *Serpents rule, OK?* Nobody knows exactly when it began – at least the early 1970s. But it has since generated thousands of variants, some of which have entered into intellectual domains light years away from the street corner or football pitch.

> Archimedes rules – eurekay!
> Absolute zero rules $O^{\circ}K^{\circ}$.
> French diplomacy rules – au quai?

My favourite is *Roget's Thesaurus rules — OK, all right, very well, you bet, certainly*. New ones are still being invented.

There is no limit to language games, because there is no limit to language. Language, it has often been said, makes infinite use of finite means. There are only so many sounds, letters, words, and grammatical constructions in English. But they can be combined in an extraordinary number of ways — ways that are to all intents and purposes unlimited, for the simple reason that each day the language changes, offering new possibilities of ludic expression. Each turn of the road, indeed, can provide a fresh source of language play.

A little further along the A3400 I passed the turning to Wilmcote. A perfect example. To most people, Wilmcote is the village where Mary Arden was born. The tour buses affirm its special status. Mary Arden married William Shakespeare's father John. You can see Snitterfield, across the fields, from Wilmcote.

But to the ludic linguist, *Wilmcote* is a first-order isogram, or heterogram. Not a very interesting one, admittedly, but a first-order isogram nonetheless.

An *isogram* is a word in which the letters turn up an equal number of times. In a first-order isogram, each letter appears just once: *dialogue* is an example. In a second-order isogram, each letter appears twice: *deed* is an example. Longer examples are hard to find: they include *Vivienne*, *Caucasus*, *intestines*, and (important for a phonetician to know this) *bilabial*. In a third-order isogram, each letter appears three times. These are very rare, unusual words such as *deeded* ('conveyed by deed'), *sestettes* (a variant spelling of *sextets*), and *geggee* ('victim of a hoax'). I don't know of any fourth-order isograms in English.

To *gegg* is in the *OED*. It is known from the early nineteenth century. The noun *gegg* means a practical joke. It is probably related to *gag*. The word is still used in parts of Scotland, and you might find it in other regional dialects too.

Wilmcote has eight letters, and each is different, so it is a first-order isogram. But there are hundreds of place-name isograms like this, with eight letters. No ludic linguist would lose any sleep over such a name. The really interesting question is: which is the longest isogrammatic place-name in English?

As far as I know – and that's an important qualification – it is a small village in Worcestershire, west of Evesham: Bricklehampton. Its fourteen letters, with no spaces, make it the longest such name in the language. Close competitors, with thirteen letters, are Buckfastleigh, Bridgehampton, and Rumboldswhyke.

That's quite a claim – not just the longest in England, note, but in the English language as a whole. Of course Bricklehampton could one day be outclassed by some tiny place in the middle of Canada, or Australia, or the USA. But nobody has yet found one.

The roads are quite narrow around Bricklehampton. It is not a good thing to be a ludic linguist and a car driver – at least, not at the same time. I don't know if anyone has ever been charged with 'driving without due care and attention for linguistic reasons', but it could easily happen. I doubt whether the magistrates would be much impressed by the defence 'I was distracted by a first-order isogram.' That's why I much prefer to be a car passenger. It's easier to write in your notebook when you haven't got to keep the other hand on the steering wheel.

There aren't many physical signs today of the Forest of Arden, which once covered a large area north-east of the River Avon, but there are several linguistic signs. Not in the name itself, oddly enough. *Arden* has nothing to do with trees. The etymology isn't entirely clear, but it's likely to come from a Celtic word meaning 'high' or 'steep'. The name *Ardennes* in France has the same origin.

The forest is commemorated most obviously in a few small towns and villages. A little further along the A3400 I went through Henley-in-Arden. A few miles further on, just before the road joins the M42, I passed Tanworth-in-Arden. As I approached the Birmingham Exhibition Centre, away on the right there was Hampton-in-Arden.

The archaeology of the area shows that the clearing of the forest was well under way in Anglo-Saxon times, and this is reflected in the many place-names ending in *–ley* or *–leigh*. In Old English, *leah* meant a 'woodland clearing', either natural or man-made. There are eighty-five such names listed in the main place-name survey of Warwickshire. All but four of them are inside the old Forest of Arden area.

I passed several of these ancient clearings on my way along the A3400. *Henley* itself, of course (a 'high leah'), with *Buckley* Green nearby (a 'leah held by charter'), then *Bearley* (a 'leah belonging to a fortified place'), and *Langley* (a 'long leah') near Snitterfield. As the road became the A34 and approached Birmingham, there were *leahs* all around – *Shirley* (a 'leah belonging to the shire'), *Saltley* (a 'leah overgrown with sallows'), *Ulverley* ('Ulfar's leah') . . .

My route along the M42 took me away from the old Birmingham Road, and away from another great source of linguistic inventiveness. If I'd carried on along the A34 I would have passed through Sarehole, now part of the Hall Green outer suburb of Birmingham. And in the early 1900s, growing up in Sarehole was J.R.R. Tolkien, who half a century later would achieve worldwide fame as the creator of hobbits and the storyteller behind *The Lord of the Rings*.

Sarehole provides another ludic distraction. It is a name in which the letters alternate between consonant (C) and vowel (V). You might think this is nothing to remark about. In fact it is quite difficult to find examples in English. The language has hundreds of ways of clustering consonants together, often just in pairs (such as *ch* and *tr*), often in much longer sequences, as in *twelfths* (CCVCCCCC). These make simple sequences of a CVCV type hard to find. Look at any page of a road map of an English-speaking country and see how many you can spot. You will be lucky to reach double figures.

I stopped for a break at *Corley* (a 'leah where there are cranes') on the M6, and tested this out on my map of the Birmingham area. I saw *Halesowen* straight away, but others were harder to spot. After another five minutes' peering I had found *Honiley* (a 'honey leah') and *Moseley* (a 'leah infested by mice'). I spent another fruitless five minutes on the task, then gave up and went in for a coffee.

There was an airline ad on a billboard outside: 'Fly Emirates'. *United Arab Emirates* is a fine example of CVCV in a country name. There could be no lengthier instance, surely?

Playing ludic linguistic games takes time. Lots of it. I never cease to be amazed at the amount of time devotees of the practice are prepared to spend exploring unusual language possibilities. And when you ask them why they do it, they give the same answer as mountaineers do, but applied to language. 'Because it's there,' waiting to be explored.

Why try to find isogram place-names? Or CVCV place-names? Why try to compose a story without using a particular letter – a *lipogram*?

Why try to compose one in which all the words contain the same vowel – a *univocalic*? Why try to compose one in which each word begins with the same letter?

To see if it can be done.

There's nothing new about this. Victorian wordsmiths invented dozens of language games, and played them incessantly. Here is a univocalic from 1875, using letter *A*. It is entitled 'The Russo–Turkish War':

> Wars harm all ranks, all arts, all crafts appall:
> At Mars' harsh blast, arch, rampart, altar, fall!
> Ah! hard as adamant, a braggart Czar
> Arms vassal swarms, and fans a fatal war!
> Rampant at that bad call, a Vandal band
> Harass, and harm, and ransack Wallach-land,
> A Tartar phalanx Balkan's scarp hath past,
> And Allah's standard falls, alas! at last.

Imagine how many hours it took to draft that!

The present paragraph is a lipogrammatic creation, though not a very interesting one. It contains no instance of the seventeenth letter of the alphabet.

Q.

Rather more challenging is the creation of a lipogram which contains no instance of one of the most frequently occurring letters in English, such as *e*, *t*, or *a*. To avoid *e* means no use of the definite article *the*, no regular past-tense forms (as they end in *–ed*), no common pronouns such as *he*, *me*, *they*, and no use of some of the commonest verbs in the language, such as *are*, *were*, *have*, and *make*. Yet Ernest Wright wrote a fifty-thousand-word novel in 1939, called *Gadsby*, which contains not a single letter *e*.

> Gadsby was walking back from a visit down in Branton Hills'
> manufacturing district on a Saturday night. A busy day's traffic

had had its noisy run; and with not many folks in sight, His
Honor got along without having to stop to grasp a hand, or
talk . . .

And so it continues, *e*-less, for several hundred pages. Imagine how
many months it took to draft that!

It's a real shame that Wright's first name was *Ernest*.

Language games continue to fascinate. They turn up in children's
Christmas annuals and Christmas crackers. They appear in daily newspapers and weekly magazines. They provide the meat for half the radio
or television quiz shows on earth. You will find thousands of ludic
linguistic sites on the World Wide Web. Type 'word games' into
Google, and you will get millions of hits.

Why are they so popular? My theory is that it is because everyone is
qualified to play them. Language games are not like (in the UK)
Mastermind quizzes or *Krypton Factor* challenges, or (in the US) *Jeopardy*
questions, where you need to have a good memory or a good body of
knowledge or just a good body – or of course all three. To play a
language game you simply have to be able to listen and speak, or, in
the case of those games based on the written language, to read and
write, and then to use your intuitions about the language. 'What word
is missing from *spick and* —?' 'What letter is likely to follow *Q*?' Faced
with such questions, we all feel able to answer because we have all been
through the same mill. In real quizzes, the questions can be much trickier,
but the intuitions we use to answer them are shared by all of us.

Tolkien played language games too, but they were infinitely more
scholarly and subtle. Before he became known as an imaginative writer
he was a philologist who spent two years, just after the First World
War, as an assistant editor on the huge dictionary project at Oxford
which would one day become the *OED*. When he turned his creative
powers to fiction, his entire *œuvre* was grounded in solid linguistic
reasoning.

He was a philologist in the literal sense of the term. A 'lover of words'. Philology has had rather a bad press at times, being associated with dry-as-dust enquiries into historical documents. When practised with Tolkienesque learning and imagination, the subject comes alive. Each word is seen as a historical adventure, an exploration, a voyage of discovery in which sound, spelling, and meaning interact in intriguing and unpredictable ways.

North Warwickshire, once covered by the Forest of Arden, is Tolkien territory. Biographers have tracked down hundreds of local allusions in his creative writing. One of Tolkien's neighbours in Sarehole was a man called Samson Gamgee. Anyone versed in hobbitlore will know that surname, and will also know that the Bagginses live at Bag End in the Shire. Bag End Farm is where Tolkien stayed for a while when he was ill with pneumonia in 1923. It is in Dormston, a small village fifteen miles west of Stratford.

From the top of the hill behind Bag End Farm you can see the Malvern Hills in the distance, with the Black Mountains beyond. Or are they the mountains of Mordor?

When I visited the four swannes at Waltham Cross, I walked through the bus station and saw the number 251 bus. It was going to Upshire.

The millions who have encountered *The Lord of the Rings* for the first time in recent years probably do not realize that they have had a lesson in Germanic philology. Tolkien's word-creations are never arbitrary or fortuitous. Each of them opens up an etymological world, typically Anglo-Saxon in character.

Take Bilbo's age, celebrated at his birthday party in the opening chapter. He is, he says, 'eleventy-one'. This sounds like a perfectly normal childlike extension of an existing counting pattern. We can imagine a child carrying on from '. . . seventy, eighty, ninety' into 'tenty, eleventy, twelvety', before being put right. 'We don't say *tenty*, we say *a hundred*.'

But Old English actually had a counting system a bit like that. The basic system didn't stop at a hundred. It went on to 120. After sixty, the numerals had an unstressed prefix, *hund–*, so we find seventy (*hundseofontig* = 'hund + seventy'), eighty (*hundeahtatig* = 'hund + eighty') and ninety (*hundnigontig* = 'hund + ninety'). It appeared as itself, *hund*, for a hundred as well as *hunteontig* ('hund + tenty'). But then the sequence continued with 110 (*hundendleofontig* = 'hund + eleventy') and 120 (*hundtwelftig* = 'hund + twelvety').

Counting in twelves is an ancient practice. We see it also in the notion of a *gross*, 144, which is twelve dozens. It is also found in the sale of certain commodities, where six score (120) is often called a 'great hundred' or a 'long hundred'.

So, when Bilbo calls himself eleventy-one he isn't just being privately clever. He is showing himself to be part of a mindset from olden times.

Farthings is another example. A farthing is one of the four regions of the Shire. The word is literally 'fourth-ing'. We find the analogy this time in Yorkshire, traditionally divided into three parts called Ridings. The word is literally 'third-ing'. Over time North Thirding became North Riding.

Tolkien is always doing this. While some of his invented words are just bits of fun – *staggerment*, *flabbergastation*, *confusticate* ('confound') – most have a derivation which takes us into other linguistic worlds. Some of these worlds are natural languages, such as Old English and Old Norse. Some are artificial languages, specially created for the stories, such as Elvish. And sometimes a word hovers uncertainly between the two.

In Elvish, the name for real silver, 'true-silver', is *mithril*. It derives from *mith* 'grey' + *ril* 'brilliance'. The word turns up in Book II, Chapter 4 of *The Lord of the Rings*, where the brave company are spending the night in the great cavernous hall of Moria. Gandalf explains what it is:

> Mithril! All folk desired it. It could be beaten like copper, and polished like glass; and the Dwarves could make of it a metal, light and yet harder than tempered steel. Its beauty was like to that of common silver, but the beauty of *mithril* did not tarnish or grow dim.

It is a good choice for an alien coinage, because it doesn't look like an English word: *–ril* is not an expected word-ending. There are probably fewer than a dozen words in English ending in *–ril*. Most are unusual words, such as *umbril* and *courbaril*. Only four – *April*, *Avril*, *peril*, and *nostril* – are at all common.

If you drive around the Midlands, however, a major exception will sooner or later jump out at you. There was an instance just along the road from Sarehole. As you approach central Birmingham, there are some old factory buildings. Several of them have Victorian advertisements etched into the old red-brick walls. And one of them is for *Bovril*.

The name has a solid, earthy, honest, hard-working ring to it. A pie and a cup of Bovril have been the survival kit for many an English football fan during cold winter games.

The word has a picturesque history. The story starts with Napoleon III, who wanted an effective way to feed his soldiers during the Franco–Prussian War of 1870–71. He ordered a million cans of beef from Britain, but there was insufficient beef to meet the demand. So a new derivative product was created, by an Edinburgh butcher called John Lawson Johnston. He first called it 'Johnston's Fluid Beef', but after reading a novel he had a better idea.

The novel was Edward Bulwer-Lytton's *The Coming Race*, a utopian piece of science fiction which was one of the most successful books of the 1870s. The narrator accompanies an engineer deep into a mine, and stumbles across a mystical, peaceful people who have learned to live without poverty, envy, or any of the other evils of human society, thanks to a mystical source of energy, which they call *vril*.

The narrator struggles to explain what vril is like, but admits that 'there is no word in any language I know which is an exact synonym for vril. I should call it electricity, except that it comprehends in its manifold branches other forces of nature, to which, in our scientific nomenclature, differing names are assigned, such as magnetism, galvanism, &c.' But the phrase which might specially have caught Johnston's attention was the way the people, who call themselves Vril-ya in honour of this force, described it: 'a great sustainer of life'.

Vril-ya means 'the civilized nations' in their language. *A-Vril* means 'civilization'. Johnston took the Latin word for 'ox', *bos*, chopped off the last consonant, and added some *vril*. The rest is history.

The drink was an instant success in Britain, and the Bovril Company was formed in 1889. In 2004 the manufacturers, Unilever, announced that they were changing the recipe from beef to a yeast extract, partly to allay fears caused by the cattle disease BSE, and partly to make the product suitable for vegetarians and vegans. But they didn't change the name. (The beef returned in 2006.)

Bulwer-Lytton's novel is fascinating for linguists, as he devotes a whole chapter to explaining how the language of the Vril-ya works. And *vril* itself, as a noun, has done rather well. Words from artificial languages do not usually have any future outside their invented context, and it is certainly unusual to find any such words entering a natural language. *Esperanto* is one. *Vril* is another. It is in the *OED*, where it is glossed rather vaguely as 'a mysterious force imagined as having been discovered by the people described in one of Lytton's novels'.

Mithril is a third. The *OED* glosses it as a 'name given by J.R.R. Tolkien to a mythical precious metal'.

There was no Bovril on sale at the service station, but Tolkien was there. In between huge piles of sweets and car accessories could be detected books and DVDs of *The Lord of the Rings*. Tolkien would be delighted that hobbits can still be found in North Warwickshire.

Etymology is the most wonderful, frustrating subject. You find yourself exploring lexical paths which are brilliantly lit with facts about earlier usage, then suddenly you are in a dimly lit passage, where it is a struggle to make your way. Often, after a struggle, you find you have ended up in a cul-de-sac. Or you are faced with the path splitting into half a dozen different ways and you don't know which one to take. Or it just stops, and you are left peering uncertainly into the darkness, wondering whether you dare take another step.

No such struggle, you would imagine, if you have the creator of a word there to ask. At least the author will know where it came from?

That doesn't necessarily follow at all.

Take *hobbit*. People did ask Tolkien where the word came from. He knew what he wanted it to mean: 'hole-dweller'. And in the first draft of the entry in the *OED* he was said to be the originator of the name. But when he saw the draft, he demurred, and the final entry says only:

> In the tales of J.R.R. Tolkien (1892–1973): one of an imaginary people, a small variety of the human race, that gave themselves this name (meaning 'hole-dweller') but were called by others *halflings*, since they were half the height of normal men.

Tolkien wasn't positive that he had invented it. He could offer no single source for the name. He saw resemblances in its phonetic shape to *rabbit* and *Babbitt* (the hero of Sinclair Lewis's 1922 novel, *Babbitt*) and *hobbledehoy*, meaning a 'youth between boyhood and manhood'. It was possible, he thought, that he had created it himself. On the other hand, he writes in a letter, maybe it came from 'buried childhood memories'. Or maybe, he once said in an interview, he picked it up 'from a nineteenth century source'.

He himself never found an earlier instance. But in 1977, after his death, somebody else did, causing great excitement in the world of Tolkien etymology. The word turns up in a nineteenth-century book of folklore compiled by a Yorkshire merchant, M.A. Denham.

He includes a long list of supernatural beings, and one of them is *hobbit*.

Of course, what we don't know is whether Tolkien ever saw this book. He might have done. A copy was certainly in his university library's folklore section – a section that he used to explore. This might be the 'nineteenth century source' he half-remembered. But we can't be sure.

Even if we do track the word back to Denham, it doesn't solve the etymologist's question. For where did Denham get it from? There are several possibilities.

Hob has been known for centuries as a name for a type of sprite. The form turns up also in *hobgoblin*. Links can be shown with other fairy beings. *Hob* is a familiar rustic form of *Rob*, the shortened version of *Robert*. From *Rob* we get a diminutive form, *Robin* – 'little Rob'. And Robin Goodfellow is famous in the fairy world as the mischievous imp, Puck.

Endings which express 'small' or 'little' are common in some languages (such as Spanish), but are unusual in English. We have –*let*, of course, as in *booklet*, *rivulet*, and *droplet*; there is –*ling*, as in *princeling* and *duckling*; and there are a few words with an –*et* or –*it* ending which reinforce the notion of small size, such as *bit*, *midget*, *snippet*, and *islet*. On this basis, a *hobbit* would be a 'small hob'.

But there are other sources for the word. It might be a shortened form of *hobbity-hoy*, a variant form of *hobbledehoy*. A *hobbit* is also an old name for a type of ordnance, derived from *howitzer*.

The obscurity of the etymology hasn't stopped people using it and basing other words upon it, such as *hobbitish*, *hobbitry*, and *hobbitlore*. And it has found fresh domains of application. In the 1960s the name received a new lease of life in California, where hippies saw in the good-natured hobbit community lifestyle an apt incarnation of their own aspirations. For a while, Americans who wore flowers in their hair also called themselves *hobbits*.

Then in 2004, in Indonesia, archaeologists discovered the fossils of a diminutive being, about a metre tall, whose status in relation to *Homo sapiens* has been hotly debated. The media immediately dubbed it a *hobbit*.

I joined the queue to pay for my coffee. Next to the till was what appeared to be a half-completed crossword puzzle. As I got closer I could see it wasn't a crossword at all. It was one of the new generation of sudoku puzzles with letters instead of numbers. When it's filled in correctly, a word or message is revealed.

Wordplay enthusiasts have a habit of 'upping the ante'. They like to make the challenge more difficult with each game. I once followed the thought processes of a wordplayer. The initial challenge was to make up a sentence in which every word began with the same letter. The sentence must make sense, and every word must be in the dictionary. He chose *H*.

Harry has hurt his hand.

Cheat. No proper names.

He has hurt his hand.

Too easy. Make it at least ten words long.

He has hurt his hand hoicking huge heavy handbooks halfway home.

Check *hoicking*. Yes, it exists. *OED* definition: 'lift up or hoist, often with a jerk or rapid movement . . . perhaps originally a regional variant of *hike*'. Still too easy. Write a hundred-word paragraph with every word beginning with *H*.

'No . . . Give me something I can get my teeth into!'

All right, then: write a whole story with every word beginning with *H*.

'No, I said something I can *really* get my teeth into.'

OK. Retell Shakespeare's *Hamlet* with every word beginning with *H*.

'Now you're talking!'

Things then went quiet for a while. Until one day, this appeared:

HAMLET

Act I Scene 1

Hamlet headquarters

> *Hamlet henchmen have had horrific haunting. Hark! Ho!*
>
> *Heck! Hair-raising hackles happen. Heebie-jeebies. Horrible.*
>
> *Horatio hazards – hallucinations? Had hallucinogens? Hangovers? Headaches?*
>
> *Henchmen howl: Haven't had hashish.*
>
> *Have.*
>
> *Haven't!*
>
> *Humbug!*
>
> *Horrendous haunter hovers hither, holding helmeted head high.*
>
> *Heavens! Historic Hamlet!*
>
> *Horatio harangues haunter. Hold! Hold!*
>
> *Horizon has half-light. Haunter hears hen hooting. Hurries hence.*
>
> *Hold! Here? Here? Hopeless.*
>
> *Have Hamlet here hereafter. Hopefully he'll handle haunter happily.*

And so it went on, for over a thousand words. The final lines are worth recording for posterity, beginning with Hamlet's dying words.

> *Hush haranguing.*
>
> *Hero Hamlet hies heavenwards, happy hunting-grounds.*
>
> *Hardarms hurries hither. Hallo. Horrific! Horrid! However, he has hankerings. Hopes he'll have homage here.*
>
> *Horatio hails him. Hamlet had hinted he'd have honours. Hardarms happy.*
>
> *Hearse Hamlet! Ho, henchmen! Have hardware hit heavens!*

Hardarms? Fortinbras.

As I finished my coffee at Corley, I reflected that this could be the start of a whole new genre. Mrs Macbeth meditates murder. Reveller Romeo reveals romantic reasons. Arden attracts amorous 'appenings. (Cheat.)

I left Corley, and Arden, and Tolkien, and Shakespeare behind and headed north along the M6 towards a totally different linguistic world. The English of creativity and play was going to be replaced by an English of rule and regulation. For I was going to Lichfield.

12

A Wheelbarrow Called Wilberforce

LICHFIELD

The reason for the change in linguistic ethos is made perfectly clear as you enter Lichfield city. On the welcome sign it says 'Birthplace of Dr Johnson'. Johnson was the man whose *Dictionary* inaugurated a new era of English lexicography. He also helped form the climate of correctness in language matters which would dominate the teaching of English for the next 250 years. There is no bigger historical language personality in Britain. But not much sign of a propensity for language play.

I drove in from the south along the A5026, the London Road, past the Shoulder of Mutton pub. At the crossroads I was presented with a choice. Either I could turn left and go around the town towards the cathedral; or I could go straight across towards the shopping precincts and – the Garrick Theatre.

I hadn't left Shakespeare behind after all. Lichfield named its fine new theatre after another eighteenth-century son of the town, actor David Garrick. And it is due to Garrick's enthusiasm for Shakespeare, as well as his prowess as a Shakespearean actor, that the modern bardic industry, including the birthday celebrations, developed in Stratford.

Garrick's house is now council offices.

Lichfield has its birthday celebrations too. Johnson was born on 18 September 1709, and close to that date each year the Johnson Society holds a weekend of events. People come to it from all over the world. I went in 2005 and met visitors from Australia, Canada, and several countries of Europe. It is totally different in scale, style, and tone from the analogous event at Stratford, but easily matches it for period recreation and enthusiasm.

On the Friday evening, I formally opened a new 'dictionary room' on the top floor of the museum, with an interactive display. On the Saturday there was a procession from the Guildhall to the Market Square. The mayor laid a wreath on the statue and there was a short service. A local theatre company performed a light-hearted play about Johnson. New artwork was unveiled in the Garrick – Johnson's face emerging out of a collage of words from the *Dictionary*. And in the evening there was a formal supper in the Guildhall for members of the Johnson Society and their guests. They rang out the old president and rang in the new one. They ate mutton, drank punch, and some smoked long pipes.

Johnson's enormous literary range is reflected in the list of the Society's presidents, whose number will reach a hundred in 2010. Leading figures from the press, broadcasting, and literature rub shoulders with the Church, industry, law, and politics. Where else would you see, on the same list, Frank Muir and John Wain, Malcolm Muggeridge and Richard Ingrams, Beryl Bainbridge and Enoch Powell? Linguists have to remember that Johnson was not only a lexicographer: he was a critic, editor, and creative writer as well.

Anyone can join the Johnson Society. The only qualification is to have an interest in Samuel Johnson.

I was staying the night at a B&B on Dam Street, which I had been told was near the cathedral, so I turned left at the crossroads. I couldn't go wrong. The three spires act as a beacon, and it is an easy matter to find Cathedral Close.

Lichfield is the only medieval English cathedral with three spires. They are sometimes called 'the three ladies of the Vale'. It is one of the smallest cathedrals around, at the opposite end of the scale from St John's in New York – 113 metres long and 21 metres wide – 370 x 68 feet. That's less than a football pitch in area. But what it lacks in size it more than makes up for in character.

People do like to name things. I don't mean just public transport objects, such as locomotives, ships, and planes, or the names given to commercial objects by their manufacturers. I mean personal, private names for every-day objects, such as fridges, lawnmowers, and wheelbarrows – or, for that matter, spires. Back in the 1980s, in a programme for the *English Now* series I presented on Radio 4, I asked listeners to send in examples of objects they had named. I was expecting a few dozen letters. I got hundreds.

A man wrote to say his wheelbarrow was called *Wilberforce*. A woman said her hoover was known as *J. Edgar*. At least two garden sheds were called *Tardis*. There was in the kingdom a waste-disposal unit called *Wally*, a teapot called *Herbie*, an ashtray called *Cedric*, and a butter-knife called *Marlon*. Maybe there still is.

The etymologies were enthralling. One man, presumably a classical music enthusiast, called his car *Simon* because of the rattle. A woman remembers calling her teddy-bear *Isaiah* – 'because one eye is higher than the other'. Another called her pocket calculator *Mr Spock* because 'it has a green face, is extremely logical, and always gives me the right answers'. One family called its yucca plant *Yorick*, anticipating its demise so that they could say 'Alas, poor Yorick!' – though since the naming, the plant had thrived. Someone called their cushion Christopher Lee 'for no particular reason'.

The principle is evidently that, if you have an object which is of particular functional or emotional significance to you, you give it a name. Often it's a name known only to members of your family. It's part of the 'house dialect' – or 'familect' – which every family has. No one from outside would ever learn about it or show any interest in it. Unless they were a nosey linguist.

Cathedrals and churches sometimes name their bells – occasionally even rename them. For instance, the original bells of Southwark

Cathedral, just round the corner from Shakespeare's Globe, were named *St Nicholas*, *Vincent*, *St Lawrence*, *Anna Maria*, *Stephen*, *Maria*, and *Augustus*. Then in 1424 an extra bell was added, and most were renamed: *Christ*, *St John the Evangelist*, *All Saints*, *Gabriel*, *St Lawrence*, *Augustine*, *Mary*, and *St Trinity*. These aren't the ones we hear today, though; new bells arrived in the eighteenth century. Only the service bell now has a personal name: *Peter*.

You might think it would always be a very serious business, naming church bells, and usually it is. The names and inscriptions they contain often remind the listeners of the transience of life. One of the bells at Exeter Cathedral is called *Doom*, probably because it was the one rung at executions in medieval times. But there are exceptions. The fourteen bells of Exeter are chiefly named after their founders – such as (A.C.) *Thomas*, (John) *Birdall*, (Thomas) *Purdue*, and (John) *Pennington*. But one is called *Pongamouth*, and nobody is quite sure why. It sounds like a nickname. A *pongo* is a type of ape with a wide mouth. Ringers call a bell 'wide-mouthed' if it rings slowly – a sense not (yet) recorded in the *OED*.

The Lichfield bells don't have names.

I drove around Cathedral Close and found Dam Street, which turned out to be dammed, or rather blocked, by a wooden gate. Pedestrian only. It needed to be unlocked before I could get through to my promised car-parking space.

The guest-house owner arrived with a key to let me through. 'You can park by our back door beside the pool,' he said. He was referring to Minster Pool, a pleasant tree-lined stretch of water running alongside the cathedral. Dam Street is so named because of the causeway which gave access to the town from the Cathedral Close. It is an ancient walkway. Its name is first recorded in the fourteenth century.

From the road I could see where he meant. But between me and the parking space, along the side of the road, was a row of closely spaced black bollards. 'You drive through the middle pair,' he said, grinning. A joke, surely? The bollards were so close together that it would have been difficult to get a Dinky car between them, let alone a Rover 75. He was going to produce another key and lower the bollards, wasn't he?

No he wasn't. 'There's plenty of room for a car like yours,' he said. 'At least a centimetre on each side.' And he added: 'Trust me.'

I recalled the excellent advice Herod gave to Claudius in Robert Graves' novel *I Claudius*: 'Trust no one.' But my car was blocking the pedestrian way, and the gate through which I had entered was now locked again. I had no choice. 'Breathe in!' people say, as they pass through a narrow opening. I always thought that was metaphorical, but I really did hold my breath as I inched the car through. The guest-house owner gave me a smug, 'Ye of little faith' look.

I walked along Dam Street into Market Square. Johnson's birthplace house is on one corner, on Breadmarket Street. You can't miss it. Facing the house is an imposing stone statue by R.C. Lucas of a brooding, seated Johnson. It was erected in 1838. Behind him, in the opposite corner of the square, is a diminutive bronze statue of his biographer, James Boswell, by the writer and sculptor Percy Fitzgerald. That went up seventy years later.

Fitzgerald was the author of many biographies, including one of David Garrick and one of Boswell. That must be fairly unusual: a statue of a biographer by his biographer.

Boswell is not looking at Johnson. He is gazing towards the cathedral. He looks slightly miffed – I like to think because Johnson was rude about Scottish accents, and Boswell was born in Edinburgh.

Boswell records, in his biographical account of the year 1776, a conversation between Johnson and Sir Alexander Macdonald:

> SIR A: I have been correcting several Scotch accents in my friend Boswell. I doubt, Sir, if any Scotchman ever attains to a perfect English pronunciation.
> JOHNSON: Why, Sir, few of them do, because they do not persevere after acquiring a certain degree of it.

This was a time in England when a prestige accent was developing, especially in the London area. Eventually it would come to be called 'received pronunciation', and all regional accents would be measured against it, and found wanting.

Johnson himself did not escape the eighteenth-century suspicion of regional accents. At one point he goes on in praise of the inhabitants of Lichfield, as being 'the most sober, decent people in England, the genteelest in proportion to their wealth, and spoke the purest English'. Boswell demurs:

> I doubted as to the last article of this eulogy: for they had several provincial sounds; as *there*, pronounced like *fear*, instead of like *fair; once* pronounced *woonse*, instead of *wunse*, or *wonse*.

He finds an ally in David Garrick, who uses his actorly skills to good effect:

> Garrick sometimes used to take [Johnson] off, squeezing a lemon into a punchbowl, with uncouth gesticulations, looking round the company, and calling out, 'Who's for *poonsh*?'

Johnson, Boswell records, 'never got entirely free of those provincial accents'.

Boswell accompanied his mentor on a visit to Lichfield that year, and found himself made very welcome by Johnson's acquaintances there. One day he records accepting an invitation to dinner from a Mrs Gastrel, who lived at Stowhill. The name at first meant nothing to him, but it would have rung bells even then with Shakespeare buffs, whether spelled with one *l* or two. Her husband was the clergyman who had cut down the mulberry tree and destroyed New Place. Boswell darkly adds:

> as Dr. Johnson told me, [he] did it to vex his neighbours. His lady, I have reason to believe, on the same authority, participated in the guilt of what the enthusiasts for our immortal bard deem almost a species of sacrilege.

No such sacrilege has attended Johnson's birthplace. The house is now a museum and – appropriately enough – a bookshop. Johnson's father was a bookseller and stationer, and he built the place a few months before Samuel was born. It has been a museum since 1901.

2005 was certainly the *Dictionary*'s year, for it was the 250th anniversary of its first appearance. Publication was 15 April 1755. The day was well remembered in 2005. Glasses were raised all over the kingdom – by lexicographers, at least. And I know of at least one secondary school that celebrated by holding a 'dictionary party', though I am not privy to what went on in it.

The *Dictionary* deserves every celebration people choose to give it. It is a remarkable work by any standards, both in its coverage and in its treatment. It was the first attempt in English at a truly principled lexicography. It portrayed the complexity of the lexicon more fully than ever before: 42,773 entries in the first edition, with 140,871 definitions and 222,114 quotations. The quotations initiated a practice of citation which has informed high-quality English dictionaries ever since.

The basic statistics are impressive enough. What is so much more impressive is the thought that Johnson performed this feat alone – apart from a small group of amanuenses who helped him write out and organize the entries on small slips of paper. Although the planning of the book began in 1746, most of the work was compiled in an intensive period of labour of less than two years. No wonder, at the end of it all, that people started to call him 'Dictionary Johnson'.

I was meeting members of the Johnson Society that evening, but had some time to spare, so I walked back along Dam Street. I had seen a plaque on the wall opposite my guest-house, and I wanted to see what it was about. The house turned out to be called Brooke House, and this is what it says:

MARCH 2ND 1643 LORD BROOKE A GENERAL
OF THE PARLIAMENT FORCES, PREPARING TO
BESIEGE THE CLOSE OF LICHFIELD, THEN GARRISONED
FOR KING CHARLES THE FIRST, RECEIVED HIS DEATH WOUND
ON THE SPOT BENEATH THIS INSCRIPTION BY A SHOT IN THE
FOREHEAD, FROM MR DYOTT. A GENTLEMAN WHO HAD
PLACED HIMSELF ON THE BATTLEMENTS OF THE
GREAT STEEPLE TO ANNOY THE BESIEGERS

It was during the first stage of the English Civil War. The Siege of Lichfield took place between 2 and 4 March 1643. The Royalists had been gaining ground in the Midlands, and had established garrisons at Tamworth, Lichfield, and Stafford. Lord Brooke was in charge of a

Parliamentarian (Roundhead) army deputed to break the Royalist hold. He won one battle at Stratford then advanced on Lichfield, an important centre, as it commanded the main north–south road through Staffordshire.

The cathedral was the focal point. Lichfield had no castle and no outer walls, so the Royalist garrison took up its positions in the Cathedral Close. Soldiers on the cathedral roof had an excellent view of the surrounding streets. But the Parliamentary attack was intense, badly damaging the towers and spires, and the garrison soon surrendered – though not before Lord Brooke was shot.

The sniper was located high on the cathedral roof, by the central spire. Standing in the spot on Dam Street and looking up at the roof, a considerable distance away, I could see that it was either one of the most brilliant shots in the history of warfare or a very lucky shot indeed. The accounts incline to the latter view. 'Mr Dyott' was John Dyott, known locally as 'Dumb Dyott', the deaf son of a local gentry family. He was a volunteer militia member. His musket would have been powerful but not especially accurate.

To annoy the besiegers. Annoy sounds odd to modern ears. That's because the meaning has changed. It's another 'false friend', like *Hooray Henry*. Today, the meaning of *annoy* is mild – 'vex, irritate'. But when the word first came into English from French in the fourteenth century, it had a much stronger sense – 'to be hateful or odious' to someone. By the time of the Civil War it had developed meanings of 'injure, harm', especially in a military context.

It turns up several times in Shakespeare in this sense. In Act I of *Julius Caesar*, Casca tells Cicero that a lion 'went surly by/Without annoying me'. He doesn't just mean that the sight of a lion failed to cause him minor irritation. He was much relieved that it hadn't gone for him.

Dyott wasn't on the roof to vex the Roundheads. He was there to kill them. Which he did.

John Dyott has another claim to fame. After the war, he married a deaf woman named Katherine. This is one of the earliest known marriages between two born-deaf people. Nobody has yet found an earlier such marriage.

Calling him 'Dumb Dyott' or 'Dummy Dyott' might have been attractive to those who like alliteration, but it is a common and demeaning misapprehension. Deaf people are not necessarily unable to speak. On the contrary, many develop excellent spoken-language ability. But the stereotype has been with us a long time, so it is difficult to eradicate. The phrase *deaf and dumb* has been known since Anglo-Saxon times. It is recorded from around the year 1000 – actually the other way round, to begin with, as *dumb and deaf*.

Just before I reached Brooke House I passed a little side-turning called *Quonians*. Now, there is nothing like a word beginning with *Q* to distract an English-language linguist. It is one of the three least frequent letters in English writing (*x* and *z* are the others). That is why it does so well at Scrabble. It is very unusual indeed in English place-names. My road atlas of Britain has about twenty-five thousand names in it. Just 102 of them begin with *Q*.

Some of them are very fine names, though. *Quob* in Hampshire – 'marshy place, bog'. *Quarles* in Norfolk – 'circle' (probably a stone circle of some kind). *Quarr* on the Isle of Wight – 'quarry'. *Quarley* in Hampshire – a 'leah with a mill'. *Quy* in Cambridgeshire – 'cow island', a collapsing of *cu + ey*.

But *Quonians* is a *Q* word *par excellence*. I have never come across it anywhere else – and neither has Google. I typed it into that search engine and got (in 2006) a mere 275 hits, all referring to Lichfield. Local records show the name *Quoniames* recorded in 1283, and a *Quoniames Lane*, also spelled *Konyames Lane*, in the fourteenth century. It looks like a Latin word, but the meaning of the adverb *quoniam* in Latin is to express sequence or cause – 'since, whereas' – which is hardly an appropriate name for a location. Streets are not normally named after adverbs.

A contributor to the magazine *Notes & Queries* in 1876 thought it must derive from a person's surname – *Kenyon*. Quonians was pronounced locally as 'Kenions' at the time, it seems. It remains a puzzle.

I walked down Quonians, past R. Bridgeman & Sons, Architectural & Ecclesiastical Craftsmen in Wood & Stone. It was less than fifty yards long, and plainly a very old street. A small plaque on one of the buildings said 1555.

There was another, larger plaque, above a hedge. It is an undated *memento mori*, which begins:

> Reader, whoever thou art. Prepare to meet thy descending God. Erelong the clod's of the valley shall cover thee: and the worms feed sweetly upon thy flesh. Be ye always ready . . .

And it concludes:

> N. Bradbury erect's this monument.

The apostrophes caught my eye. Today these would be considered mistakes, examples of the so-called 'greengrocer's apostrophe' – a name first applied to the practice of using an apostrophe before the *–s* marking a plural noun in words ending in *–o*, as in *potato's* and *tomato's*. It then spread to other noun endings, such as *pea's* and *plant's*, as well as third-person verb endings, such as *happen's*. Quite plainly, a large number of people have never learned the modern rule, which is that the apostrophe is used to show possession (as in *cat's paw*) or to identify an omitted letter (as in *I'm*), with just a few exceptions.

Ire built up in middle England during the later decades of the twentieth century, eventually culminating in 2001 with an Apostrophe Protection Society and, two years later, with Lynne Truss's *Eats, Shoots and Leaves*, advocating 'zero tolerance' of abuses of punctuation.

It is, however, a slander on greengrocers. I know a greengrocer who is an excellent speller, *and* who plays Scrabble. The problem is more deep-rooted.

The apostrophe was in fact one of the last punctuation features to come into English orthography, and it has never settled down. In texts from around Shakespeare's time we see it being used repeatedly for plurals and third-person singulars in verbs. In the opening plays of the First Folio we find *fellow's, et cetera's, it's lips, how fare's my lord, answer's* (the verb), *go's* (the verb), and *dilemma's*.

Even as late as Johnson's day, the system was still developing. There are no longer any plural apostrophes after a consonant, but there are several after nouns ending in *–o* or *–a*. In the *Dictionary* we find him allowing such spellings as *grotto's, innuendo's, supercargo's, virtuoso's, volcano's,* and *echo's,* as well as *comma's, opera's, cupola's, savanna's, vista's,* and *toga's*.

In the nineteenth century, printers and publishers attempted to standardize the system, but they still left some anomalies. They applied the rule about possession rigorously to nouns, but forgot about pronouns, so that the possessives *his, hers, its, ours, yours,* and *theirs* don't have an apostrophe. They banned the apostrophe from plurals, but allowed a number of exceptional cases, such as after numerals (*the 1860's*), abbreviations (*the VIP's*), and individual letters (*P's and Q's*).

Anyone who refuses point-blank to allow an apostrophe before a plural has to surrender when they are asked to punctuate 'dot the i's and cross the t's'. (Alternative solutions exist, but they are cumbersome.)

People found it difficult to apply the rules consistently, right from the start. There was a great deal of inconsistency around the turn of the century as to whether it should be *St Pauls* or *St Paul's*, or *Harrods* or *Harrod's*.

To begin with, Charles Henry Harrod was perfectly satisfied with his grocer's apostrophe when he opened his shop in Knightsbridge in 1849. A tea merchant and grocery wholesaler, his shop was apostrophized from the outset. An advertisement in 1895 for a Bradbury's Wellington hand sewing-machine, retailing at £2, informs readers that it can be purchased from the first floor of 'Harrod's Stores, Brompton'. But as the century progressed, variation crept in. Manufacturer marks on metalware products made for the firm show a mixture of *Harrod's* and *Harrods*. By the early 1900s, the apostrophe had largely disappeared. An advertisement in *The Times* for 9 December 1907 says: '15 acres of Christmas gifts at Harrods.'

The trend affected other firms. Around the same time, *Lloyd's Bank* became *Lloyds Bank*. And in 1890 the US Board on Geographic Names made a far-reaching decision, which is still in force:

> Apostrophes suggesting possession or association are not to be used within the body of a proper geographic name (Henrys Fork: not Henry's Fork).

Why?

> The word or words that form a geographic name change their connotative function and together become a single denotative

unit. They change from words having specific dictionary meaning to fixed labels used to refer to geographic entities. The need to imply possession or association no longer exists.

You might have thought that would settle the matter. But no. There are hundreds of names with apostrophes in the official US repository, the Geographic Names Information System. These exceptions are administrative names, such as schools, churches, cemeteries, hospitals, airports, and shopping centres. Such names, the Board concluded, 'are best left to the organization that administers them'.

But even with natural locations there are exceptions. In fact there are five of them. *Martha's Vineyard* was approved in 1933 after a big local campaign. *Ike's Point* in New Jersey was approved in 1944 because 'it would be unrecognizable otherwise'. *John E's Pond* in Rhode Island was approved in 1963 to avoid confusion with *John S Pond*. *Carlos Elmer's Joshua View* was approved in 1995 at the request of the Arizona State Board on Geographic and Historic Names to avoid having a sequence of three apparently given names. And *Clark's Mountain* in Oregon was approved in 2002 at the request of the Oregon Board to reflect the personal preferences of the explorers Lewis and Clark.

I suppose a history could be written about each one of these names. For instance, who was Martha, and why a vineyard? The vineyard bit is easy, for the island was covered with wild grapes when it was discovered. The other bit is more complicated. The discoverer was the English explorer Bartholomew Gosnold, who arrived there in 1602, and he had a daughter – as well as a mother-in-law – called Martha. Tradition has it that the island was named after one or other of them. However, for some time after the discovery, the island was actually called Martin's Vineyard, presumably after the captain of Gosnold's ship, John Martin. The two names must have been in competition for a while before Martha triumphed.

The English writing system today is full of apostrophe anomalies. London Tube stations *Earl's Court* but *Barons Court*. *McDonald's* but *Starbucks*. In the USA, a chain of drive-through hamburger outlets has two brands: one is called *Checkers*, the other *Rally's*. The *Nathan's* eatery is associated with *Kenny Rogers Roasters*. And so it goes on. But even the firms which insist on apostrophes have to bow before technology. The website of *McDonald's* restaurants is *www.mcdonalds.com*.

Anyone using an Internet search engine knows that whether you type in an apostrophe or not makes little difference to the results. On the other hand, with some satellite positioning systems, the apostrophe can be critical. If you are looking for a *McDonald's* and the system only has that form, then typing in *McDonalds* will get you precisely nowhere.

A website for the development of the King's Cross area of London has (in 2006) a big heading: *King's Cross Online*. Immediately under-neath is the heading *Welcome to Kings Cross*. The name is repeated several times on the home page without an apostrophe. But click on the next page, about Development, and every use has an apostrophe.

It is hardly surprising that people are confused.

But that doesn't stop apostrophes playing a very important part in forming relationships. When Lynne Truss's book first came out, she was invited to appear on the *Richard and Judy* television chat show. There the nation learned that Richard and Judy were first attracted to each other in part 'because they both cared about apostrophes'.

My meeting with the Johnson Society was in Cathedral Close, just round the corner from the house of another famous Lichfield resident, Erasmus Darwin. He was another great eighteenth-century intellectual, but younger than Johnson, born in 1731, when Johnson was twenty-two. He settled in Lichfield in 1756, living in a large house on Beacon Street, by the West Gate entrance to Cathedral Close, where he started a medical practice. He was also a poet, teacher, polymath, and inventor.

Charles Darwin was his grandson, and wrote a biography of him. He comments that Erasmus and Johnson rarely met when the latter came to Lichfield, and when they did 'they seem to have disliked each other cordially, and to have felt that if they met they would have quarrelled like two dogs'. It is hardly surprising. Two intellectual heavyweights in one small town are hardly likely to get on. In any case, their religious views – Darwin's radical, Johnson's conservative – were also at opposite ends of the scale. Darwin's name is conspicuously absent from Johnson's correspondence.

Erasmus Darwin seemed to want to invent everything. And for linguists, what is fascinating about him is that he invented a speaking machine. It was a small vertical construction in a wooden frame. A head at the top, with leather lips, overlay some bellows. It was capable of producing [p], [b], [m], and the vowel [a], and apparently it was realistic enough to have fooled some first-time listeners into thinking that it was a real person saying *mama* and *papa*, or *map* and *pam*.

It certainly impressed the engineer Matthew Boulton. In 1771, at one of the meetings of the Birmingham Lunar Society, he promised to pay Darwin £1,000 if he could deliver to him within two years 'an Instrument called an organ that is capable of pronouncing the Lord's Prayer, the Creed, and Ten Commandments in the Vulgar Tongue' (that is, in everyday speech) – in exchange for the commercial rights, of course. (Boulton was an astute businessman.)

Darwin didn't win the bet. It would take another two hundred years before the science of phonetics would come up with such a device.

Whether this was a serious proposition or a joke is unclear. Given the rather unusual constitution of the Lunar Society, it could have been either. It was formed in 1765 in Birmingham by a small group of leading scientists, inventors, and polymaths. The name came about because they scheduled their meetings on the Monday nearest the full moon. This was nothing to do with witchcraft. It was simply that the extra light made their journey home in the dark easier and safer. There was no street lighting in those days.

With ludic wisdom, they called themselves *lunaticks*.

The members read like a roll-call of inventiveness. As well as Boulton and Darwin they included James Watt, Josiah Wedgwood, William Herschel, and Joseph Priestley. In its creative range it was second only to the Royal Society. But it lasted only as long as most of its founding members were alive, and it was formally wound up in 1813.

A reincarnation of the Society took place in Birmingham in 1991. It is important to distinguish it from another Lunar Society, formed in Birmingham in 2002. That is a six-piece indie/pop/alternative band.

Darwin was also one of the first to use a speaking tube outside London. He had one in his study, leading down to an earpiece near the back of the kitchen fireplace. Charles Darwin recounts the story:

> A countryman had brought a letter and sat waiting for an answer by this fire, which had become very low, when suddenly he heard a sepulchral voice, saying, as if from the depths of the expiring fire, 'I want some coals.' The man instantly fled from the house, for my grandfather had the reputation amongst the country folk of being a sort of magician.

As I rounded the corner into Cathedral Close, a group of cherubic young lads – choirboys, possibly? – were running along the pavement, one shouting 'Exterminate, exterminate,' in a Dalek voice. Not good for the vocal cords, I reflected. The original Dalek voices were processed electronically, using the services of the BBC's Radiophonic Workshop. Replicating that tinny harangue without electronic help is a sure recipe for developing a voice disorder.

The last thing in the world a voice-over artist wants is to develop friction-induced nodules on the vocal cords.

In fact there were two voice-over men involved in the Dalek voices created for *Dr Who*. One was Peter Hawkins, who died in 2006. The other was David Graham.

When you read the CV of a venerable voice-over artist, it can be like having your past life – or, at least, the lives of your children – passing in front of your eyes. David Graham was the voice of Parker, Brains, and several other characters in *Thunderbirds*. Peter Hawkins was the voice of the original Flowerpot Men. He invented their *flobbadob*-type speech – he called it *oddle-poddle* (not yet in the *OED*). *Flobbadob* meant 'flowerpot'. Later he did all the characters in the pirate cartoon *Captain Pugwash*. And his urgent tone of voice as the announcer at the beginning of another television series has virtually become a phonetic catch-phrase: HERGÉ'S ADVENTURES OF TINTIN.

The Daleks weren't his only science-fiction vocal creation. He was also the first voice of the cybernetically augmented humanoids known as Cybermen, which competed with the Daleks for the title of who can scare the most daylights out of children. To make the distinctive voice, he was fitted with a dental plate containing a microphone, originally designed to help people who have had their vocal cords surgically removed. Could there ever have been a more unusual application of the technology of clinical phonetics?

Whenever a children's television programme does something un-usual with language there are always anxious letters. When *The Flower-pot Men* was first shown in the 1950s, some mothers were reluctant to let their children watch it in case it retarded their linguistic develop-ment. Exactly the same response greeted the arrival of the *Teletubbies* in the 1990s.

Such reactions hugely overestimate the linguistic influence of tele-vision and hugely underestimate the extraordinary language-learning ability of the young child. A child who can learn to distinguish two or three languages by the age of five – and over half the children in the world are bilingual or trilingual – is hardly going to be bothered by a bit of flobbadob or the occasional 'Uh-oh'.

After my meeting with the Johnson Society I walked back to my guest-house in Dam Street. I found myself thinking of the enormous circle of acquaintances Johnson had while living in London. People used to fall over themselves to be introduced to him. Johnson used to say that he never sought after people himself.

As usual, Boswell picks him up on the point, and suggests that there were in fact some people that Johnson had gone out of his way to meet. Johnson reluctantly agrees, adding, 'I sought after George Psalmanazar the most. I used to go and sit with him at an alehouse in the city.'

I had already come across that name on my travels. George Psalmanazar had been a tenant of Hay Castle for a while. He was an adventurer who became one of the most notorious impostors of the eighteenth century. He arrived in London from Europe in 1703, claiming to be a native of the island of Formosa (present-day Taiwan). He invented a religion, culture, and language, and in 1704 published *An Historical and Geographical Description of Formosa, an Island subject to the Emperor of Japan*. It contained some remarkable claims, and was a tremendous success.

Nobody knows what his real name was. The name he adopted when he 'arrived' in the West was an allusion to the biblical king of Assyria, Shalmaneser.

Psalmanazar's stories were fantastic. The society of Formosa was polygamous, and men were allowed to eat their wives if they were unfaithful. Twenty thousand children were sacrificed annually to the gods. There were whole villages built on board boats. People gobbled it up. An expanded second edition was published in 1705.

He was a brilliant liar. When challenged that he had fair skin and hair, he said that, as an upper-class member of Formosan society, he did not have to work in the sun; and in any case he had lived underground. When asked – by none other than astronomer Edmond Halley at the Royal Society – whether the sun shone all the way down chimneys, he said it didn't – whereupon Halley said it would have to do so, as Formosa was between the tropics. Psalmanazar had an answer: Formosan chimneys are twisted in shape, so the sun never reaches the bottom.

The language itself was an amateurish affair, which wouldn't have stood up to a philologist's scrutiny for five minutes – but it would be another sixty years before a scientific philology developed. The word for 'king' was *bagalo*; 'nobles' *tanos*; 'governors of cities' *os tanos soulletos*; 'son' *bot*; 'daughter' *boti*. It is all very European. The Lord's Prayer is *Koriakia Vomera*, and it begins:

> *Amy Pornio, dan chin Ornio vicy, Gnayjorhe sai Lory, Eyfodere sai Bagalin, jorhe sai domion apo chin Ornio kay chin Badi eyen . . .*

It is all very *vril*-like.

Slowly, suspicions grew, and after a while Psalmanazar confessed to the deception. He became a literary hack in London's Grub Street, and – after an illness some years later – a reformed character. By the time Johnson got to know him, he was a pious man of letters. A memoir, published after his death in 1763, revealed all.

Grub Street. It is defined in Johnson's *Dictionary*:

> Originally the name of a street in Moorfields in London, much inhabited by writers of small histories, dictionaries, and temporary poems; whence any mean production is called *grubstreet*.

The street is in EC2, just round the corner from the John Keats pub in Moorgate. It isn't called *Grub Street* any more. The name was changed to *Milton Street* in the nineteenth century – after a local builder, not the writer. But the old name lives on in literary parlance. An article in *The Times* in 2006 was headed 'Is Grub Street Dead?'

Johnson inserted 'writers of dictionaries' into his list of the hack writer inhabitants of Grub Street. That was an in-joke. Dictionary Johnson did have a sense of humour, after all. It's just that you have to know where to look for it.

13

How do You Like Your Eggs?

SAN FRANCISCO

Lichfield is in the heart of Roman England. Thomas Telford's A5 trunk road passes close by, on its way to Holyhead. It was one of the easier sections for him to build, as all he had to do was follow a long straight section of the Roman road, Watling Street.

As I approached the A5 I went past the village of Wall, the site of a Roman staging post. There are well-preserved foundations of a Roman inn and bath-house. The place is called *Letocetum*. It would make a fine film location – but I don't know of any Roman epic made in the Lichfield area.

Lichfield is typical of the Roman place-names from the Anglo-Saxon era. An Old English word is added to a Celtic name. The commonest ending of the time was *ceaster* 'town', producing the many names illustrated by *Doncaster*, *Lancaster*, and *Cirencester*. Another was *burh* 'fort', as in *Salisbury*. And a third was *feld*, as in *Lichfield*.

The earliest manuscripts of Bede's *Ecclesiastical History* tell how Chad, the first Bishop of Lichfield, had his seat *in loco qui vocatur Lyccidfelth* (or *Licidfelth*) – 'in a place that is called Lyccidfelth'. The events recounted took place in the seventh century, so the name presumably dates from around that time or a bit before.

The meaning of the first element in the name has been much disputed. In the 1880s, philologist Henry Bradley suggested that Bede's *Lyccid* was an Anglicization of the early Welsh *luitcoit*. In modern spelling that would be *llwyd goed*, 'grey wood'. *Letocetum* seems to be a Romanized version of the Welsh name.

The arrival of the French spelling system for English in the early Middle Ages caused some long-standing problems. One of the substitutions they made was to replace Old English *c* with *ch*. As a result *lic* became *lich*. And this gave rise to a number of misconceptions about the meaning of the name.

Lic in Old English was the word for 'corpse'. During the Middle Ages, several words came into English with this meaning, such as *lich-gate* ('the roofed gateway to a churchyard which receives a dead body before burial'), *lich-bell*, and *lich-rest* (a 'burial place'). With this build-up of instances, it was only natural to assume that *Lichfield* was a 'field of corpses'.

The only problem was: there was no historical field of corpses. But that doesn't stop the popular mind when it comes to proving a desired etymology. A legendary story of the death of a group of Christian martyrs in the area was resuscitated, and it soon became thought of as fact. Johnson – whose etymologies are not his strong point – presents it without comment in his *Dictionary*:

> **lich** A dead carcase, whence *lichwake*, the time or act of watching by the dead; *lichgate*, the gate through which the dead are carried to the grave; *Lichfield*, the field of the dead, a city in Staffordshire, so named from martyred christians. *Salve magna parens*.

'Hail, great mother,' adds the Lichfield-born Johnson.

'Grey wood' is nearer the truth.

I took the A5 away from Lichfield, heading for North Wales again. There is a sort-of signpost showing the way. A short distance along, the road crosses the Anglesey Branch Canal, part of the Birmingham canal system. It started life as a feeder from Cannock (now Chasewater) Reservoir, but it was widened and deepened in the 1850s when the Marquess of Anglesey began to exploit the coal reserves nearby.

A little further down the road is Chasewater Country Park. The sign says it is part of the Forest of Mercia – ninety-two square miles of woodland and parkland in southern Staffordshire. I had left Offa's Dyke and Leominster and Earl Leofric sixty-five miles behind me. The name was a reminder of just how large Offa's kingdom was.

Another old forest? Another set of 'leahs' likely. And sure enough, I passed by *Muckley Corner* (a 'great leah'), *Chorley* (a 'leah for peasants' – 'churls'), *Leomansley* (a 'leah with elms'), and *Great Wyrley* (a 'bog-myrtle leah'). Today, Great Wyrley is achieving fame as the 'M6 Toll Leah', for that is where they built the toll plaza you pass through when you're travelling westbound.

The modern toll isn't as fastidious as the one on Madocks' cob, or the one built by Telford at Llanfair in Anglesey. The Llanfair one has such regulations as:

> For every Horse, Mule or other beast drawing any Waggon, or Cart, the Wheels being less than 3 inches breadth or having Wheels with Tires fastened with Nails projecting and not countersunk to pay double Toll.

Checking all that would slow things down a bit on the M6. Not that I've seen a mule on the M6 recently . . .

It's funny how place-names can take on a completely different set of associations as a result of social change. Having travelled along the M6 Toll Road several times since 2004, I knew Norton Canes as a services area only. That day, travelling back towards Anglesey, and using the A5 for the first time in several years, I passed through the village of Norton Canes. I had forgotten about the village.

Norton is a *tun* – 'farmstead, homestead' – to the *nor* – 'north' – of somewhere. In this case, associated with *Canes* – 'Cannock'.

The village probably grew around the church, mentioned in Domesday Book. It is called *St James*. St James is the patron saint of pilgrims. And Norton is about a day's walk from St Chad's shrine in Lichfield.

Another fire. In 1887 bells were put in the tower to celebrate Queen Victoria's jubilee. A few weeks later, on 17 January 1888, St James burned down. An organ had recently been installed, and people think that the fire was caused by an oil lamp burning in the organ chamber to keep away the damp. Amazingly, a new church was built and ready for use within nine months.

The chemist's in Burntwood Road in Norton Canes was the UK's first drive-through pharmacy when it opened in 1995. Without a toll, presumably.

Norton Canes is but the latest in a long line of places known today primarily for their transport associations. Who now standing in Terminal 3 at Heathrow is aware that beneath their feet is the site of the village of *Heath Row*, cleared when the airport was built in the 1940s? The 'heath' in question was the western end of Hounslow Heath.

Gatwick is an ancient name, recorded from the thirteenth century. The airport is on the site of a manor owned by the Gatwick family. In 1890 it was converted into a racecourse. The Grand National was held there during World War I. The site became an airport during the 1930s.

At least there is still a village in Stansted – an Old English name meaning 'stony place'. The full name of the village is *Stansted Mountfitchet* – the name adopted by a Norman baron some time after the Conquest, presumably a nostalgic reference to Montfiquet in Normandy. It boasts a splendid reconstruction of a Norman castle. Nearby is the House on the Hill toy museum, with the largest private toy collection in Europe.

In the twelfth century, the Mountfitchets founded the Augustinian priory of St James. The patronage passed to the de Veres, the Earls of Oxford, in 1320. It is now an unoccupied listed building close to the airport perimeter and under the current flight path. The government thought it would make a good immigrant centre a few years ago, then changed its mind.

Another Shakespearean echo. Edward de Vere, the 17th Earl, is one of several alternative candidates for authorship proposed by people who can't stomach the thought that the plays could have been written by someone as (extra)ordinary as Shakespeare.

An airport for me is a gateway to languages. And these days, it is also a gateway to the worldwide varieties of the English language. It was once thought that, as English became used internationally, everyone would end up speaking and writing in the same way. The reality is much more complex and interesting.

Certainly, everyone who learns English within an educational setting ends up with roughly the same system of sounds, spellings, words, and grammar. That system is called 'Standard English'. Its standardness is maintained by a tradition of writing in print, overseen by the editors, copy-editors, and proof-readers of the world's publishing houses, and formalized by English-teaching syllabuses, textbooks, and examination boards everywhere. Whether you learn English in Kolkata, Athens, Singapore, or Rio de Janeiro, you will emerge from your course with, broadly speaking, a command of the same 'thing'. You are reading it now.

But that 'broadly speaking' is important. If you learn English in a part of the world where British influence is historically predominant, you will end up speaking a variety of English which has a distinctively British character. By contrast, if you learn it in a US-influenced part of the world, your English will display American characteristics. These are the two major world varieties. There are others, with more local influence, such as Australian English in parts of the southern Pacific, or South African English in southern Africa.

Just how much difference is there between British and American English? The most noticeable differences, thanks to Noah Webster, are in the spellings, but even there we are talking about only a few dozen common alternatives, such as *color* vs *colour*, and only a few hundred in all.

Next comes vocabulary – encountered more sporadically than spellings, but cumulatively much more important. My daughter Lucy has married Vicente, from Venezuela. They live in Amsterdam, and his recent visit to Britain was his first close encounter with British English on home soil. It proved necessary to introduce him to *boots* and *bonnets* (of cars), *skirting boards* and *curtains*, *taps* and *telegraph poles*, *pushchairs* and *nappies*, *tea towels* and *prawn cocktails*. He was used to *trunks* and *hoods*, *baseboards* and *drapes*, *faucets* and *telephone poles*, *strollers* and *diapers*, *dish towels* and *shrimp cocktails*.

In driving around, he noticed GIVE WAY, where he was expecting YIELD. We went over a *flyover* (*overpass*). We passed some *caravans* (*trailers*) and *estate cars* (*station wagons*). We ended up in a *tailback* (*traffic jam*). At one point we called in to a *chemist's* (*drugstore*). We paid in *notes*, not *bills*.

Americans do have the word *flyover*. But they would be talking about what in Britain would be called an aeroplane *fly-past*. That's one of the 'false friends'. The two varieties share a number of words, but give them different meanings. *Football* is a classic example, meaning 'American football' in the US, not 'soccer'. An American *first floor* is a British *ground floor*.

On the other hand, the influence of American English on British English is also very noticeable. I hardly noticed when Vicente said *elevator* (*lift*), *gas* (*petrol*), *can* (*tin*), and *trash* (*rubbish*). Nor when he talked about *bathtubs* (*baths*), *bathrooms* (*toilets*), and *bookstores* (*bookshops*).

But at least in these cases we share the concepts. Far more difficult is when we don't, as in the alien lexical world (to British ears) of baseball and the correspondingly alien world (to American ears) of cricket. Of the two, the British lexicon is weirder, with its *silly-mid-offs* and *long legs*.

Even with sport, though, mutual cultural influence helps. And the influences seem to be growing in both directions. When I was in San Francisco recently, I went past the Chieftain Irish *Pub* on Fifth Street. There are pubs all over the USA now. And, thanks to the 1993 film, I now know about Groundhog Day.

I wasn't so linguistically confident when I first visited San Francisco. It was in the 1960s, during my very first trip to the USA. I stayed in a downtown hotel and came down in the morning to a diner-style break-fast. I sat up against the bar and looked at the menu, I asked for orange juice, toast, and some ham and eggs. The chef looked at me: 'How do you like your eggs?' he asked.

I did not know what to reply. I had never been asked that question before. It simply wasn't a British question at the time. If you asked for 'bacon and eggs' in Britain, it would have automatically been taken to mean fried eggs. If you wanted a 'boiled egg' you would have asked for one using those words.

How did I like my eggs? I replied: 'Cooked?'

He looked at me strangely, and said, 'Limey, huh?' And then he rattled off a string of alternatives: I remember *sunny side up* and *once over lightly*. 'Once over lightly?' I said, and presumably I must have asked a question, at least in my facial expression. 'Sure, over easy,' he said. I nodded. It sounded good, and so it was.

These days, the British lexicon of eggs has changed. You could hear these phrases in the Savoy.

That wasn't my only mealtime problem. I had to forget about *rashers* of bacon and think of bacon *slices*. *Lean bacon* turned out to be *Canadian bacon*. But don't try asking for Canadian bacon in Canada. There, it is simply *back bacon*, or sometimes *peameal bacon*.

Then there was *eggplant* (*aubergine*), *zucchini* (*courgettes*), *navy beans* (*haricot beans*), *raw beets* (*beetroot*), *scallions* (*spring onions*) . . . *Puddings* were a problem too. For a start, they were *desserts*.

Limey is a strange name for a Briton. In the USA it emerged during the First World War. It arose because of the Royal Navy's practice of prescribing lime juice to help protect sailors against the vitamin-C deficiency, scurvy, a routine risk on long journeys. English ships came to be called *lime-juicers*, and English sailors *limeys*. Within a decade, the term was being applied to anyone from Britain. The *Chicago Tribune* for 18 October 1924 has a headline *Midway Signs Limey Prof to Dope Yank Talk*. *Dope* in this context means 'find out about'. *Midway* is a name associated with the University of Chicago.

The Limey Prof was Sir William Craigie, the co-editor of the *Oxford English Dictionary*. He was very impressed by this headline when he visited the USA in 1925. It's an example in the *OED* now.

Actually, you have to be careful in thinking about the name *Midway* when you visit Chicago. On the one hand you see it in relation to *Midway Plaisance*. On the other hand, it is the name of one of Chicago's airports. The two are not at all the same.

Midway Plaisance is an open space connecting Washington Park and Jackson Park. The World's Columbian Exposition – celebrating the four hundredth anniversary of Columbus's landing in America – was located there, a year late, in 1893. It led to the general use of *midway* for an amusement arcade within a big show such as a trade fair or exhibition. All sorts of places have midways now.

The University of Chicago is located nearby, hence the newspaper headline. *Monsters of the Midway* is the nickname of the Chicago Bears (American) football team.

Midway Airport was originally called *Chicago Air Park*. It was renamed in 1949 in honour of the US victory at the Battle of Midway in World War II, a turning point during the war in the Pacific. That *Midway* is the name of a small island in the middle of the Pacific Ocean, roughly halfway between North America and Asia.

Plaisance, by the way, is a variant spelling of *pleasance* 'pleasure ground'. There is a Pleasance in Edinburgh, and the Pleasance Theatre is one of the main Fringe venues at Festival time.

The last time I visited San Francisco was in 2004, when I had a series of meetings in and around Silicon Valley. I'd spent the morning wandering round colourful Fisherman's Wharf, taking in the honking seals, Alcatraz, and some clam chowder, and trying not to spend too much time being a linguist.

But it was impossible. The Pier 39 area had so much ingenious language play, my notebook and camera were always in use. The store names, especially, took my fancy. Quite plainly the only reason there were rules in the English language was to bend and break them, to maximum effect.

Several played with spelling and puns. *Krazy Kaps* sold novelty headwear. *Bare Escentuals* sold cosmetics. *Shirtique* sold casual men's wear. *Le Beastro* was a dog boutique.

The cat boutique relied on a different strategy – adopt a familiar expression: *Here Kitty Kitty*. Similarly conversational was an art shop run by a Michael Godard: *Oh My Godard*. And several stores relied on everyday allusions. *To Herb With Love* sold aromatherapy bath salts. *Charms by the Bay* sold charms. The *San Francisco Sock Market* sold, well, socks.

Not even grammar could escape. Collectible knives were sold at *We Be Knives*.

I had to leave, as I'd arranged to meet some colleagues after lunch, at the café on the corner of the psychological heart of downtown San Francisco, Union Square. It was early November, and when I reached the square they were in the process of erecting a giant eighty-foot Christmas tree. A man in a box at the end of a crane was trimming the tree into a perfect triangular shape. The ground was littered with discarded branches.

It was a pleasantly warm day – this was northern California, re-member – and the square was packed with tourists and shoppers. A group of diminutive children walked past all wearing sweaters that said *Giants*. 'Why giants?' I asked someone at the next table. I got a

withering 'limey'-like look. San Francisco Giants is the local baseball team.

Actually, Americans shouldn't be too quick to condemn Brits, seeing as the name of the game is a British import in the first place. The earliest recorded usage is from England in 1744, when a children's alphabet-book includes 'B is for base-ball', and describes a game in which a ball is hit with the hand and the hitter runs to the next post.

Probably the most famous early reference is from a totally unexpected source. We would not associate baseball with Jane Austen, but there it is, in the opening chapter of *Northanger Abbey*, where the charmingly imperfect heroine, Catherine Morland, is described as preferring 'cricket, base ball, riding on horseback, and running about the country at the age of fourteen, to books'. That was written in about 1799.

Another British import was being read at the next table – a Harry Potter book. At least, an Americanized edition of Harry Potter. I could tell by the title: it read *Harry Potter and the Sorcerer's Stone* – not *Philosopher's Stone*. Evidently, the American publisher felt that US children would have some difficulty with the notion of a philosopher.

If you compare the British and American editions, you find over two hundred substitutions. The children eat *crumpets* and *crisps* in the UK; they eat *English muffins* and *chips* in the US – *potato chips*, that is. A *dustbin* becomes a *trashcan*, a *cooker* becomes a *stove*, *Sellotape* becomes *Scotch tape*. It is a mini-dictionary of transatlantic differences: *candy-boxes* for *sweet-boxes*, *jell-O* for *jelly*, *mommy* for *mummy*, *sweater* for *jumper*.

A lot of school terminology varies. People tend to forget that every-day notions such as *GCSEs* or *A-levels* are British English. And as Harry and his friends are at what is essentially a British school, there are several changes here – such as *study schedules* for *revision timetables*, *course books* for *set books*, *public school* for *comprehensive*, and *had the best grades* for *came top*.

A couple arrived at a nearby table. 'Do you want a sandwich?' asked the man. 'No, I just ate,' said the woman. That's one of the few gram-matical differences between American and British English. I would have said 'No, I've just eaten.' Within a few minutes I heard *gotten*, where I would have said *got*, and *quarter of two*, where I would have said *quarter to two*.

Well, what else can you do when you're sitting in a sunny square with nothing to do but wait for someone to arrive? Linguists don't eavesdrop. They just overhear. They are programmed to. They can do nothing about it. Think of it as a handicap, and sympathize.

Later on I bought a US edition of *Harry Potter* and went through looking for American English grammar. I found very little. There was a *gotten*, a *shan't* replacing a *won't*, *on weekends* instead of *at weekends*, a few places where American English prefers a *the* where British doesn't – as in *got the flu* – and a sprinkling of other changes. Occasionally an idiom was altered. 'Bit rich coming from you!' says British Harry to

British Ron in Chapter 2 of *The Chamber of Secrets*. 'You should talk!' says American Harry to American Ron.

At another table, two youngsters were text-messaging furiously. I was surprised. Although texting had been around in the UK for several years, it hadn't taken off in the US, mainly because of the problem of sending messages between different telephone networks. Things were evidently changing. And indeed, when I looked up some statistics later, they showed that 2004 was a year when American texting grew by over 100 per cent.

My colleagues arrived and we set off in a car to visit some companies in the area south of San Francisco now known as *Silicon Valley*. This is another name – like *blurb* – whose origin can be pinpointed. It was coined in 1971 by a journalist, Don Hoefler, referring to the growing concentration in the area of firms manufacturing or using silicon chips. Software and Internet companies dominate the Valley now.

As we drove south, we passed familiar name after familiar name. Apple, eBay, Google, Hewlett-Packard, Adobe, Yahoo!, Intel, Logitech ... Each seemed to be trying to outdo the others in looking different. eBay was one of the most striking, with its four large letters in bright red, blue, yellow, and green at the entrance gate.

It was difficult to think of an Internet company whose name wasn't somewhere here. The headquarters of the larger organizations looked like mini-cities. I visited one. It had a gym, spa, games room ... more like a hotel than an office. My visitor's pass was called a 'passport' and at the top a message said 'Enjoy your travels' – meaning, around the company. It was like entering a foreign country. The security was just as intense.

Well, actually, not quite. On that same US trip I flew from New York to San Francisco. At the security check in New York, even after going through the detector gate, I was taken on one side and frisked with a device which would buzz if it detected anything suspicious on me. They paid special attention to my beard.

I looked at my beard later in the hotel room mirror. It couldn't have hidden anything, except a chin. But I suppose you can't be too careful.

There are several other Silicon Valleys now. The M4 corridor between London and Reading has been dubbed *Silicon Valley*. So has the area around Dublin, and the Bangalore region of India, and the Campinas–São Paulo region of Brazil. Route 128 in Massachusetts is sometimes called the *Silicon Valley of the East Coast*.

There are a number of others. All you need is a high concentration of software or Internet firms in one place, and away you go. You certainly don't have to worry about whether there is an actual physical 'valley'. That is an irrelevance now.

The Californian original is definitely a valley, however. As we went south along Route 101, I looked to the right and could see we were within the coast mountain range. Huge banks of fog were rolling down the slopes. We drove through a saintly litany of suburbs – San Bruno, San Mateo, San Carlos . . . with San José in the distance.

The Internet needs a patron saint. The book/fireman St John of God has a church dedicated to him in Fifth Avenue, San Francisco. Maybe he would take it on?

Too late. A front-runner has already emerged. In 1999, the proposal was made to give the patronage to St Isidore of Seville, a bishop of the early seventh century. It was an appropriate choice. A prolific compiler of knowledge, his works include a dictionary, an encyclopedia, and a history of the world. His encyclopedia was later divided into twenty volumes, and its structure in many ways resembles the kind of comprehensive classification we see in contemporary databases, recognizing such domains as law, medicine, agriculture, building, and so on. The worlds of the Internet could not be in better hands.

As we turned off the expressway into Sunnyvale, where we were to have our meeting, a huge billboard swung into view. It was advertising a new type of car, available cheaply from an Internet source, and it said *.COM AND GET IT*.

I'd come across that joke before. *Dot.com all ye faithful* had been the headline in a newspaper situations-vacant column a couple of years earlier. And exactly the same piece of wordplay had been used once to persuade people to buy Christmas cards from an Internet site. But it still felt fresh.

I am alternately impressed and unimpressed by the linguistic impact of the Internet. On the one hand it is a revolutionary medium – a genuine third means of human communication, supplementing the two traditional modes of speaking and writing and offering radically different opportunities for self-expression. On the other hand, its influence on the actual words and sentence-patterns of individual languages has so far been rather limited.

Why is this medium – computer-mediated communication, as it is often called – so revolutionary? Because it allows us to communicate with each other in novel ways.

There was never anything in traditional written language like the cutting-and-pasting which we can routinely perform in emails and downloads. You send me an email, and I can chop bits out, rearrange it, add bits at the beginning, in the middle, or at the end, and send it back to you. You can then do the same to my message. This was never possible in the days when we just sent letters to each other.

Nor was there anything like the hypertext link – the piece of text on a web-page, usually in blue, which we can click on in order to get to another part of the Internet. I can move from one part of a page to another, from one page to another, or from one site to another, just by pressing a mouse button. The nearest thing to that in traditional writing was our ability to track footnotes or cross-references. But the analogy is very limited. It is perfectly possible to have a book without any footnotes or cross-references. It is not possible to have a World Wide Web without hypertext links. That is why it is called a 'web'.

The animated nature of the written language on screen also takes it away from traditional writing. The one thing you can say about a page of print is that it is permanent. The present page doesn't change as you look at it. That sort of thing only happens in 'Harry Potter' movies. It is so very different on screen, where text can move in front of your eyes, ads jump out at you, and you can add or delete words at will.

The Internet has many different functions. In addition to looking things up on the Web and sending each other emails, we have the option of entering a chatroom, playing interactive games, having an instant-messaging conversation, and maintaining an online diary, or blog (= 'web log'). Each of these is a radically new communicative skill.

Take chatrooms and gamerooms. Here we can be having a conversation with dozens of people simultaneously. We can see their messages scrolling down the screen. It has never been possible before to talk to so many people at once. And the new generation seizes the opportunity. Following half a dozen different on-screen threads is easy meat for the teenagers of today. And the pre-teenagers. I have seen an eight-year-old switch to and fro between a screenful of windows with unselfconscious ease.

Or take blogging, in 2006 the fastest-growing area of Internet use. It is a veritable renaissance of the genre of diary-writing. Millions of people are now putting their daily thoughts, feelings, and creations onto their own individual sites, telling their friends about them, and being read as a result. Some of the most popular blogs are read by countless numbers.

With so much communicative novelty, we might have expected the language of the people who use the Internet to have changed dramatically. Change there certainly has been. Dramatic it isn't – yet.

Vocabulary is the area where language change is usually most easily noticed, and there really hasn't yet been that much new lexicon in English as a result of the Internet. A few years ago I collected as many novel words and expressions as I could find, related to the Internet as a new technology, and managed to get a few hundred. This sounds like a lot, until you realize that there are over a million words in English, and a few hundred new ones is really neither here nor there.

There were dozens of new applications of old words, such as *spam*, *menu* and *mouse*. There were dozens of new coinages, especially using new prefixes and suffixes, such as *e-books* and *e-voting*, *webcam* and *webcast*, *spybot* and *mailbot*.

The *–bot* is from *robot*; it refers to a bit of software that automatically performs a certain task.

There were a few dozen new abbreviations, several of which have become popular in text-messaging, such as *cu* ('see you'), *afaik* ('as far as I know') and *thx* ('thanks'). And new spellings could also sometimes be seen. Pirated material, for instance, is often identified by replacing the noun plural *–s* by a *–z*. What is the difference between *tunes* and *tunez*? The latter is a pirate download.

Some of the innovations have been a delight to the eyes of an English-language historian. The *–en* plural ending on nouns is virtually dead. It turns up in *oxen*, *children*, and *brethren*. But on the Internet it has had a new lease of life. Any noun ending in *–x* might appear with the ending. Thus we find users of the VAX computer system called *vaxen* and users of the BIX information exchange system called *bixen*. *Matrixen* are lots of matrixes. *Boxen* are lots of boxes. It is all a bit of a joke, but it illustrates the playful, innovative world of Internet usage. And you never know which innovation is going to become fashionable and one day, perhaps, enter the standard language.

An unexpected orthographic innovation was the use of middle capital letters within a proper name. This is not a total novelty, because of such names as *McManus* and *O'Malley*. But it was surprising to see how many companies decided to adopt the convention, such as *eBay*, *AltaVista*, and *CompuServe*. *eBay* in fact has two innovations, by also not beginning with a capital. *Yahoo!* has an exclamation mark as part of the name, which makes it difficult to know what to do when it appears as the last word in a sentence.

Again, such things may not last. The novelty might wear off. Or it mightn't.

But when you add all this up – every new word, ending, spelling – it doesn't amount to very much. A thousand or so linguistic novelties, possibly. That is a few drops in the linguistic ocean of English.

The interesting question is: is it going to stay like that?

We pulled into the Internet company car park, and went into the reception area. I was solemnly given my entry passport. It really did say 'passport'. I looked around the waiting room. Given that it was a leading Internet organization, the signs and notices were all very conventional. Standard English ruled.

I think we ain't seen nothin' yet. I believe we are living through a period in which the foundation for major linguistic change is being laid. Perhaps 'climate' is a better word than 'foundation'. All languages that use the Internet will be affected, and English, because of its global reach, probably most of all. The effects will be seen not so much in relation to vocabulary, but in relation to the writing system and in relation to grammar.

The Internet has allowed us to depart from the monopoly that Standard English has had on written usage over the past three hundred years. The kind of English I am using now, in writing this book, is standard in relation to spelling, punctuation, capitalization, and grammar – apart from conscious deviations such as *we ain't seen nothin' yet*. All four of these areas are already demonstrating departures from Standard English norms – and showing that the language can nonetheless survive.

In email, chatrooms, and instant messaging in particular, we see people dispensing with punctuation and capitalization, sometimes slightly, sometimes seriously. Marks which are critical for meaning, such as the question mark and the exclamation mark, are maintained – and even increased, to express emotional intensity. Sentences such as *No!!!!!* or *You believe that????* are common. But commas, semi-colons, inverted commas, full stops, apostrophes, and other features of precise pointing are readily dropped. Sentences do not begin with capital letters, and proper names and even the pronoun *I* can appear in lower-case.

Most chatroom sentences are short – the average length is six words – so the need for complex punctuation to preserve meaning is absent. The same point applies to instant messages and to texts on mobile phones. The meaning of

i think its time we changed the subject

is perfectly clear, despite the non-standard orthography. When English first came to be written down, that was in fact how it was done. There were no modern punctuation marks, no modern capitalization conventions. Not even a standardized spelling.

Internet users are currently exploring the tolerances made available to them by the new medium. Obviously, if everyone punctuates, capitalizes, and spells just as they want, then mutual intelligibility is likely to break down. On the other hand, the grammarians and lexicographers who formulated Standard English overdid it, rather, in the number of artificial rules they introduced. And the spelling system, as several people have suggested, could usefully be simplified without loss.

So we may be working our way towards a new happy medium. It is early days. Most people have been online for less than a decade.

Blogging will be the test-bed, it seems to me. This is a genre which is making people write much longer texts than in chatrooms. The ideas being expressed are more complex. So it is not possible for bloggers to dispense with the traditional rules so readily. At the same time, this is writing which is totally spontaneous, put up on a screen without the intervention of an editor or proof-reader, so it is much more like 'speaking in print' than anything before. And it shows many of the properties of spoken language, such as loosely constructed sentences and unexpected changes of direction. Bit like this book, really . . .

After the visit to Sunnyvale I travelled back to San Francisco, and spent a day as a tourist. It wasn't so much that the place had changed since the 1960s, as that my imagination about the place had changed. I could hardly go anywhere without being reminded of a scene from a film.

I walked from Union Square over Russian Hill towards Fisherman's Wharf. I crossed Filbert Street. The hills are dramatic. This was one of the streets where Steve McQueen was engaged in some spectacular car-chasing in 1968, in *Bullitt*.

Later, I walked in the other direction, towards the Mission district. Mission Dolores is the oldest building still standing in San Francisco, dating from 1776. It has a small cemetery. That is where Madeleine (aka Kim Novak) visits the grave of Carlotta Valdes in Hitchcock's *Vertigo*.

It is not, I discovered, where she falls to her death. I always thought everything happened at Dolores. But no, the final scene takes place in a different Mission, ninety miles to the south – Mission San Juan Bautista.

Or rather, it would have done if things had gone according to plan. Hitchcock first visited the Mission in the 1940s, and was impressed by the high tower there. When he came back in 1958 to film *Vertigo*, the tower was gone. It had been demolished because of dry rot. That didn't stop him. He added the tower with special effects and shot the action scenes in the studio.

To the north of the city is Bodega Bay. That's where they filmed *The Birds*.

The list of films made wholly or partly on location in the San Francisco area goes on and on. *Never Die Twice*, two *Doctor Dolittles*, *Being John Malkovich*, assorted *Star Trek* and *Indiana Jones*, *Mrs Doubt-*

fire, *Basic Instinct*, *Pretty Woman*, *The Towering Inferno*, *Escape from Alcatraz*, *Superman*, *Herbie Rides Again*, *Dirty Harry*, *The Graduate*, *Pal Joey* ... A film called *Fisherman's Wharf* was made there as early as 1897. North Wales, eat your heart out!

A distinct absence of Roman epics, though. Maybe there is a chance for Lichfield yet.

14

My Husband is Without

LODZ

It isn't possible to follow the A5 all the way to Holyhead any more. As it enters Shropshire it joins up with the M54, which seriously outranks it, and for a while it ceases to exist. It then re-emerges on its way towards Shrewsbury. The Roman road carries on, a short distance to the north, ignoring such modern distractions as the motorway.

I stayed on the Roman road, on one of its straightest stretches. It led me to another one of those English place-names which seem quaint at first sight, but turn out to be ordinary upon reflection: *Weston-under-Lizard*. The 'lizard' in question is only indirectly a reptile. It is Lizard Hill, a mile or so south-west, between the A5 and the motorway. In summertime its slopes are covered in bright red poppies.

Why bother with a cumbersome 'under' addition? Because there is another Weston not far away, south of Derby, near the East Midlands airport. That one is called *Weston-upon-Trent*. There are dozens of Westons around the country – unsurprisingly, as all the name meant originally was 'homestead to the west' (of somewhere). A well-known one is *Weston-super-Mare*. There's also a *Weston-in-Arden* north of Coventry.

Weston Park is nearby, a seventeenth-century building that much impressed Disraeli – and, for that matter, the leaders who attended the

1998 G8 summit meeting, who used it as a retreat. It may also have impressed P.G. Wodehouse. Enthusiasts of the 'Blandings Saga' have long speculated about the real identity of Blandings Castle, the home of Lord Emsworth. Weston Park is one of the leading contenders.

The hill called *The Wrekin* (pronounced 'ree-kin') is nearby. That's important. Wherever Blandings is, Wodehouse says you can see The Wrekin from the battlements.

It's impossible to miss it, as you drive north along the A5 or M54. There it is, on the left, a huge mound of volcanic rock, 1,335 feet high. From the top, on a clear day, you can see fifteen counties.

Such a prominent feature, inevitably, came to be used as a hill fort. It was the headquarters of the Celtic tribe the Cornovii, until it was taken by the Romans in AD 74.

It also had an effect on the language. In local dialect, if someone says 'They went all round The Wrekin,' it means that they went the long way round. There is a metaphorical use too. 'You're going all round The Wrekin' means you're speaking in a roundabout way.

The fort is one of the few in England whose original name is known: *Uriconion*. The modern name, and its curious spelling, is an adaptation: it is found as *Wrocene* in the tenth century. *Wroxeter*, to the west, shows the same spelling and origins. It is the site of the Roman fort of *Viriconion*, or *Viroconium*. It was one of the largest Roman settlements of its time, covering some two hundred acres and holding a population of around five thousand. It is the largest ancient city to have survived in England without being obscured by modern town planning.

There are legends that King Arthur (of course) had a base here. And there are other legends about how The Wrekin came to be. Most involve giants. The favourite story is that it was built by a Welsh giant who wanted to teach the nearby town of Shrewsbury a lesson, so he dug a spadeful of soil to dump into the nearby River Severn, which would cause the town to be flooded. But he lost his way, and stopped for a rest near Wellington. He asked directions from a local cobbler who was passing by, and told him what he was intending to do. The cobbler, realizing he would lose his livelihood if the town was flooded, showed the giant his sack of worn-out shoes, and told him he had worn them out himself by walking the long distance from Shrewsbury. The giant believed him, decided it was too far to carry on, and went home, leaving his spadeful of soil behind, in the form of The Wrekin.

It could be a story out of *The Lord of the Rings*.

Tolkien in fact lived not far away at one point in his life. After enlisting in the army in 1916, he was stationed at Cannock Chase, in Staffordshire, and his wife lived in the nearby village of Great Haywood. Sent to the Somme, he was invalided home after a few months with trench fever, and there he started to write the collection of mythical stories called *The Book of Lost Tales*, a precursor to *The Silmarillion*. He also lived in Penkridge, south of Stafford, and used to walk The Wrekin.

The Roman road from Cannock to Wellington must be one of the longest stretches of straight road in the country. For thirteen miles to the middle of Oakengates, just north of Telford – so a local man told me – it is nowhere more than two hundred yards out of a straight line.

His remark reminded me of another time people had proudly told me that a straight stretch of road was unique. It was in the very centre of Poland, in the city of Lodz. Through the middle of that city, running north to south in a straight line for over four kilometres, is Piotrkowska Street. It is said to be the longest commercial street in Europe – some say in the world. It is one of the few streets I've ever come across with a nickname – Pietryna.

Shortened forms are common enough. A street with a long name often motivates an abbreviated form. In Manhattan, Lexington Avenue is often called *Lex*. Massachusetts Avenues in several cities are called *Mass Ave*. But real nicknames are unusual. There's a famous case in Dublin. *O'Connell Street* was sometimes naughtily known as 'The Street of the Three Adulterers' – a dig at the three main people statued there: Parnell, O'Connell, and (until the IRA blew it up in the 1960s) Nelson.

I have anglicized the spelling of the name of *Lodz*. In Polish it has three distinctive letters – a capital *L* with a small slanting line through it, and acute accents on the *o* and *z*. The pronunciation is nothing like 'lodz'. It is more like 'woodge'. It means 'boat' in Polish. A boat and oar appear on the city coat of arms. A river flows through the city.

I was in Poland talking about – and at the same time finding out about – Euro-English. New varieties of English have come into exist-ence all over the world, as a reflection of new cultural identities. We have seen it happen repeatedly on both small and large scales. A regional variety might affect only two or three million people, such as Irish English in Ireland. Or it might affect 250 million people, such as American English in the USA. Is there a new variety emerging in Europe? People have divided views.

In between these extremes, at different periods of history, we have seen local varieties of the language emerge as a reflection of new political identities – in Australia, Canada, South Africa, India, Ghana, Nigeria, Singapore . . . indeed, there are clear signs of regional dialects of international English in at least fifty countries or territories around the world. They are not all equally clear-cut, in their stage of develop-ment. And they are not all equally recognized by local people. Nor are they all equally liked. But they are there.

Not long ago I was part of a radio discussion about whether a variety of Canadian English exists. The debate focused on how many local words, expressions, pronunciations, and spellings there were which were known across the whole of Canada. Several examples were cited – such as *auditor-general* and *butter tarts* – and there are hundreds more. Some Canadianisms are internationally known, even if they are not recognized by outsiders as such. *Mounties* is a case in point. And ice-hockey enthusiasts everywhere know of the *Maple Leafs* team, but may not appreciate how regionally distinctive the name is. Type *leafs* into Google, and you see the focus on Canada straight away.

'Sens edge Leafs on first NHL shootout', said a Toronto news report in 2005. Or, more explicitly: 'The Ottawa Senators beat the Toronto Maple Leafs 3–2 after the first shootout in National Hockey League history.'

The contributors to the programme disagreed over whether a variety of Canadian English was a good thing or a bad thing. The arguments soon ceased to be linguistic and began to be political – all about Canada's self-image and identity. It's no business of mine how this should develop. But I do know that, whatever direction Canadians choose to take, there will be immediate linguistic consequences.

It doesn't take much to make a variety of English regionally distinctive. And once the urge – conscious or unconscious – to create a local identity is there, it is not long before a little becomes a lot. When people start compiling dictionaries of language-isms – Canadianisms, Australianisms, Ghanaisms, and so on – the collection soon runs into thousands.

It would be surprising if it were otherwise. No two regions have the same local geography, fauna and flora, myths and legends, food and drink, or indigenous peoples and practices. And each of these areas generates large numbers of individual words, idioms, sayings, catch-phrases, and other expressions. Not everyone in the country knows them all, of course. Nor is it necessary that everyone should know them all. It suffices that everyone knows some.

The places are especially important. Every country has local expressions which refer to its places, adding nuances of meaning over and above the literal physical entity. In Britain, we have a huge number of places which, for historical reasons, carry associations that are often missed by people from outside the country. The famous ones are likely to be recognized, of course, such as *Whitehall* ('civil service'), *Soho* ('red-light district'), *Wimbledon* ('tennis'), *Wembley* ('football'), and *Scotland Yard* ('police'). But it is surprising how many people from outside the country have no idea what to suggest when asked for the 'cultural meaning' of these places:

Aldermaston, Ascot, Balmoral, Billingsgate, Broadmoor, Chelsea, Chequers, Cowes, Dartmoor, Eton, Euston, Glyndebourne, Henley, Holloway, John o'Groats, Lambeth, Mayfair, Sandhurst

Or of these streets:

Baker Street, Bond Street, Carnaby Street, Chancery Lane, Downing Street, Fleet Street, Great Ormond Street, Harley Street, Oxford Street, Petticoat Lane, Piccadilly Circus, Sloane Square, Wardour Street

Every country can compile a similar list. Indeed, every city can. Everywhere has its shopping malls, red-light districts, political centres, law courts, and sports stadiums. It applies as much to Toronto and Vancouver and Quebec as to Sydney and Melbourne and Perth. Similar things happen in the countryside too, of course, but there the words tend not to be so well known. City words rule.

The names don't exist in isolation. They feed into the language in all kinds of subtle ways, forming idioms and social expressions. What do these mean?

> It's like Clapham Junction in there.
> Her earrings are more Petticoat Lane than Bond Street.
> Fleet Street will be up in arms.

The first refers to a chaotic state of affairs, alluding to the complicated layout of lines and platforms that comprise the railway station. The second is a rather catty remark, for Petticoat Lane contains a street market, while Bond Street is known for its expensive shops. The third is interesting. There are no newspapers printed in Fleet Street any more. But the idiom lives on.

Moreover, the language never stands still. It only takes a tragedy to alter the resonance of a place-name. *Lockerbie. Dunblane.* Or, in other parts of the world: *Bhopal. The World Trade Center.*

Nor is it just place-names which form the cultural linguistic identity of a region. Local social institutions, political parties, prominent people, and radio or television programmes – to name just four domains – add elements which contribute to the uniqueness of a regional variety of English. For Britain, think about *Alf Garnett*, *Jackanory*, and *The Archers*.

The names do not always travel. *Alf Garnett*, as a working-class stereotype, is meaningless in the USA. But everyone there knows *Archie Bunker*. Correspondingly, few British people have ever heard of *him*.

Also, the names change their connotations as you go from place to place. *Soho* in London is very different from *SoHo* (i.e. *So*uth of *Ho*uston Street) in New York. And if you visit *Oxford Street* in Sydney, don't expect the same array of services as are provided by *Oxford Street* in London.

The uniqueness of a country lies most obviously in its individual history and geography. Canada has a special historical ethnic and cultural mix, involving Britain, the USA, France (especially in Quebec), and indigenous Indian groups from the Plains to the Arctic. No other country has such a mix. And as each of these elements influences the way people speak and write, the result is bound to be distinctive. Canadian spelling, for example, is like no other, thanks to the dual influence of American and British systems. There is a *tire centre* in Toronto, different from what would be a *tire center* in New York and a *tyre centre* in London.

The uniqueness of South Africa lies, similarly, in its particular mix of European, African, and (to a lesser extent) Asian cultures. And similar mixes can be found in India, Singapore, Fiji, and all the other parts of the world where English has come to be used as a daily medium of communication. When I visited Singapore, I heard all around me on the streets the distinctive blend of English and Chinese that has come to be called *Singlish*.

The question I was exploring, on my European trip, was how far the same thing was happening in Europe. To what extent was the 'new Europe' of the European Union showing any signs of a new 'Euro-English'. When people from different European cities speak English to each other, have they yet begun to localize it? Have they started to translate local names into English equivalents, writing them down using English spellings, and pronouncing local names in an English way? Have they developed new shared ways of speaking that would identify them as coming from 'Europe' – as opposed to North America, or Africa, or Asia? Or even 'Europe' as opposed to the UK?

There are signs. I have visited about fifteen European countries in the past five years, and the evidence is accumulating that a Euro-English *is* growing. It is being shaped by two forces, one 'top-down' and the other 'bottom-up'.

The top-down force comes from the rules and regulations of the European Union. There is an influential *English Style Guide* issued by the European Commission. This makes recommendations about how English should be written in official documents from the member states. On the whole it follows standard British English usage, but in cases where British English has alternatives, it makes decisions – such as recommending the spelling *judgment*, not *judgement*.

Hundreds of decisions have made. If a personal name has an accent (e.g. *Wallström*), this should be retained; but non-British titles should be avoided (e.g. the German practice of saying *Prof Dr Schmidt* should be replaced by *Prof Schmidt*). The twenty-four-hour clock should be followed: so, 3 o'clock in the afternoon is *15:00*.

There are more subtle stylistic points. Minutes and summaries of meetings should be written in the past tense, as is normal in English. 'Mr Smith said that things were getting worse.' The point here is that in French and some other languages, minutes are usually written in the present tense. 'Mr Smith: Things are getting worse.'

A large amount of new English vocabulary and idiom is now routinely heard in the corridors of power in Brussels, Strasbourg, and

Luxembourg. It is the language of decisions, joint actions, and amendments. Each has its specific mode of expression. A preamble to a document always begins with 'Having regard to . . .' and continues with a series of clauses beginning 'Whereas . . .'. The *Euro-* prefix is everywhere. You can encounter everything from *Eurofighters* to *Euro-butter*. I have even encountered – though admittedly not in the pages of the *English Style Guide* – *Eurosex* and *Euroviolence*. I speak as a linguist, you understand.

New expressions are in use. *The Twenty-five*, meaning 'the twenty-five member states'. Or, referring to earlier periods, *The Fifteen*, *The Twelve*, *The Ten*, *The Nine*, *The Six*.

There are hundreds of new abbreviations, too, such as the names of the various departments of the Commission. The main administrative departments are *DGs* – 'Directorates-General'. Each has its own abbreviation, such as *EMPL* for 'employment'.

There is a telling remark in the *Style Guide* about these abbreviations. The authors say:

> These are supposed to be for the Commission's internal use only but some of them are becoming current elsewhere.

This is a sign that usage is spreading. And indeed, when I typed *DG EMPL* into Google in 2006 I got 200,000 hits, only some of which were 'internal'.

There is a wonderful acronym used by the EU called *NUTS*. It stands for Nomenclature of Territorial Units for Statistics. It provides a uniform naming of territories so that information from different countries can be easily related. Is it *Picardie* or *Picardy*? *Catalunya*, *Cataluña*, or *Catalonia*? NUTS recommends *Picardy* and *Catalonia*.

I don't know how far these trends will eventually percolate into everyday use. They may stay restricted to the world of political discourse. Most of the distinctive usages are formal in style, used only in writing, and would not transfer easily into everyday conversation. And in any case, not everyone likes them. I know several people who go out of their way to leave Euro-jargon behind at the Euro-office.

More important than these 'top-down' linguistic pressures, I suspect, are the 'bottom-up' trends which can be heard around Europe these days. Ordinary Europeans who have to use English to each other every day are 'voting with their mouths' and developing their own preferences. In Amsterdam, where Lucy and Vicente live, their circle of English-speaking friends includes people from a dozen or more countries. German, Dutch, French, Spanish, Bulgarian, Arabic, and other accents interact and influence each other. In sociolinguistics, the technical term for this interaction is 'accommodation'. People who get on with each other find that their accents move closer together. They accommodate to each other.

In Lucy's coterie, everyone uses a clipped, syllabic style of speech, reflecting the rat-a-tat rhythms that are heard in many European languages. The vowels waver uncertainly between British and American. They use word-orders that are not normal in standard British English, such as *You have really the answer?* They use plural forms that would be considered to be an error in the standard language, such as *informations*. They have a preference for certain expressions, such as *For sure*, meaning 'I agree with you.' And they have their own colloquial English forms for local place-names.

I heard exactly the same sort of thing in Lodz. And in Stockholm. And in Paris.

People are sometimes horrified when they hear such usages. '*Informations* is not English,' they say. But actually it was, once. In the sixteenth century, we find such usages as *an information*. In the eighteenth century, we find Lord Chesterfield writing a letter which says 'The informations I have received . . .' It could one day be plural again. And in contemporary Europe, it already often is.

I don't think Euro-English exists yet, as a variety comparable to American English or Indian English or Singlish. But the seeds are there. It will take time. The new Europe is still an infant, linguistically.

When so many languages come into contact with each other, usage becomes somewhat unpredictable. As I walked along Piotrkowska Street I was continually being surprised by the unexpected choices of English made in shops and advertisements. I wasn't surprised to see such signs as *Hamburger*, *Hot-Dog*, and *Sex-Shop*. These are loan-words which have entered most languages. What was eye-catching was to see signs entirely in Polish except for one untranslated phrase or sentence.

A huge billboard had an ad for a cigarette brand entirely in Polish, except for one English sentence: *TEST IT*. A shop had all its displays in Polish except for the name *Sports-Tourist*. On the wall above the shop was an ad for a hair salon, also entirely in Polish except for its brand name, *Pretty You*.

Unexpected language mixings appeared. In another Polish city, Wroclaw, I visited an Internet café called Salon Dziel Udarych. Underneath it said in English: *Cyber & Tea Tavern*. So far so good. But in between it also said *Dla Niepalacych* – 'for non-smokers'. And the English equivalent alongside said '*For Non Fumers*'.

Books have been compiled listing the 'fractured English' encountered abroad. I have a personal collection of my own. But many of the examples you read in books – of the type 'You are invited to take advantage of the chambermaid' and 'The manager has personally passed all the water' – are of uncertain authenticity. The genuine ones tend to be rather more boring.

If *non fumers* had been an isolated instance, I would have let it pass without comment. But I have seen it in other places too. It is not French – that would be *non-fumeurs*. It seems to be an imagined borrowing into English. It is the kind of thing that could catch on.

Crazy usages do sometimes catch on. There was a chatroom a few years ago in which one of the members inadvertently typed *comptuer* instead of *computer*. Everybody thought it very funny, and copied him. Within days it had become the standard usage of that chatgroup. New members who spelled the word as *computer* were criticized.

I have no idea whether, one day, *fumer* will become Euro-English for 'smoker'. But it is the kind of thing which *could* happen. Everything influences everything, and slowly a consensus emerges.

Even artificial sentences have their day. Some of us have waited years to find an opportune moment to say in conversation the sentences used in Victorian phrase-books that taught English to foreigners. 'Coachman, stop, the postillion has been struck by lightning' was a famous one. Another was 'Unhand me, sir, for my husband, who is Australian, awaits without.'

The story is told that, during the Lord Mayor's Procession in London a few years ago, the weather was awful. The procession takes place on the second Saturday of November. One of the coaches had two postillions at the back. There was a flash and a clap of thunder, and the coachman had difficulty controlling the horses. One of the postillions fell off. The other hung on like grim death.

And throughout the crowd the foreign tourists offered thanks for being able to say, at last, 'Ah look, the postillion has been struck by lightning.'

I made that last bit up. The sentence will never be used in modern times.

Wrong. It was used by film star Dirk Bogarde as the title of a memoir, *A Postillion Struck by Lightning*, the first of his autobiographical books.

I am still waiting to hear that somebody has been able to use the sentence about the Australian husband.

Lodz is one of those places where, although I was only there for two days, I kept discovering things. It has a nickname: 'the Polish Manchester'. This is because of the rapid development of the textile industry there in the nineteenth century. Eventually it turned Lodz into the second-largest city in Poland.

It has the largest film studios in the country, and is the seat of the Polish Film Academy. Roman Polanski passed through its doors. So did another Oscar-winning director, Andrzej Wajda. The pronunciation of the city name cries out for the pun, and there it is: *Hollylodz*. You have to remember the 'woodge' pronunciation to get it.

A stretch of the street by the Grand Hotel has been laid out, Hollywood style, as a walkway of fame. Stars in the pavement honour stars of the Polish cinema. I stood on Roman Polanski.

And along the middle of the street is a millennium monument – a paved section containing about thirteen thousand blocks, each engraved with the name of a Lodz citizen. Buying a brick helped pay for street renovation.

The piazza outside Shakespeare's Globe in London is also covered with paving stones engraved with the names of early Globe supporters and donors. I've stood on Laurence Olivier too.

As I wandered along Piotrkowska Street, by no. 78 I met a bronzed Arthur Rubinstein, playing a grand piano, with a huge wing emerging from the top of the instrument. There is space on his stool to sit by him. The piano is in fact a huge musical box. Put a coin in the slot at the front and you can hear a Rubinstein recording of various pieces by Chopin or Tchaikovsky. I was told that, while listening, it is traditional to pat his right hand and make a wish. I did.

And my wish came true. I hoped to have a reason for writing about Lodz one day.

I passed a huge colourful piece of graffiti in a car park by no. 152 – though 'mural' might be a better description. It features one of the town squares, a monument, the old town hall, an old tram, and – leaping out of the frame – the Lodz heraldic boat under full sail. Later, I learned that it was claimed to be the largest such piece in the world – at least, according to *The Guinness Book of Records*.

Then I turned a corner and found myself surrounded by linguistic echoes. I was in Zamenhofa Street. The founder of Esperanto, Ludwig Zamenhof, is remembered here, as he is in many Polish cities.

But my main discovery was to come. I got into one of the bicycle rickshaws that run up and down Piotrkowska Street. I chose a bright red and green one. There was also a bright yellow one shaped like a Lodz boat, but as I get seasick I thought better of that. I asked the driver (driver? rider?) to take me to the Old Cemetery off Ogrodowa Street – an ecumenical cemetery for people of all Christian backgrounds and from many countries.

There, in an unpretentious plot, with a stone cross above a dark green marble slab, was the grave of Ira Aldridge. He was an actor, born in 1807, who defied the constraints of an African-American racial background to become one of the century's leading Shakespearean performers. He couldn't get work in the USA, so he emigrated to England, where he made his debut.

He got a mixed reception. The *Times* review condemned what it called his terrible pronunciation, blaming the shape of his lips. The *Globe* reviewer, however, found his speech pleasantly sonorous. But his colour held him back in the London society of the day, so he ended up performing mainly in Europe, where he achieved international fame for his performances as Othello, Macbeth, Lear, and Shylock. He would often sing an anti-slavery song at the end of a performance.

And then, while on tour, he died. He had been invited to perform

Othello at a new theatre, the Paradyz, at Piotrkowska 175. The first performance was scheduled for 6 August, but Aldridge didn't feel well. They postponed the opening, but he died in his lodgings the next day.

The town gave him a splendid funeral. His tombstone has an enamelled picture of him in the role of Othello. The date reads 7.VIII.1867. He is still remembered. A local appreciation society ensures that there are often fresh flowers or lit candles on his grave.

On the way to Lodz, I had made a small detour to visit the small manor house in the village of Zelazowa Vola, where Chopin was born. Or, at least, what is left of it. Fire destroyed much of the original property in the nineteenth century. It houses a museum now, in six rooms on either side of the hall. The furnishing shows the style of the period, but sadly nothing belonging to the Chopin family has been preserved. There is a delightful garden. All-Chopin recitals take place there on Sundays during the summer.

Chopin statues and streets are everywhere in Poland. There is one of each in Lodz. But the composer's body is not in Poland. That is buried in the cemetery of Père Lachaise in Paris.

Apart from his heart. He left instructions that it should remain in Poland. And that is where you will find it, sealed in a pillar in the Church of the Holy Cross in Warsaw. As you face the altar it is on the left, with a Chopin bust marking the spot.

Père Lachaise cemetery, where the rest of him lies, is another amazing place. It has been a cemetery for over two hundred years, and now contains over seventy thousand burial plots. At 188 acres, it is the largest park – if that is the right word – in Paris. Father François de La Chaise d'Aix – known as 'Le Père La Chaise' – was confessor to Louis XIV.

It attracts thousands of tourists – most of them, it sometimes feels, visiting the grave of Jim Morrison, the charismatic lead singer of The Doors rock group. He is buried in Poets' Corner.

Walking through Père Lachaise is like browsing through a chronology of the arts. Bizet, Rossini, Poulenc . . . Delacroix, Ingres, David . . . Wilde, Apollinaire, Balzac, Molière . . . Sarah Bernhardt, Simone Signoret, Yves Montand . . . Piaf, Bécaud, Callas . . . It is a 'Who's Who' of the artistic dead.

Linguists are there too. A tall monument in the style of Cleopatra's Needle marks the grave of Jean-François Champollion, the man who first deciphered Egyptian hieroglyphics.

And William Madocks is there. The man who built the cob at Porthmadog. He died in Paris on his way home from a holiday in Italy.

Madocks's Italian visit included several of the places where his old acquaintance Shelley had lived. At Hay one year I found Thomas Medwin's account of Shelley's visit to Pisa to see his friend Lord Byron. Medwin stayed with Byron during 1821–22. And according to Medwin, Byron pronounced his own surname as 'Burn'. That possibility had never occurred to me.

A number of words were pronounced very differently in the early nineteenth century compared with today. We know this because dictionaries after Johnson were beginning to include transcriptions to tell readers how words were pronounced; and even though these were usually only rough respellings, they yield important clues.

They couldn't have been anything else but rough. Accurate phonetic transcriptions, of the kind used by the professors behind Henry Higgins, didn't emerge until towards the end of the century.

Thanks to these respellings, we know that *oblige* was pronounced 'obleege', *daughters* was 'darters', *gold* was 'goold', *seven* was 'sivin', and *china* was 'chayney'. We also know that there were often differences in the way a word was stressed. *Compensate* today has the stress on the first syllable. In the early nineteenth century, it was on the second. And the battle we now call *Trafalgar* was, when it was fought, *Trafalgar*.

One of Admiral Nelson's naval surgeons is buried in Père Lachaise. Leonard Gillespie was an Ulster-born surgeon who served on the

Victory in 1805, but he missed the Battle of Trafalgar by a couple of months, due to ill-health. He lived in Paris for many years.

Balcony was *balcony* – bal-<u>coh</u>-nee. Dictionaries before 1800 show the older stress pattern only. Dictionaries after 1850 show the modern pattern only. In between, there is uncertainty.

It is a bit like the modern uncertainty over such words as *research*. It used to be only *re<u>search</u>*. Today, we often hear *<u>re</u>search*. In fact, I've never heard anything else in recent years among young people in Europe.

The nineteenth-century banker, poet, and conversationalist Samuel Rogers couldn't stand *bal<u>co</u>ny*. It 'makes me sick', he said, in his *Table-Talk*. Some people say the same about *<u>re</u>search* now. But in fifty years' time the reaction will probably seem as antiquated as Rogers' seems today.

Even word order has changed a bit since Samuel Rogers' day. In Sheridan's play *The Critic* (1779), there is the line: 'Speaking from within has always a fine effect.' Keats in an 1818 letter wrote: 'My passion gets entirely the sway.' We would relocate the adverbs *always* and *entirely* today. Either of these quotes could be taken for modern Euro-English.

And adjective order preferences have changed. Mrs Gaskell writes in her letters of *an old curious seat* and *some old mysterious stone steps*. That was in the late 1830s. Today we would say *curious old seat* and *mysterious old stone steps*. Like *three old pigeons*.

This last one came to mind as I drove along the A5 through the village of Nesscliffe. You pass a pub called *The Old Three Pigeons*. I wanted to regularize it to *The Three Old Pigeons*.

There are lots of interesting place-names along this stretch of the A5. *Ness* itself meant 'ridge' in Old English. You can see it clearly – an escarpment of red sandstone overlooking the Shropshire Plain. There's an old hill fort at the top.

A few miles further along and the road passes by a truly remarkable name: *Ruyton XI Towns*. I have never come across another name, anywhere in the world, which has a Roman numeral in the middle. It's pronounced 'Roy-ton eleven towns'. *Ruyton* is the easy bit: 'rye farm'. The strange second half dates from 1308, when the Earl of Arundel brought eleven townships together into one borough: Coton, Eardiston, Felton, Haughton, Rednal, Ruyton, Shelvock, Shotatton, Sutton, Tedsmore, and Wykey. Buildings from all eleven still exist, though only some of them are part of modern villages.

During the summer of 1878, Arthur Conan Doyle worked in Ruyton for a few months as a medical assistant with a doctor in general practice. That was the year he began to write stories for magazines.

I was still in territory which would have belonged to Mercia. The next big town along the A5 was Oswestry, and Offa's Dyke passes about three miles to the west. If I turned left I would find myself back in Welshpool. But it was time to reconnect with my 'Voices' project in Rhyl, on the North Wales coast, so I turned right at Oswestry and headed north.

There are many legends surrounding Oswestry. King Arthur surfaces again – this time through Guinevere. The story goes that she was born at Caer Ogyrfan, the old hill fort that is at the edge of the town.

Rather more historically, Oswald, the Christian king of Northumbria, was killed during a battle here against Penda, the pagan king of Mercia, in 642. Penda dismembered Oswald's body and hung the pieces from a tree. The place became known as 'Oswald's Tree' – and hence, *Oswestry*.

There are remains of old Marcher forts everywhere in this part of Britain, most of them built in the 1200s. I'd passed Whittington, and was about to pass Chirk, and ahead of me, up the north-east Wales coast, were Holt, Caergwrle, Hawarden, Ewloe, and Flint.

Chirk is an English version of the Welsh name *Ceiriog*, which meant 'favoured one'. It is the name of the local river. The town has a different Welsh name today: *Y Waun*, which means 'The Moor'. As I crossed the border, the signposts changed into two languages. After a mental journey through the multilingual graveyards of Europe, I was back in bilingual Wales.

15

I'm Jack

LLANGOLLEN

There is a huge roundabout outside Chirk. Drivers in a hurry go straight across, north along the A483 past Wrexham, eventually joining the dual-carriageway A55 across North Wales to Holyhead. Drivers in less of a hurry, or who simply want to enjoy some scenery, turn left and follow the A5 through the town, entering the Vale of Llangollen. They are the wise ones.

In 1833, in *A Topographical Dictionary of Wales*, Samuel Lewis had this to say:

> the Vale of Llangollen is deservedly celebrated as containing, in proportion to its extent, a greater variety of interesting objects, and a more beautiful and striking combination of the milder and nobler features of pleasing and majestic scenery, than probably any other in the Principality.

I agree. I have driven all over Wales, and have yet to see anywhere which quite beats it for variety, linguistic (at least in July) as well as visual.

It is the juxtaposition of ancient and modern which is so striking. As I entered the Vale I could see ahead of me on the right the steep hill above Llangollen with the remains of Castell Dinas Bran – 'Crow

Castle' (if you take the first and third words) or 'Crow City' (if you take the last two). Arthur turns up again. In one legend this is said to be the burial site of the Holy Grail.

Look right and you see Thomas – Telford, that is. The Shropshire Union Canal runs calmly alongside the A5 for several miles; but when it reaches the village of Froncysyllte it turns north and is carried straight across the River Dee, 126 feet high. It is the longest and highest cast-iron aqueduct in the world.

Telford was asked to build it in order to link the ironworks and collieries of the Wrexham area with Chester and Shrewsbury. The bridge section was made entirely from cast iron. It is eleven feet wide, just over five feet deep, and just over a thousand feet long, and supported by nineteen arches. He started to build it in 1795, and it was opened ten years later, the month after the Battle of Trafalgar.

It is called Pontcysyllte – 'the connecting bridge' – because it connects to the River Dee, which feeds it at the Horseshoe Falls just outside Llangollen.

If you have a good head for heights you can walk along it. In fact, the towpath next to the canal forms part of the Offa's Dyke footpath. The views are spectacular – though, not having the required good head, my experience of them is virtual only, thanks to a helpful website.

It is spectacular enough from below, looking up at the bridge from the foot of the arches. I've done that, and still felt dizzy looking up towards the top of the huge arches. The colourful narrow-boats seem to be sailing across the sky.

Llangollen is home to the International Musical Eisteddfod, which is held at the beginning of July each year. When I said earlier on that there were more English accents packed into Portmeirion than anywhere else I know, I was forgetting Llangollen in July.

Eisteddfod is pronounced 'eye–*steth*–vod', with the *th* sounding as in *thy*. It is a combination of *eisteddd* 'sit' + *bod* 'to be', and is loosely translated as a 'sitting together' or 'gathering'. It is a competitive festival of music and literature, with ancient origins in bardic tournaments. Wales has a national eisteddfod in a different location each year, and there are regional ones too. Welsh is the official language of these events.

The Llangollen Eisteddfod is unique. It is held there every year, and it is firmly international in character. Welsh has its place, but English is the lingua franca. And with visiting choirs, singers, musicians, and dancers there from fifty or so countries, from all parts of the world, it is an accentologist's paradise.

In 2005 there was a World Music Zone, with performers from Africa, Jamaica, Brazil, and Japan. In a Spoken Word Zone you could hear Malaysian poetry, Indian storytelling, and Jamaican rap, as well as home-grown Celtic variants.

I couldn't get to the 2005 Eisteddfod, but I remembered from earlier years the fascinating accent mixes which evolved as people from totally different language backgrounds, and with widely differing levels of expertise in English, talked to each other. Sometimes the conversations collapsed into giggling confusion. But usually people survived. If nothing else, everyone came away with their musical vocabulary much enhanced.

Are there common features among this welter of world accents? I think the most noticeable thing is the rhythm. I had heard it in Kolkata and in Amsterdam and in Lodz. It is a syllable-by-syllable way of talking, reflecting the natural rhythms of the mother-tongues. Imagine this sentence spoken with every syllable given an equal stress. *I-ma-gine this sen-tence spo-ken with ev-ry syl-la-ble gi-ven* . . .

You hear that kind of speech occasionally on English television. Antoine de Caunes of *Eurotrash* is a great exponent, as French is a 'syllable-timed' language, and his speech rhythms reflect it. Also, aliens use it. *Ex-ter-mi-nate*.

You would have heard that last example in Llangollen a few years ago. There was a 'Dr Who' Museum here between 1996 and 2003.

During that blissful period, on the brown tourist sign in Castle Street you could see a Welsh dragon pursued by a Dalek.

I'm not sure the Dalek would have won, in any confrontation. By all accounts, Welsh dragons were formidable foes.

Traditionally, English is not spoken in a syllabic way. It is a language where the main stresses fall at roughly regular intervals in the stream of speech. The technical term is 'stress-timed'. It is a 'tum-te-tum-te-tum' way of talking.

It is sometimes called the 'heartbeat' of English poetry. 'The curfew tolls the knell of parting day . . .', 'Shall I compare thee to a summer's day . . .', 'I wandered lonely as a cloud . . .', 'Is this the face that launched a thousand ships . . .' But it is not restricted to poetry. If I were to read this chapter aloud, you would hear the tum-te-tum beat all the time in the prose – though not as strictly metrical as in these poetic examples, of course.

English hardly ever gravitates towards a syllable-timed speech rhythm – apart from occasions when a foreign accent motivates it. The nearest cases aren't really speech at all. Children learning to read, painfully sounding out syllables. Chants and raps. And popular song. 'There may be trouble ahead', wrote Irving Berlin in *Follow the Fleet*, and as it is sung we hear the even beat on many of what would normally be unstressed syllables – *There may be trou-ble a-head . . . But while there's moon-light and mu-sic and love and ro-mance . . . Let's face the mu-sic and dance*.

One of the commonest conversational topics when people from different countries get together using English as a lingua franca is the eccentricity of English idioms. It only takes one person to use an ear-catching idiom, and someone will ask about it. 'Time to face the music,' said one eisteddfod participant to another, making a joke of the idiom, as Irving Berlin did, as someone was about to go on stage.

Her less fluent listener's brow furrowed. 'What means *face the music*?'

The first speaker explained. 'It means to be brave when you're faced with a difficult situation.'

'But why?'

The *why* question. In so many cases, with English idioms, if only we knew! In this particular case, two origins have been suggested. One is from the theatre, where a performer had to go on stage and face an audience that was not always going to be friendly. The musicians in the band would be in front of the stage, so the performer would, quite literally, be facing them.

The other is from the military situation where a soldier was being dismissed in disgrace. The event would be accompanied by a beating drum, often with a fife which would play something appropriate, such as 'The Rogues' March'. Hence the other expression of being 'drummed out' of the army.

The timing seems much better for the first explanation. The earliest recorded usage of the phrase *face the music* in the *OED* is 1850. And the first 'music halls' appeared in suburban London following the Theatres Act of 1843, which allowed a licence to saloons that offered variety acts and alcohol only if they became theatres.

'Drumming out' is recorded much earlier, from 1766. It seems unlikely that it would take the best part of a century to make someone think of using *face the music* as an idiom. If there is an idiomatic or metaphorical meaning lurking within a word, people sniff it out very quickly.

Some of the clearest evidence about the speed at which figurative meanings emerge has come since the arrival of the Internet. That's a medium where you can't write anything without it being logged, with date and time. As a result, if you decide to use a word in a new way on your website, nosy linguists will one day be able to track its first use down more precisely than ever before. There has never been so much data available on the history of words. The Internet is a lexical goldmine.

It is already possible to see new uses of words that arrived in the early days of the Internet. Take *spam*, in its sense of an unwanted email sent to many recipients. The phenomenon developed in the early 1990s. The *OED* has a reference from 1994. People started saying such things as 'I got twenty emails this morning, and eighteen of them were spam,' and 'That firm spams me every day.'

It's a word where the source is known, but not the originator. In 1970 the *Monty Python* comedy team ran a sketch set in a café. Every dish on offer included large quantities of the tinned meat, Spam. That seems to be the inspiration for the Internet usage. But who first used the word with reference to email is a mystery.

During the 1990s use of the word increased in frequency along with the phenomenon. Then I heard someone say, 'I can't stand the spam they put into those commercial breaks.' He was talking about television, not computing. He meant 'unwanted utterance'. Soon after, I heard someone else say, 'I asked for my money back, but he just gave me a pile of spam and told me to come back next week.' Here it meant 'evasive utterance'.

Both those remarks were made within five years of the first Internet usage. And several other computing or Internet terms have been adapted – at least, in the slang of young people – in the same speedy way. 'I've hacked it.' 'I'll ping you later.' 'Give me a download about what's going on.' 'They're just a click away from getting together.'

As I drove into Llangollen, I passed the sign to Plas Newydd ('new place'), the home of the celebrated 'Ladies of Llangollen', who got together at the turn of the nineteenth century, and both fascinated and scandalized Regency society. It is a black-and-white timbered house, surrounded by gardens and trees, on a hill looking down on the town.

They were two upper-class women from Ireland: Lady Eleanor Butler and the Honourable Sarah Ponsonby. The first was born in 1739, the second in 1755. They met in 1768, became firm friends, and rather than face unwanted marriages, decided to leave Ireland and set up house together. They succeeded in doing so, despite much family opposition, eventually settling in Plas Newydd in 1780. There they stayed for fifty years. Eleanor died in 1829; Sarah two years later.

Ponsonby is an interesting surname. It's actually a place-name. Ponsonby is in Cumbria, near the coast south of Whitehaven. It is literally *Puncun's by* – the (Danish) 'village of Puncun'. 'John, son of Puncun' is mentioned in early records in 1177 as the owner of the place. *Ponsonby* as a surname is known from the early fourteenth century. It is related in meaning to the word *puncheon*, 'awl, punch'. One of those *eo* spellings.

The two ladies lived in pastoral seclusion, reading, writing, gardening, and walking, and becoming widely admired among Romantic writers as what was thought of as a symbol of romantic friendship. Their literary visitors included Shelley, Byron, Scott, and Wordsworth. Edmund Burke visited them, as did Josiah Wedgwood and the Duke of Wellington. So did the poet Anna Seward – 'the Swan of Lichfield' – and Dr Johnson's friend Hester Thrale, who lived nearby for a time. Wordsworth was so moved by his visit in 1824 that he wrote a sonnet to the two ladies while he was there, calling them 'Sisters in love'. Seward wrote a poem too, after her visit in 1795: 'Llangollen Vale'. The ladies have an iconic stature in feminist literary history.

In the garden of Plas Newydd is the font from the ruined Cistercian abbey, Valle Crucis (pronounced 'valley croo-chis', 'Vale of the Cross'), north of the town along the A542 just before the climb up to the Horseshoe Pass. That was my route, for I had to visit Rhyl before returning to Holyhead.

The road took me past the abbey, with its striking remains. It was founded in 1202. Despite Henry VIII's destructive efforts, the west end of the abbey, with three fine windows, is still standing. So are the dormitory, sacristy, and chapter house. And the monks' large fishpond is still there too.

Some think the Holy Grail might have been in Valle Crucis. Eliseg's Pillar is nearby, from the ninth century, a high cross memorial to

Prince Eliseg of Powys. This is the cross commemorated in the name 'Vale of the Cross'. Only part of the shaft survives, some eight feet high. It has a Latin inscription, faded now, which lists the names of the rulers of Powys, one of whom was 'Guorthigirn' (Vortigern). In the stories, Vortigern meets the child Merlin. And he is killed by King Arthur's father, Uther Pendragon. Arthur is never far away in this part of the world.

I looked back down at Llangollen. It was St Collen who started it all. He founded the church here in the late sixth or early seventh century. The town name breaks down into *Llan + Gollen* – 'the church of Collen', with that typical Welsh change in the first letter of the name which I'd seen in *Llanfair* a few days before. The church has a fine fifteenth-century carved oak roof. No other church in Wales is named for Collen. But there is a *Langolen* in the west of Brittany and a *St Colan* near Newquay in Cornwall. He's a real Celt, behind the variations in spelling.

Spelling. That reminded me of a visit to the Eisteddfod one year when I saw the name *Ye Olde Cake Shoppe* outside a stall. Ye olde spellinges can work, if they suit the subject-matter. Cakes, I suppose, fall into that category – as long as the reference is to the shoppe and not to the time since the cakes came out of the oven.

The next year I saw *Vitamin Shoppe*. That seemed less right, somehow.

I started looking out for uses of *Shoppe*. There does seem to be a trend to use it in contexts which you wouldn't consider to be 'olde' in a million years. In India I saw a *Computer Shoppe* and a *Technoshoppe*. In Singapore I saw *International Shoppes*. And in Melbourne there was one which really made my brain hurt: *Anti Skin Cancer Shoppe*.

I wonder at the connotations sometimes. Do they do only old-style haircuts in *Murphy's Barber Shoppe* in Swansea?

Driving through the Cotswolds once, I came across *The Olde Bakery Tea-Shoppe* in the High Street in Winchcombe. But even there I found linguistic surprises. It is now *Juri's Olde Bakery Tea Shoppe* – and Juri

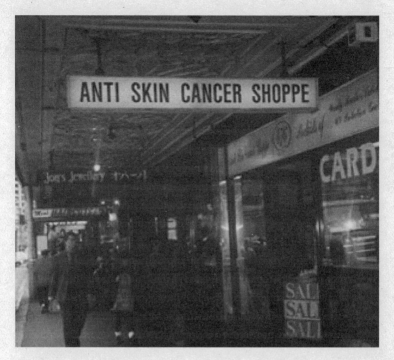

is Japanese, the daughter of a family who fell in love with the Cotswolds and moved to the area in 2004.

Winchcombe does something which other towns ought to emulate. The stories behind some of the street-names are told on plaques around the town. One of them is in Juri's restaurant garden; another is on the Castle Street wall outside.

My road north to Rhyl took me through Ruthin, Denbigh, and St Asaph. If I had stopped, I knew I would hear a variety of accents that would tell me I was definitely in North Wales. But when I got to the seaside town, it was very different. For Rhyl is an 'accent island'.

Rhyl became a fashionable seaside resort in the mid-nineteenth century. In 1879, *Black's Picturesque Guide to North Wales* talks about it as 'altogether a modern creation, and still rapidly extending . . . Its

recommendations are, easy access, good hotels and lodging-houses, and some agreeable objects within moderate drives.'

Easy access it certainly had. People from the rapidly growing cities of Liverpool and Manchester found it a convenient destination, and many settled in the area, especially after World War II. Older residents today remember the area as very Welsh in character. Several had Welsh-speaking grandparents. But within a couple of generations, the accent shifted markedly. When you hear people from Rhyl talking today, they sound more Lancashire than Welsh.

As part of the 'Voices' project, I interviewed one man whose family had lived in Rhyl for four generations. They used to run the donkey rides on the beach. When he was a child he would earn money by carrying the cases of the visitors from the train station to their hotel in a wheelbarrow. There was no trace of Welsh in his voice. There was no pronunciation of *r* after vowels and he had a noticeable northern *a*. He said 'ah-land' for *Ireland* and 'lahk' for *lark* and 'fahter' for *fighter*. Words like *definitely* and *Wembley* ended in an 'eh' rather than an 'ee'. He pronounced the *g* in *singer* and *wrong*.

I then spoke to some of the stallholders at the fairground. I might have been in Southport or New Brighton, over in north-west England. But in the middle of the conversation one of them quite unconsciously referred to his *nain* and his *taid* – pronounced like 'nine' and 'tide' – the colloquial Welsh words for 'grandmother' and 'grandfather'. You wouldn't get that in Southport. And as I got used to the accent, I realized that it wasn't as broad as Lancashire. In particular, the rhythm was a little more clipped, and the intonation more lilting. There were hints of traditional Welsh here, after all.

Then I got a fright. As I was talking to the hoop-la man, another stallholder came over, and introduced himself to me. 'I'm Jack,' he said. I nearly fell over. For it was the voice of the Yorkshire Ripper.

The fake Ripper, of course. By 1978, the police had made little progress in their search for the serial killer who had been murdering women, mainly in the Leeds–Bradford area, over the previous four years. Then a series of handwritten letters arrived, claiming to be from the killer, followed in June 1979 by an audio cassette. 'I'm Jack,' the tape began. 'I see you are still having no luck catching me.' And it went on for three minutes and sixteen seconds.

The detective in charge of the case was convinced the tape was genuine, and valuable time and resources were devoted to following it up. He set up Dial-the-Ripper phone-lines. The public could ring in and listen to the voice, in the hope that someone would recognize it. It was all a waste of time. When Peter Sutcliffe was caught, in 1981, his accent was not at all like the one on the tape.

The police had turned to phoneticians for help, to establish where the tape voice came from. It's something that detectives do quite often, looking to a branch of my subject called 'forensic phonetics'. Just a few months before my trip to Rhyl I had myself been approached by Holyhead police to listen to a tape of someone making threats over the phone, to advise on whether it was the same voice as a tape recording they had made of a suspect. If there is enough material, and the acoustic quality of the recording is reasonable, you can usually make judgements with some confidence. And if necessary you can run the extracts through special acoustic equipment to provide some objective evidence.

In 1979 the Yorkshire police approached Stanley Ellis and Jack Windsor Lewis at the University of Leeds – an excellent choice. Leeds had long been the centre of dialect studies in Britain. The Survey of English Dialects was organized from there. I remember Stanley Ellis years ago travelling around the country in a caravan in search of accents. Nobody had more hands-on phonetic experience than he had. I've never met anyone with a better ear for regional accents.

The Ripper tape had 257 words in it, and the recording was good. That would be plenty.

You didn't have to be a phonetician to sense that the speaker came from the north-east of England. The media dubbed him 'Wearside

Jack', because it sounded as if he came from around the River Wear. But which part, exactly? Ellis spent months analysing the tape. He quickly identified the voice as coming from Sunderland, and then visited the pubs and clubs of the town to narrow it down. He concluded that the voice was of someone who had been brought up in the Castletown or Southwick districts, just north of the river.

That supported the letters which had been received by the police from the supposed Ripper, which had been postmarked Sunderland. But there was no point in looking there. The first one, received in 1978, took pains to explain the obvious: 'You probably look for me in Sunderland dont bother I am not daft just posted letter there on one of my trips.'

Was the tape genuine? The Geordie accent is one of the most difficult to mimic, if you are not from the area. Even Peter Sellers kept away from it. There was no indication that the voice on the tape was disguised. Unless you are a brilliant impressionist – or an expert phonetician – disguised voices tend to be rather inconsistent. Even then, they are not usually accurate. Impressionists tend to exaggerate certain features in order to make an effect. The tape voice wasn't like that. Moreover, there were certain idiosyncratic features of articulation. One word had an unusual quality for the sound of *l*. Another word, *sorry*, had a lengthened *s*. Might the speaker have had a speech problem as a child, such as a stammer?

The tape contained nine silences of three seconds or more. Four of them were at least six seconds. One was thirteen seconds. Stammerers do display long pauses in their speech. But the phoneticians weren't convinced. We all elongate sounds on occasion. And in recording a taped message, we might well pause excessively while thinking what to say next, to avoid giving the game away. The police held on to the stammering theory, but from a linguistic point of view it was dismissed as speculation.

The phoneticians were puzzled. The voice was certainly distinctive, and they were sure it would be quickly recognized. If this man had been living in Yorkshire, where the murders took place, his voice would have stood out a mile. The man had to be living on Wearside, where the voice would not have been so identifiable. They were sure it was a hoax.

The phoneticians wrote to the police, stating this view, but their warning went unheeded. Suspects continued to be eliminated from enquiries if they had no Wearside accent. Angry that their warnings had been disregarded, Jack Windsor Lewis went public in the *Yorkshire Post* on 3 December 1980. But it proved unnecessary to take the consequences of his article into account. Sutcliffe was caught a month later. He was from Bradford. The tape had definitely been a hoax.

After years of speculation about his identity, the hoaxer was finally caught through DNA evidence in 2005, and pleaded guilty at his trial a few months later to a charge of perverting the course of justice. He had been living in Flodden Road, just south of the river, less than a mile from Castletown. And he had gone to school in Castletown. The phoneticians had been right in their analysis. Henry Higgins would have been proud of them.

It still surprises me that the voice wasn't identified in Sunderland at the time. We all have a good auditory memory for voices, and can recognize someone over the phone, even if we haven't heard them for some time. Almost everyone must have heard the tape, for it was widely played on radio and television. Given the relatively low population of the Sunderland area, the phoneticians felt that the combination of geographical and personal characteristics would have reduced the number of possible candidates to just a few hundred. Yet nobody singled him out, not even members of his family.

On the other hand, the very fact that hundreds of people *did* have this accent would make it difficult for anyone to be so certain of the speaker's identity that they would be prepared to call the police about it. And non-linguistic factors always outweigh linguistic ones. The hoaxer had a brother and four sisters. You might think they would have recognized him. But they would know that their brother didn't drive, so he couldn't possibly have managed to travel rapidly throughout the territory that the Ripper covered. That fact alone would have been enough to make them discount any vocal similarities on the tape as just a coincidence.

I wasn't involved at all in the forensic phonetic investigations in 1979, but I remember doing a transcription of my own at the time, out of interest. So the voice has stayed with me. That's why Jack, my new fairground acquaintance, caught me by surprise. He was from Sunderland. I wasn't expecting this accent in Rhyl.

My work done, I bade farewell to my BBC friends. They were heading back down to Cardiff, with a lot of editing to do. By the end of the 'Voices' project we would have filmed the best part of forty hours of material. They would have to reduce this to a programme of fifty minutes. I didn't envy them.

I pointed the car towards Holyhead. The road out of Rhyl took me onto the A55, past Colwyn Bay and the Great Worm of Llandudno, and along the coast to Bangor, the Telford bridges, and Gaerwen. That was where my travels had begun, several linguistic journeys ago.

I reflected on my trip around Wales. Apart from the places in North and Mid Wales I'd visited during the past week, I had talked to people across South Wales too. I recalled another accent island, in Pembrokeshire, in an area often called 'little England beyond Wales'. Rhyl wasn't alone.

And there were accent islands still emerging, especially in the capital, where groups of immigrants had settled and melded their mother-tongue with the local way of speaking. One woman, from Yemen, had lived in Cardiff for several years, and spoke in an accent which I could only describe as Yemeni-Cardiff. Her way of speaking was the norm in some parts of the city.

What is happening in Wales is happening everywhere else too. You can hear Chinese Scouse and Jamaican Scouse in Liverpool now. And there are hundreds of new dialects, with associated accents, in London. Hardly any of them have been recorded and studied. The search for English goes on, all over the world. My reminiscences in this book are wide-ranging, but they have hardly made a dent in the extraordinary range and variety of the language.

And yet, while everywhere is different, in many ways everywhere is the same. Innumerable linguistic echoes reverberate around the places visited in these chapters. People ask similar questions, have similar interests, worry about similar issues, and express similar attitudes towards language acceptability, variation, and change.

No encounter with language is purely intellectual. There is always an emotional underpinning. It has always impressed me how we so readily lapse into the vocabulary of 'love' and 'hate', when talking about language. 'I love my language.' 'I like his accent.' 'I hate it when some-one says . . .' 'I was appalled to hear on the radio . . .' 'It's a gorgeous name.'

That is why, in the 'Voices' project, I spent so much time asking people how they felt about things. I didn't want to rely only on my own impressions. I wanted to get their own perception of the way they spoke. 'So how do you think you sound to other people?' I would ask. 'What do you *feel* about your accent?'

Every single one of the people I interviewed in Wales claimed to be Welsh, and to be proud of it. They all had a strong sense of identity. And, notwithstanding the at times considerable influences from outside the principality, they felt their accent could be described as 'Welsh'. I am certain that, if my journey had led me to explore the English of Scotland or Ireland, or the English of Trinidad or Jamaica, I would have heard the same kind of variation and received the same kind of reaction, with 'Welsh' replaced by the appropriate alternative.

People and places have countless language stories to tell. Wherever you go, whatever you see, whoever you meet, there is a fresh linguistic world awaiting you. You may have to tease it out, by hook or by crook, but it is there. All you have to do is ask. And be prepared to dig a little.

'So, what do you feel about the way you speak?'

It was the last question I put to my Rhyl informant with the case-carrying, donkey-riding childhood, before I went home. He was in no doubt. In his broad quasi-Lancashire lilt he told me quite firmly: 'It's a Welsh accent, you see.'

I had heard that somewhere before . . .

REFERENCES AND SOURCES
INDEX OF PLACES
INDEX OF PEOPLE AND CHARACTERS
INDEX OF TOPICS

ON THE WAY

References and Sources

Internet addresses in this section were live at the beginning of 2007, but unfortunately there is no guarantee that they will stay that way.

CHAPTER 1
Anglesey place-names:
    Gwilyn T. Jones and Tomos Roberts, *Enwau Lleoedd Môn/The Place-Names of Anglesey*. Isle of Anglesey County Council, 1996
Long words:
    Examples of this kind of wordplay can be found at http://wordways.com

CHAPTER 2
Bee sources:
    Karl von Frisch, 'Dialects in the language of the bees' in *Scientific American*, August 1962; J.R. Riley, U. Greggers, A.D. Smith, D.R. Reynolds and R. Menzel, 'The flight paths of honeybees recruited by the waggle dance' in *Nature* 435, 2005, 205–7
Britannia bridge fire:
    There is an account with an interview at http://www.bbc.co.ik/wales/walesonair/database/bridgefire.shtml
Dylan Thomas quotation:
    'Conversation about Christmas', in *Quite Early One Morning* (London: Dent, 1954), p.14

CHAPTER 3
History of Portmeirion:
    Clough Williams-Ellis, *Portmeirion: The Place and its Meaning* (Penrhyndeudraeth: Portmeirion, revised edition, 1973), p.45

George Eliot quotation:

'A difference of taste in jokes is a great strain on the affections,' in *Daniel Deronda* (1876), Book 2, Chapter 15

Prisoner Appreciation Society:

http://www.sixofone.org.uk

Runes:

R.I. Page, *Runes* (London: British Museum, 1987), p.32

Bengt Odenstedt, *The Inscription on the Undley Bracteate and the Beginnings of English Runic Writing* (Umeå: Umeå University, 1983)

George Steiner quotation:

'The Idea of Europe', in *The Liberal* (Hay Festival edition), 2006, 4–8. *The Liberal* originally ran for four issues only between 1822 and 1824. It was founded by Lord Byron, Leigh Hunt and Shelley

CHAPTER 4

Shaw quotation:

The Preface to *Pygmalion* can be read at http://www.readbook online.net/read/902/10935

Burgess quotation:

In *A Mouthful of Air* (London: Hutchinson, 1992), II, Epilogue

Daniel Jones background:

Beverley Collins and Inger M. Mees, *The Real Professor Higgins: the Life and Career of Daniel Jones* (Berlin and New York: Mouton De Gruyter, 1999), pp.97–103

Off the wagon:

Reference to serial killing: *The Spokesman-Review*, Spokane, 26 October 2000

CHAPTER 5

Florence Nightingale:

The voice can be heard at www.bl.uk/collections/sound-archive/history.html

Bird-names source:

J.C. Maycock, 'Survey of bird-names in the Yorkshire dialects', in *Transactions of the Yorkshire Dialect Society* (1953), ix–x

Coal-mining terms:

An early collection is *Glossary of Terms Used in the Coal Trade of Northumberland and Durham* (Newcastle: Bell, 1849)

CHAPTER 6
Inn-signs:
> Jacob Larwood and John Camden Hotton, *English Inn Signs* (London: Chatto and Windus, 1951)

Robert Graves quotation:
> Letter to *The Times*, 1961

CHAPTER 7
Godiva hymn:
> An extensive collection of verses can be found at http://godiva.skule.ca

Webster quotations:
> From *Dissertations on the English Language* (1789)

Orrm source:
> Extracts can be read in Bruce Dickins and R.M. Wilson, *Early Middle English Texts* (London: Bowes and Bowes, 1951), pp.82–5. The Ormulum project is at: http://www.english.su.se/nlj/ormproj/demo

CHAPTER 8
Industrial Locomotive Society:
> Index of names at http://www.industrial-loco.org.uk

John Bradburne website:
> At http://www.johnbradburnepoems.com

CHAPTER 9
Linguamón website:
> At http://www.linguamon.cat

Shakespeare Ghost Town:
> At http://www.shakespeareghostown.com

CHAPTER 10
Indian English:
> Henry Yule and A.C. Burnell, *Hobson-Jobson* (London: Routledge and Kegan Paul, 1886)

Suhayl Saadi quotation:
> From *Psychoraag* (Edinburgh: Black and White Publishing, 2004), pp.60–1

Shakespeare's Globe:
> At http://www.shakespeares-globe.org

CHAPTER 11
Language-play:
> David Crystal, *Language Play* (London: Penguin, 1998)

Tolkien's words:
> Peter Gilliver, Jeremy Marshall, and Edmund Weiner, *The Ring of Words: Tolkien and the Oxford English Dictionary* (Oxford: Oxford University Press, 2006)

CHAPTER 12
Johnson Society:
> At http://www.lichfieldrambler.co.uk

Boswell quotations:
> From James Boswell, *The Life of Samuel Johnson* (London: Penguin Classics, edited by Christopher Hibbert, 1979)

Quonians theory:
> Hirondelle, 'Quonians Lane, Lichfield', in *Notes & Queries*, 1877, s5–VII, 393

Geographic names:
> US Board of Geographic Names: http://geonames.usgs.gov

King's Cross development:
> At http://www.kingsx.co.uk/kx7.htm

Darwin biography:
> Charles Darwin, *The Life of Erasmus Darwin* (1879; edited by Desmond King-Hele, Cambridge: Cambridge University Press, 2002)

Psalmanazar extracts:
> At http://www.romanization.com/books/psalmanazaar/index.htm

CHAPTER 13
American English:
> Gunnel Tottie, *An Introduction to American English* (Oxford: Blackwell, 2002)

Pier 39:
> Index of stores at: http://www.pier39.com:80/Shopping/index.htm

Harry Potter:
> Examples of US/British differences at http://www.uta.fi/FAST/US1/REF/potter.html

US texting statistics:
> At http://www.funsms.net/sms_in_statistics.htm

CHAPTER 14

Wrekin panorama:

> At http://www.bbc.co.uk/shropshire/content/panoramas/
> wrekin_panorama_360.shtml

Cultural meanings:

> The cultural meanings of English place-names are summarized in
> David Grote, *British English for American Readers* (Westport, CT:
> Greenwood Press, 1992)

European Union English style guide:

> At http://ec.europa.eu/translation/writing/style_guides/english/
> style_guide_en.pdf

Lodz graffiti:

> At http://www.travelblog.org/Photos/431019.html

Pronunciation of 'Byron':

> Thomas Medwin, *Conversations of Lord Byron* (London: Henry
> Colburn, 1824), p.32

CHAPTER 15

Pontcysyllte panorama:

> At http://www.bbc.co.uk/shropshire/content/panoramas/
> pontcysyllte_aqueduct_360.shtml

Llangollen Musical Eisteddfod

> At http://www.international-eisteddfod.co.uk/

'Voices' project:

> The BBC 'Voices' project is at http://www.bbc.co.uk/voices. The
> programme The Way That We Say It, which motivated my journey
> round Wales, was broadcast on BBC Wales in August 2005. A few
> extracts can be heard at: http://www.bbc.co.uk/wales/northwest/sites/
> voices/pages/tvclips.shtml

Index of Places

Index of People and Characters

Index of Topics

Bees and Fires

Travis Elborough talks to David Crystal

Although you say a little about this elsewhere, I wondered if we could start by talking briefly about how *By Hook or by Crook* came into being. You write that it was your editor who suggested you read W. G. Sebald – and there's a lovely scene where you describe scraping mud off a copy of Sebald's *Rings of Saturn* – I take it he was not a writer you'd read before, then? What was it that appealed to you about his writing and the idea of a linguistic travel book?

No, this was a first encounter with Sebald. When I first saw his book I was appalled by his long paragraphs, and thought I would hate it, but I went with his flow and found it enthralling. What I took out of it mainly was that sense of flow, and also of the ambiguity in his account – did these things happen or not? Was I reading fact or fiction? The distinction didn't seem to matter. *By Hook* blurs that boundary too. Everything that I describe in the book happened, but not always in the order I say. And the mental shifts to other parts of the world and into various topical domains are of course timeless. I sensed a great deal of artifice and structure beneath the Sebald flow, and there is certainly a great deal of that in *By Hook*.

This book is very different in many ways from your others, but would it be fair to say it represents a development from *The Stories of English*? That book, after all, was full of anecdotes and, as the title suggested,

incredible 'stories' about English much like this one.
Yes. *Stories* was chiefly a journey through time; *By Hook* chiefly through space. And it's interesting to see some of the personalities appearing in both, such as Orm, Shakespeare, Webster and Daniel Jones.

You write that in your previous books you've always had a tight structure and known where you were going, but how exactly did you decide where you were going? Were there any places, perhaps, that you wished you had gone to or that you visited but didn't in the end include in the finished book?
'Where' means two things in *By Hook* – geographical destinations and linguistic destinations. My hope was that one would evoke the other, in either direction, and that's how it turned out. Usually I was spoilt for choice. A geographical location would yield half a dozen possibilities – interesting names, phrases, objects, personalities . . . My basis for choice was to avoid duplication of content (e.g. collective nouns turn up only in Chapter 11) but to keep a theme going whenever possible. I didn't know whether readers would notice that bees and fires keep turning up, for example, as do Shelley and Telford. Sometimes the encounter was quite unexpected – Shelley at Lechlade, for instance. And finding Madocks in Père Lachaise cemetery was a wonderful moment.
　As for the journey itself, I had the last ▶

LIFE
at a Glance

BORN

1941 in Lisburn, Northern
Ireland, but brought up
in Holyhead, North
Wales

EDUCATED

St Mary's College, Crosby,
Liverpool; BA and PhD in
English from University
College London

CAREER

Research assistant on the
Survey of English Usage
at UCL; lecturer in
linguistics at Bangor
then Reading, becoming
professor there in 1975;
now honorary professor
of linguistics at Bangor;
left the full-time academic
world in 1984 to work as
an independent writer,
editor, lecturer and
broadcaster

FAMILY

Married first to Molly
Stack (children: Steve, Sue,
Timmy, Lucy) and now to
Hilary Norman, who is ▶

4

Bees and Fires *(continued)*

◀ line in mind from the very beginning, along
with the first, so I knew the journey would be
a circle, but that was all. The general direction
in the UK was dictated by the BBC Voices
project, plus the other events that took me
into Gloucestershire and Warwickshire that
year. The coverage was really dictated by the
size of the book, which in turn was dictated by
the publisher, who (thinking of foreign sales,
doubtless) asked that I take the journey to as
many parts of the world as possible. My trip
to New Zealand was too late to include, but
this PS has remedied that.

**Over the course of your travels what were
you most surprised to discover?**
The unity within the infinite diversity of
language. The stories vary immensely, at
different times and places, but ultimately
they illustrate quite a small range of issues.

**Since you argue that literature is one of the
best places to look if you want to find out
about the varieties of English around the
world, have you ever been tempted to write
a novel yourself?**
I like to try my hand at all literary genres.
It teaches you so much about how the real
literary geniuses do it, and it's great fun –
a nice foil to academic writing. In fact my
very first publications were two short stories,
when I was 17. I wrote a novel when I was in a
TB sanatorium when I was 21, and burnt it a
few years later when I reread it. I've had two
books of poetry published. But my favourite
genre is drama. I've written several plays for
radio and television, though none of them

ever got produced. And I've written one theatre play, *Living On*, about the last speaker of a dying language, which had a rehearsed reading in London in 2007.

If we can have a rash of dermatologists, what is the collective noun for linguists?
A loquacity? Collocation? Assimilation?

You write quite positively about blogs and the internet – how in a generation there will be a huge corpus of regional accents and dialects of English online and that the internet is freeing us from the monopoly of Standard English. But do you ever worry that over time, almost by a process of attrition, there's a danger that regional differences might actually get rubbed away and replaced with a kind of Google-sanctioned English? Or, should we just accept this as a natural part of the language's evolution?
Well, anything can happen, certainly. But all the evidence suggests that the internet is exposing us to a huge amount of linguistic diversity, and this is steadily increasing. Type 'Geordie' into Google and you'll get 200,000 hits, with several sites displaying dialect words and offering audio recordings. International dialects are also readily available. My feeling is that the attempts by internet pedants to make us all write in the same way will have only a limited effect.

You say that you've spent a career trying to make valid statements about language and languages and about the English ▶

LIFE *at a Glance*
(continued)

◀ also my business partner (children: Ben)

LIVES
Returned to live in Holyhead after leaving Reading

5

Bees and Fires *(continued)*

◄ language in particular. Given the rapidity with which the language currently appears to be changing, is it a difficult time to be a linguist? Or do we, if anything, need linguists more than ever right now?

It's the most exciting time to be a linguist. But it's the most difficult time to be a language teacher.

There is a major reason why we need linguists more than ever. With half the world's languages likely to die out this century, the need to document the endangered cases is really urgent – and that needs linguists, and money.

Are you surprised by the success of books like *Eats, Shoots and Leaves*? And what do you think their popularity says about our attitudes to the written and spoken word?

I was amazed. I had been the consultant for Lynne Truss's original Radio 4 series on punctuation, and I recall expressing my doubts to her about the viability of books on punctuation. How wrong I was! Evidently she touched a deep nerve of linguistic insecurity in readers. But I've told this story in *The Fight for English*.

And, finally, will we see more 'stream of consciousness' language books from David Crystal?

I hope so. I do have a sequel in mind, but whether the idea ever comes to fruition really depends on how well *By Hook* does, in terms of sales. Certainly there are plenty of places in the world still left to visit, and each of them tells a unique linguistic story. ■

Top Ten Favourite Films and Television Shows

1. *The Third Man*
   (Carol Reed)

2. *Last Year in Marienbad*
   (Alain Resnais)

3. *The Prisoner*
   (Patrick McGoohan)

4. *Day for Night*
   (*La nuit américaine*: François Truffaut)

5. *Shooting the Past*
   (Stephen Poliakoff)

6. *Perfect Strangers*
   (Stephen Poliakoff)

7. *Powaqaatsi*
   (Godfrey Reggio)

8. *Black Orpheus*
   (*Orfeo Negro*: Marcel Camus)

9. *Shakespeare in Love*
   (John Madden)

10. *Uprising*
    (Jon Avnet)

Longing to Visit

by David Crystal

'A place in New Zealand is longer ...' (p. 3)

WHEN I WROTE THAT, in the middle of 2006, I hadn't been to New Zealand, but a trip was in the pipeline for September that year. I had been booked to give a lecture series at the University of Wellington and a talk to a Community English conference in Napier, about 335 km to the north, on the coast at Hawke's Bay. So we hired a car.

It was on the drive back that things got interesting. We were heading down the east coast road, State Highway 2, past some of the vast wineries, and reached the town of Waipukurau. The map told us that the main road would make a sharp right turn there, so we were keeping a close eye on the signs. As we approached the bend, I noticed a sign telling us that if we wanted to go to Porangahau, we should keep straight on along route 52.

The name rang a bell. That was where the longest place name was, surely? Yes, definitely. Or near there, at any rate. It was nearly 50 km away, though, and we would have to follow what looked like a tortuous route through the hills before we could rejoin the main road. Did we have the time? The hire car was due back in Wellington that evening. Logic said no, but linguistic curiosity won. I couldn't possibly miss this. Hilary was already indicating right. 'Go straight on,' I squawked. 'But the main road is that way!' 'I know, I know, trust me, all will become clear!'

And so it did. We hadn't travelled far along route 52 when the New Zealand tourist board confirmed my memory. There was a sign saying 'Longest Place Name' and a distance in kilometres. I was impressed. There was nothing like this on the roads leading to Llanfairpwll.

Twenty minutes later, and I was even more impressed. There was another sign, then another. Longest Place Name 20 km. We passed through Wanstead. Longest Place Name 10 km. We passed through Wallingford (we began to wonder which country we were in). We reached a junction. A signpost now, pointing down a road to the right: Longest Place Name 4.3 km. What a build-up! I appreciated the thought behind the .3. They don't leave anything to chance, these Kiwis.

We were nearly there. There would be a chance to stop, pit-stop, eat, buy cards, pick up some souvenirs, take some photos, and explore the site. We drove along the side road. We passed a farm. Sheep. Fields on both sides. The ground fell away to the left. Low hills to the right. Trees here and there. More sheep. A barn. Then another sign:

LONGEST PLACE NAME IN THE WORLD, 500 M ON RIGHT.

We rounded a bend, and ahead of us was a long, straight stretch of road. In the distance, on the left-hand side, we could see another signpost, pointing across the road. We got nearer. It said: Longest Place Name. ▶

> ❛A signpost now, pointing down a road to the right: Longest Place Name 4.3 km. What a build-up! ❜

Taumatawhakatangihangakoauauotamateaturipukakapikimaungahoronukupokaiwhenuakitanatahu

> ◄ And there, in a lay-by, it was. The Longest Place Name in the World. On the longest sign I had ever seen. All 85 letters of it.

❝ And there, in a lay-by, it was. The Longest Place Name in the World. ❞

But nothing else. Not a thing. No ice-cream van. No café. No postcard stall. No loo. Nothing. Just a sign, by a field, on a hillside, in a lay-by.

We parked the car, got out, and looked at it. It said in Maori (I add some sense-breaks to make it easier to read):

Taumata-whakatangi-hanga-koauau-o-
Tamatea-turi-pukaka-piki-maunga-horo-
nuku-pokai-whenua-kitana-tahu.

Fortunately, there was an explanation. A notice behind the name briefly told the story:

Tamatea was a well-known chief, warrior and explorer of his time. He is the ancestor of the Ngati Kahungunu people of Porangahau, and acquired many names to commemorate his prowess. Whilst passing through the inland district of Porangahau, Tamatea encountered the Ngati Hine people and had to fight them to get past. In the battle known as 'Matanui', his brother was killed. Tamatea was so grieved at his loss that he stayed for some time at that place and each morning he would sit on the knoll to play a lament on his koauau.

Hence the name indicating the hill on which Tamatea, the chief of great physical stature and renown, played a lament on his flute to the memory of his brother.

A rather more vivid translation runs: 'The hilltop where Tamatea, the man with the big knees, conqueror of mountains, eater of land, traveller over land and sea, played his koauau to his beloved.'

After reading that, the bare, lonely setting seemed just right. An old tree stump. Grass. A few fallen branches. We stood by the sign and looked up to the top of Tamatea's hill. It was quite a distance, and we didn't have the time to walk all the way up. The sheep munched on, ignoring us. There wasn't a sound. I'm glad there weren't any ice-cream vans.

I practised saying the name. Local people, I learned later, call the place *Taumata* ('hilltop') for short. But the full form is a remarkable creation, including the splendid *koauau* – a wonderfully expressive word for the Maori flute.

We needed some lunch, so we resolved to stop at the first village we came to. With luck, we thought, we would find a place with an equally resonant Maori name and perhaps a local old-timer who could tell us something more about Tamatea. ▶

> The bare, lonely setting seemed just right. An old tree stump. Grass. A few fallen branches.

Longing to Visit *(continued)*

◀ But we were out of luck that day. For the next township was called Wimbledon. And its sole pub was run by an émigré Dutchman.

However, there is an upside to everything. If we liked, said our host, we could take some tennis rackets and go into the back garden. He would then issue us with a certificate saying we had 'played tennis at Wimbledon'.

As we thought, it took a while to get back onto the main road. But when we did, route 52 waved us farewell with a final linguistic experience. We rejoined highway 2 at a place with the totally unexpected name of Dannevirke. It was founded by Danish and Norwegian settlers in 1872, and the town is proud of its heritage. They have a Scandinavian Club, and a Viking stands guard on the town's welcome sign. The name means 'Dane's work'. And as we drove through Dannevirke, travelling south, on the left we passed Hamlet Street. ◼

❛There wasn't a sound. I'm glad there weren't any ice-cream vans. ❜

Have You Read?

Other Books by David Crystal

The Stories of English, Penguin, 2004

Pronouncing Shakespeare: the Globe Experiment, Cambridge University Press, 2005

The Cambridge Encyclopedia of the English Language, Cambridge University Press, 2nd edition, 2003

The Fight for English, Oxford University Press, 2006

Words, Words, Words, Oxford University Press, 2006

Think on my Words: Exploring Shakespeare's Language, Cambridge University Press, 2008

Read on

If You Loved This,
You Might Like ...

Spoken Here: Travels among Threatened Languages
Mark Abley

Mother Tongues: Travels through Tribal Europe
Helena Drysdale

Blackfoot Physics: a Journey into the Native American Universe
F. David Peat

Talking for Britain: a Journey through the Nation's Dialects
Simon Elmes

Travels in an Old Tongue: Touring the World Speaking Welsh
Pamela Petro